WEALTH WITHOUT RISK
FOR CANADIANS

Charles J. Givens

WEALTH WITHOUT RISK
FOR CANADIANS

HOW TO DEVELOP A
PERSONAL FORTUNE WITHOUT
GOING OUT ON A LIMB

Canadian edition first published in 1991 by
Stoddart Publishing Co. Limited
34 Lesmill Road
Toronto, Canada
M3B 2T6

Second printing November 1991

U.S. edition first published in 1988 by
Simon & Schuster Inc.

Canadian Cataloguing in Publication Data

Givens, Charles J.
Wealth without risk for Canadians

Includes index.
ISBN 0-7737-2391-9

1. Finance, Personal.   2. Investments.   I. Title.

HG179.G58 1991   332.024   C91-093421-5

Cover Design: Brant Cowie/Art Plus Limited
Typesetting: Tony Gordon Ltd.
Indexing: Heather Ebbs

Printed and bound in the United States of America

The author has researched all sources to ensure the
accuracy and completeness of the information contained
in this book. Nevertheless, we assume no responsibility
for errors, inaccuracies, omissions, or any inconsistency
herein. Readers should use their own judgment and/or
consult a financial expert for specific applications to
their individual situations.

To Chuck and Rob, my sons, and Adena
My greatest supporters

Contents

Acknowledgments

This book was written on six continents, including Antarctica. Adena, my wife, was always there with encouragement and patience.

Buddy and Jo Hewell, ATAP Financial Services, provided tremendous insights into the insurance sections. Buddy is one of North America's foremost authorities on insurance, retirement plans, and the associated tax laws.

Special thanks go to Fred Hills of Simon and Schuster for his initial recognition of the importance of this material and his patience while it was being organized.

I appreciate the efforts of Ron Lane, President of Charles J. Givens International, and his son, Ron Jr., for monitoring the research needed for me to write my book for the Canadian reader. Special thanks to my Canadian experts in mutual funds, taxes, banking, and insurance, specifically: Robert Appel, Hartley Nathan, and Barbara Chernin.

Countless hours of typing, editing, and research were spent by Beth Webley, Elaine Wilson, Jennifer Griffith, Debby Kirkpatrick, Grace Yohannan, Jane Martinez, Randy Van Sickle, Cathie Epperson, Kristine Petterson, and Dawn Douglass.

MY STORY
Charles J. Givens

While I was still a young man my father died. Even after owning his own business for 15 years, he died absolutely broke. There wasn't even enough money to pay his funeral expenses. I will never forget wondering, "How, in a great country like the United States, can anyone work so hard an entire lifetime and end up with nothing?" With half-formed tears I promised myself that would never happen to me. No matter how long or hard I had to search, how many books I had to read, or how many people I had to ask, I was determined to find the answers. I wanted to be rich and nothing was about to stop me.

What I learned about money over the next 15 years enabled me to build my personal and business fortune. The determination and single-mindedness of purpose paid off. If you read the financial articles in *Time, Canadian Business, The Financial Post, Newsweek, The Wall Street Journal, Profit*, or *Venture* magazine you know the story. I feel fortunate to have been able to share my strategies with my Canadian readers by the medium of print and also through radio and television.

I have found that there is no downside to having a lot of money. Money is freedom, and freedom is the ability to do whatever you want when you want to do it.

The path I followed in building my wealth was certainly not the easiest. Every possible mistake was made, for one reason — no one was around to show me how.

At age 25, I was a millionaire for the first time through the creation of a Nashville music, business conglomerate, Colony International. At

26, I was broke. No one had ever told me that I, and not my insurance agent, was responsible for being certain that I had enough of the right kind of insurance. My recording studio and office building burned to the ground and I never collected a dime.

During the next three years I moved from the bottom to the executive suites of Genesco, a major apparel conglomerate, by designing management computer systems in an era when computers were new and computer professionals almost nonexistent. The job gave me the leverage to use borrowed money to finance my way into almost a million dollars of stock market wealth. New companies, new issues, and new profits to borrow against. Then in 1968 the market turned. No one had ever told me that stocks can go down. Instead of continuing to follow my own instincts and common sense which had created the paper fortune, my emotions led me to a vested, fast-talking stockbroker. "Here. You watch my money," I said, almost relieved. He must still be watching it because I never saw another cent. I traded my Cadillac for a mortgaged Volkswagen, sold my house to pay off the margin calls, left Corporate America and Nashville with a bankroll of $200 in my pocket.

My third fortune was made and lost through the creation of a luxurious yacht club. Cashing in a $3,000 insurance policy, I put a 60-day option on a million-dollar estate previously owned by a Pittsburgh steel magnate on the banks of the Indian River in Florida. With no extra money and no income, the next few months were financed by a wallet full of credit cards.

The $50,000 required to close on the property was obtained only at the last possible minute. Everything seemed to be working. Plans to convert the estate to a yacht club were drawn up, and soon the club would be finished. No one, however, had pointed out that it was probably better to complete the docks before the club. The governor of the state of Florida signed a bill prohibiting dredging in the river until a five-year ecological study was finished. No docks — no boats; no boats — no yacht club. The trustee for the project neglected to make a mortgage payment, and the third mortgage holder foreclosed. The balance sheet showed my net worth had jumped from the minus columns to $1,000,000 in one year. It was gone in one day.

Three times in eight years I had created a million-dollar fortune in less than 18 months starting with nothing. I knew how to make money, I just didn't seem to be able to keep it.

Beginning in 1971, through a combination of leveraged business and real estate investments, I managed to build and keep the fortune I now enjoy. In 1986, *Success* magazine for the first time chose the 20 living Americans who they felt had started with the least chance, made the biggest mistakes along the way, and built the biggest fortunes. I felt very honored to be one of those 20. Why is that important to you? Because when it comes to money, yours or mine, I know what I'm talking about. If I tell you a strategy will work, you can bank on it. You can use these strategies to open financial doors never before available to you, to compress the time it takes to build your dreams. Most importantly, enjoy every moment of the journey as I have learned to do. That's what separates the real winners from the losers.

This book is simply a composite of the money strategies I have discovered over a lifetime of financial experience. You will find them both easy to understand and easy to apply.

Making financial decisions is like standing in a room full of doors, knowing that behind one is the financial reward you seek but behind the others are financial perils you seek to avoid. Without additional knowledge your alternatives are not appealing. Through trial and error you may make a choice detrimental to your wealth or you could refuse to choose at all, as most do, letting fear create financial stagnation. An unseen third alternative is the one you have chosen through reading this book — making your financial decisions by knowing in advance what lies beyond each door, a form of X-ray vision that will connect predictable financial results to your choices. You cannot fail in a plan that allows you to choose results instead of only the processes or paths to be followed. That, my friend, is the power you now hold in your hand.

Without knowledge, personal and business financial decisions are made using an ounce of logic peppered with a pound of emotion. Money does not behave according to the rules of common sense. Instead, wealth building has its own set of principles — principles that work, work all the time, and work for anyone. These principles, or money strategies, add to your wealth, compress time, and endow you with what most refer to as the Midas Touch.

I feel fortunate to have the financial success coupled with good people to run my businesses so that I can afford to devote most of my time to teaching my strategies. It was for that purpose that I created my nonprofit educational foundation in 1975. Today, it has grown into the Charles J. Givens Organization with 350,000 members — families who depend on us for all their financial help and advice. It was also for that purpose that I have written this book. My money strategies are safe, practical, and they can be applied to every aspect of your financial life. Better yet, you don't have to be a financial wizard to put them to work for you.

To Your Success

Charles J. Givens

You will see all the elements of our secrets. The conclusion will be yours to draw. We can help you learn it, but not to accept it.

The sight, the knowledge, and the acceptance must be yours.

Ayn Rand
Atlas Shrugged

Part I

PERSONAL

FINANCE

STRATEGIES

Chapter 1

DEVELOPING
YOUR FINANCIAL
BLUEPRINT

I expect to spend the rest of my life in the future, so I want to be reasonably sure what kind of future it is going to be. That is my reason for planning.

Charles Kettering, industrialist, 1950

Objective: Turn dreams into realities.

There are three strategies we were never taught in school:

- How to run a successful marriage
- How to raise successful children
- How to build wealth successfully

The purpose of this book is to show you how to overcome the third of these educational gaps: how to build your wealth quickly and easily by making your financial decisions correctly and with confidence.

Everyone with self-earned wealth will tell you that money is not complicated. The confusing trade terms, buzz words, and complex explanations that are thrown around by investment counsellors and financial people are not necessary. They just muddy the waters, and sometimes hide the fact that the so-called experts don't really know what they're talking about.

In the course of my life, I have discovered a success principle that has enabled me to accumulate tens of millions of dollars while maintaining a constant state of happiness, emotional balance, and zest for life.

3

Strategy #1:
ACHIEVE SUCCESS IN ANY AREA OF LIFE
BY IDENTIFYING THE OPTIMUM STRATEGIES
AND REPEATING THEM UNTIL THEY BECOME HABITS.

Success with money, family, relationships, health, and careers is the ability to reach your personal objectives in the shortest time, with the least effort and with the fewest mistakes. The goals you set for yourself and the strategies you choose become your blueprint or plan.

Strategies are like recipes: choose the right ingredients, mix them in the correct proportions, and you'll always produce the same predictable result: in this case financial success. The success strategies for managing money and building wealth are called Money Strategies.

Canada, like other countries, is chock full of financial victims — those who fall prey to financial hucksters whose advice, in the long run, benefits only themselves.

Every one of us makes two or three major money-management decisions every month. Through lack of training, or misdirection, these decisions often turn out to be major financial errors. Guessing at financial decisions — or simply relying on bankers, brokers, and insurance salesmen — may cause you to throw away an easy $1,000 a month.

Your first line of defence? Knowledge. For every financial decision there is an optimum strategy — the "right" strategy.

On the other hand, money strategies mean little unless they are part of a greater plan. Strategies are only tools, not ends in themselves. Your dreams are the true destinations; your goals are the signposts of accomplishment that define your path.

By incorporating my Money Strategies into your day-to-day life, by making the right decisions at the right time, financial frustration and failure will become things of the past.

Why, then, do so many people find it so difficult to accumulate wealth and, more important, to enjoy the journey? There are two reasons: not being clear about what they are after, and not knowing the strategies for achieving it.

The starting point in any plan is where you are right now. Where you are is where you are. Period. Your first objective is to accept yourself and your current status as an O.K. place to be without making excuses as to why you don't know more or aren't doing better. Excuses become the limiters that can transform realistic dreams into idle wishes. Lack of action and lack of willingness to effect true change are almost the only things in life that create frustration and depression.

When it comes to excuses for not taking financial control, I hear the same ones again and again:

"I can't even balance my chequebook."   "I'm too young."

"I'm too old."   "I'm too tired."

"I'm too broke."   "I'm too dumb about money."

"I can't get my husband (or wife) to listen."   "I'm too busy."

"I don't want much."   "I'm too scared."

Excuses never produce results. All they produce are more excuses. You can find unlimited excuses for failure but no one ever makes an excuse for success. There is no reason to!

So, right now, figure out where you want to be — your goals in life — and write them down. Your written plan will set the tone, speed, and most important, the direction for the rest of your life.

Have you ever attended a rousing motivational lecture and been impressed by the spirit, humour, and drive, yet walked out of the room thinking, "What the hell am I supposed to do now?" Enthusiasm, but NO DIRECTION.

Direction can turn the power of a light bulb into a laser beam. Lasers are nothing more than sharply focused light. Lasers have the power to cut through steel and destroy missiles in space. Same light as the light bulb — just more focused and directed. Clearly establishing objectives and defining up-front your direction will turn the power of your mind into the laser beam it was meant to be, drawing to you the opportunities, people, knowledge you will need, empowering you to cut through the obstacles that hinder your path to success and financial independence.

Power to accomplish also lies in knowing how to compress time — to do in one year what it takes everyone else ten years to accomplish. As you will discover, the strategies in this book are powerful time compressors. Use them.

Success also requires an understanding and use of the Momentum Principle.

Strategy #2:

SUCCESS REQUIRES FIRST EXPENDING TEN UNITS OF EFFORT TO PRODUCE ONE UNIT OF RESULTS. FROM THEN ON, YOUR MOMENTUM WILL PRODUCE TEN UNITS OF RESULTS FOR EACH UNIT OF EFFORT.

Direction and control begin with a written plan spelled out in two parts. Part A lists "dreams" — what you are after both financially and personally. Part B lists your "strategies" — the specific financial and personal road map that will take you from where you are to where you want to be. By clearly defining your direction, and by adopting the correct money and attitude strategies for control, you will automatically establish the shortest possible route.

When I was 18, I sat down with a pad of paper and, without exactly realizing what I was doing, wrote an action blueprint for my life. I called it my dreams list. The following exercise will do the same for you, clearly defining at one time and in one place your goals, dreams, objectives, and even your fantasies.

Choose a totally quiet spot where you will not be interrupted. At the top of the pad of paper write the following:

DREAMS LIST

If I had unlimited . . .

TIME
TALENT
MONEY
ABILITY
SELF-CONFIDENCE
SUPPORT FROM FAMILY

Here's what I'd do . . .

Relax and let the ideas bubble up from both your conscious and subconscious. Do not at this point consider your potential or probability of achieving each item as you write. Go with the flow. What you will write will excite you, motivate you, inspire you, make you laugh, and most of all, define desires and dreams that are ready to surface but all too often are held back by the complexities of daily living.

Write each down no matter how silly each seems, no matter what each costs. The ideas will come slowly at first, gaining speed as you leave behind the self-imposed constraints and limits within your life.

My first list was 181 dreams long, of which 170 have already become reality. Since that time I've added dozens of others — as you will probably find yourself doing also once you enter your new financial reality.

Each of us has dreams. The first step for turning dreams into reality is to get those dreams out in front of you where you can see them, feel them, and become them.

Having taught my students this dreams-list strategy for over 15 years, I have personally seen some truly wonderful things happen that might never have occurred otherwise:

A 66-year-old Ph.D. spent his birthday hang gliding with me off the huge sand dunes at Kitty Hawk, North Carolina.

A 14-year-old boy started his own successful business.

A 45-year-old, recently separated housewife, with no previous sense of adventure, rappelled straight down a 200-foot cliff, then rode a zip line 60 feet in the air, 300 yards across a valley at 40 miles per hour hanging from only wrist straps — resulting in more self-confidence in two days than she had achieved in her entire lifetime.

Through the dreams-list strategy a 35-year-old mother swam and played with dolphins at Kings Dominion Park in Virginia — a dream she had had since she was a child.

A 28-year-old European immigrant, who barely spoke English, built a $5,000,000 fortune in five years starting with a $6.00-an-hour job. I will never forget the tears of joy in his eyes as he sat in my office in Orlando telling me the story of his success and the part my strategies had played in his life.

Once you have made your list with no limits, choose those objectives that are the most important to you. Some will be individual objectives, others will include and require the support of your family. Encourage your spouse and children, if you have them, to create their own lists also.

After you define your dreams, the things you want to do, places you want to go, what you want to be and accomplish, the next logical step is to build your personal road map — your strategies list.

The rest of the chapters in this book will show you all of the safe alternatives for creating the wealth to live out your dreams.

Chapter 2

BECOMING YOUR OWN

FINANCIAL EXPERT

The easiest job I have ever tackled is that of making money. It is, in fact, almost as easy as losing it.

H.L. Mencken, 1922

Objective: Take control of your financial future.

The two most important words in managing money and building wealth are "take control." No one will ever watch your money or your financial future as well as you — no broker, financial planner, or insurance agent. Control begins with your written plan and is exercised through your choice of money strategies. The correct strategies turn wealth building, like walking, into a series of small, easy-to-accomplish steps.

Unless you were fortunate enough to be left a million dollars by a rich uncle, you must begin by learning to transform your income into wealth. There are only three types of money strategies needed to transform income into wealth, but you must use all three — none is optional. Omitting any one from your plan would have the same effect as removing a leg from a three-legged stool.

PERSONAL FINANCE STRATEGIES

Personal Finance Strategies are those day-to-day personal and family decisions you make unrelated to your job, taxes, or investments. Personal Finance Strategies enable you to save money as you spend it. The objective of Personal Finance Strategies is to increase your spendable income each year by thousands by getting rid of financial waste.

Personal Finance Strategies will:

A. Cut the cost of your life insurance by up to 60%.
B. Cut your automobile, mortgage, and homeowner's insurance premiums by up to 50%.
C. Reduce your lifetime mortgage payments by up to 50%.
D. Cut your MasterCard and VISA interest by up to 20%.
E. Turn your home equity or insurance policy cash values into income.
F. Restore your credit in 60 days.
G. Send your kids to college free.

TAX-REDUCING STRATEGIES

Income taxes are the biggest expense you'll encounter in life, bigger than the mortgage on your home or the cost of getting your kids through college. You can never build any real wealth without first getting your tax life under control.

One third of all the wealth you will or won't accumulate is dependent on whether you have a good tax plan. My experience in working with over 300,000 families during the past 14 years indicates most families are paying twice as much in income taxes as necessary. Why? Lack of a good tax-reducing plan. Your objective is to pay no more than 5% of your income in taxes.

The biggest taxpayer in recent history was Elvis Presley. I remember from my days in the Nashville music business how Elvis prided himself on the massive amount of taxes he paid. He had no tax plan, no tax shelters, and got little or no tax advice. He was also in a unique position. He couldn't outspend his income; money literally came in faster than he could get rid of it. After the excessive income and estate taxes were paid, and because of pitiful planning, Elvis's estate was incredibly small; the government got it all.

You, on the other hand, are probably having no difficulty in outspending your income and, if so, a good tax plan will begin to plug the dike. Every dollar you save in taxes is one dollar added to your tax-free wealth. Under the current tax laws, $1,000 of additional tax deductions will save you approximately $250 in taxes, assuming that you are taxed at the lowest federal marginal rate. The figure may change because the provincial tax rates vary.

There are two steps in reducing your taxes:

A. Make money you spend tax deductible as you spend it.

In this book I have listed special strategies that may turn your day-to-day expenses into tax deductions; you may make your education, automobile, videotape recorder, money you give to children, interest on loans, and entertainment tax deductible. A good tax plan may make up to 60% of your income deductible as you spend it.

B. Use the power of retirement plans and investment tax shelters. Tax-free compounding is one secret to financial success. Retirement plans and tax shelters give you the power of tax-free compounding.

POWERFUL INVESTMENT STRATEGIES

Investing money and saving money are not at all the same strategies. Savers are those who earn less than 10% per year and do little more than make financial institutions wealthy. Successful investing, on the other hand, requires knowledge and not risk to accomplish the following three-pronged objective:

1. To earn 20% per year safely,
2. with no commissions, and
3. with no taxes.

How can you safely earn up to 20% a year in a world that expects only 7% from banks and bonds? By using any of what I consider the best investment opportunities in Canada — those that you won't find advertised in the financial pages or sold through brokers and financial planners. All are uncovered in Section III, Powerful Investment Strategies.

THE EIGHT BEST INVESTMENTS

INVESTMENT	STRATEGY	ACTIVE/ PASSIVE	AVERAGE YEARLY RETURN
1. No-load mutual funds	Money movement	Passive	12%–25%
2. Mutual fund margin accounts	Leverage	Passive	25%
3. RRSP accounts	Self-directed accounts	Passive	15%–20%
4. Your own home	Leverage, & personal use	Passive	20%
5. Asset management chequing accounts	Legal float and debit card	Active	8%–14%

6. Employer's pension plan	Money movement and payroll deducted	Passive	20%
7. Discounted mortgages	Guaranteed interest tax deferral	Active	30%
8. Investment real estate	Leverage, and Equity growth capital gains	Active	30%

I will also show you how to reduce the cost of your investment program. Paying unnecessary fees and commissions on your investments is like throwing $20 bills into the fireplace to heat your home. You'll get the job done but the method is extremely ineffective. You cannot be splitting your money with everyone else and expect to have much left for yourself. By learning to work directly with financial institutions you can eliminate the middleman, the commissioned salesman, and keep 100% of your money working for you.

On October 19, 1987, the stock market and most investors' stock portfolios dropped by 20%. The one-day drop shocked the world and crowded other news items from the headlines. Yet every day millions of investors turn over billions of dollars to investment salesmen, and experience a one-day drop in their investment capital of 8%. Although no headlines are made, paying commissions is the same kind of investment loss.

To start your Wealth Without Risk program you need only income. It doesn't matter whether you have $1.00 or $100,000 in your investment plan. Making big money does not take big money, only knowledge and a little time.

It might surprise you to know that the average couple in Canada earns $50,000 per year and lives paycheque-to-paycheque with little hope of breaking the cycle.

WHERE THE MONEY GOES*

(Average Annual Family Income $50,083**)

HOUSEHOLD EXPENSES

FOOD	$5,013
CLOTHES	860
UTILITIES	1,861
HOUSEHOLD	2,857
CAR	570

GIFTS	710
PETS	320
	12,191

INSURANCE

CAR	1,700
LIFE	1,500
CHILDREN	499
DISABILITY	500
CREDIT LIFE	360
MORTGAGE	730
HOMEOWNERS	711
	6,000

TAXES

FEDERAL	7,000
PROVINCIAL	3,500
PROPERTY TAXES	1,000
CPP	1,012
	12,512

PAYMENTS

MORTGAGE	11,000
CAR LOAN	3,400
CREDIT CARDS	1,680
PERSONAL LOANS	1,200
	17,280

FOR SELF

FUN	700
VACATION	1,400
	2,100

NO SAVINGS
NO RRSPs
NO INVESTMENTS
TOTAL   **$50,083**

*Charles J. Givens Organization Research Study
**Statscan Nov. 90

Now here is a chart showing where the money goes before and after Money Strategies are used:

USING THE CHARLES J. GIVENS
PERSONAL FINANCE AND TAX STRATEGIES

Family Income—$50,083

	BEFORE	AFTER	DIFFERENCE
INSURANCE	$ 6,000	$ 2,850	$ 3,150
TAXES	$12,512	$ 7,800	$ 4,712
CREDIT CARDS	$ 1,680	$ 980	$ 700
TOTAL	$20,192	$11,630	$ 8,562

New Money for Investments, Fun, Vacations: $8,562

After applying just the Personal Finance and Tax Strategies the typical Canadian couple may now have as much as $8,000 to $10,000 extra tax-free dollars to spend and invest each year. Same income, but a new lifestyle and outlook for the future. You will save thousands each year in all of these areas by using the Personal Finance and Tax Strategies. Coupled with Powerful Investment Strategies, you will automatically and systematically achieve your objective: Wealth Without Risk.

Chapter 3

CASUALTY INSURANCE — CUTTING YOUR PREMIUMS BY UP TO 50%

By promoting insurance on the basis of what people think about uncertainty, instead of what they would be correct in thinking, by exploiting the fallacy that one buys insurance to collect for a loss instead of showing that the purpose of insurance is to avoid uncertainty, we have invited a plague of problems upon the insurance industry.

Henry K. Duke, letter to *Harvard Business Review*, 1955

Objective: Save up to 50% of your premiums on automobile, homeowner's, mortgage, disability, liability, and rental-car insurance.

Casualty insurance covers most everything life insurance doesn't cover. There are a dozen types of casualty insurance policies and coverages salesmen will try to sell you. Half no one needs, yet everyone buys; the other half everyone needs, but few know how to buy. This chapter will clear up the mystery of what you need, what to avoid, and how to save thousands of dollars per year in the process. Have your current automobile, homeowner's and other policies in front of you and make notes on the items you wish to change as you learn the correct strategies.

AUTOMOBILE INSURANCE

Auto insurance laws were enacted to protect innocent victims of accidents from serious financial loss. Every province requires that registered car owners have insurance. Automobile insurance is one of

14

your biggest expenses, yet you'll find you can cut your premiums by 30% to 50% with these strategies. There are eight different automobile coverages you must understand.

LIABILITY COVERAGE

The liability portion of your policy covers your legal liability for damage you do to other people or to their property. There are three types of liability coverage available on your policy.

1. **Bodily injury liability,** the first type, covers injury to people in other cars, pedestrians, and passengers in the policyholder's car. The policyholder and family members are also covered while driving someone else's car, including rental cars if the policy has been endorsed to include this additional coverage. Bodily injury liability covers legal defence and any damages up to the limits stated in the policy, whether determined by negotiation or by trial.

Strategy #3:

CARRY ENOUGH BODILY INJURY LIABILITY TO COVER YOUR NET ASSETS PLUS ALL POTENTIAL LEGAL FEES.

How much liability protection should you carry? Enough per person to cover the net value of your assets, plus an extra one-third for lawyers' fees. If you rent your home and are living paycheque-to-paycheque with few assets, the minimum protection is probably enough. If you have $100,000 equity in your home, $50,000 of personal assets and money in retirement plans, you will want to carry a minimum of $250,000, even up to $1,000,000, of liability insurance.

Strategy #4:

CARRY A MINIMUM OF $1,000,000 PROPERTY DAMAGE LIABILITY COVERAGE.

---

2. **Property damage liability**, the second of the three types, covers damage to someone else's car or property caused by the policyholder's car. Family members and others driving with

permission are also covered. Limits should be at least $1,000,000 because of the current high cost of automobiles and the possibility of multiple car damage. The limit applies per accident.

Strategy #5:

BUY $1,000,000 OF UMBRELLA LIABILITY COVERAGE FOR UNDER $150 PER YEAR.

---

3. ***Umbrella liability*** is the third type of coverage. Instead of raising the limits on both automobile and homeowner's policies and paying double premiums, you can buy an inexpensive "Personal Umbrella Liability Policy" that covers all personal liabilities. You can buy $1,000,000 of protection with an umbrella policy for only $100 to $150 per year. You must ask for umbrella liability insurance by name. Since the premiums, and therefore, commissions are so small, your insurance agent/broker may neglect to mention it, although a good one should.

Before selling you the umbrella liability policy, most companies require you to:

1. Carry a minimum required limit on your homeowner's and automobile policies, usually $1,000,000.
2. Place both your automobile and homeowner's policies with the company issuing the umbrella policy. A discount may be available if you comply with these requirements.

COMPREHENSIVE AND COLLISION COVERAGE

4. ***Comprehensive insurance*** pays for losses due to theft, damage from fire, glass breakage, falling objects, explosions, etc. The deductible ranges from $50 to $500. Ordinarily, banks and finance companies require you to buy collision and comprehensive before approving you for a car loan.

5. ***Collision insurance*** covers damage to your car in the event of a collision with another vehicle or object no matter who is at fault. Your insurance company will seek reimbursement from the other driver's insurer if the policyholder is not at fault, and

then reimburse the policyholder for the deductible. Deductibles usually range from $100 to $1,000. Collision insurance is expensive. It typically represents about 33% of your total premium.

Strategy #6:

WHEN THE VALUE OF YOUR CAR DROPS BELOW $1,500, DROP THE COLLISION AND COMPREHENSIVE COVERAGE.

If your car is damaged, you can't collect more than the car is worth no matter how much you've been paying in premiums. When your car is older and not worth much, it no longer pays to carry comprehensive and collision coverage at all. Thieves don't tend to steal old cars; the penalty is no greater for stealing a new car.

Strategy #7

UNLESS REQUIRED BY LAW, DROP DUPLICATE COVERAGES LIKE MEDICAL PAYMENTS AND NO-FAULT INSURANCE.

---

6. ***Medical payments coverage*** pays for medical expenses caused by a car accident to your family members, or another person riding in your automobile. You and your family members are already covered under your provincial health insurance plan, and others riding in your car are covered by the liability portion of your policy or by their own provincial health insurance plan. Typical premiums for this coverage are $40 per year for $5,000 of insurance. You cannot collect twice for the same medical expenses, so if you have a provincial health insurance plan, medical payments coverage is a complete waste of your money.

7. ***No-fault insurance*** is based on provincial laws that are supposed to lower the cost of automobile insurance by allowing an injured party to collect without litigation. No-fault laws allow you to recover losses from your own insurance company even if someone

else is at fault, but require you to give up your right to sue. These laws vary by province, but the common features include:

- partial reimbursement for medical expenses,
- partial reimbursement for lost income,
- partial compensation for death, permanent injury, or disfigurement, and
- partial reimbursement for property damage.

No-fault is more duplicate or unnecessary coverage, and should not be taken unless required by provincial law. Medical expenses are covered under your provincial health insurance plan, and property damage is covered under the collision portion of your policy.

8. *Uninsured motorists coverage* covers you and your family members by your own insurance company for bodily injury caused by an uninsured motorist or hit-and-run driver. UMC also pays if your medical bills are in excess of the other driver's liability limits. This coverage is automatically included in the policies in some provinces. Double-check with your insurance agent/broker.

Notice that the liability portion of your insurance policy covers only injury you do to others; the uninsured motorist's coverage is for injury others do to you. UMC is just a high-priced combination life insurance and hospitalization plan and thus is a complete waste of money. If you have other hospitalization and medical coverage, you cannot collect the medical benefits twice even though you paid both premiums.

STRATEGIES FOR INSURANCE DEDUCTIBLE

Strategy #8:
RAISE THE DEDUCTIBLES ON YOUR AUTOMOBILE AND HOMEOWNERS POLICIES TO $500 OR MORE.

The deductible is the amount you agree to pay before the insurance company has to kick in. Most policyholders opt for the lowest possible deductible — usually $50 on automobile comprehensive and $100 on collision coverage, and $200-$250 on homeowner's policies. Lower deductibles may make you feel good, but they do you no good. Each year, less than 10% of all automobiles and homes will be involved in accidents or losses, and only half of those policyholders will have to pay any deductible. Choose the deductible with which you feel most comfortable, $500 or even $1,000. As your assets and income increase, increase your deductibles accordingly. Increasing your auto insurance deductible to $500 will reduce your comprehensive and collision premiums as much as 15%. Increasing the deductible to $1,000 will cut those premiums by up to 20%.

The following two strategies will show you why low deductibles don't make sense.

Strategy #9:
NEVER FILE AN INSURANCE CLAIM FOR UNDER $500.

Smart policyholders don't file small claims. The insurance company will raise your premiums next year by 25% or more, or worse yet, cancel or not renew the policy if there are frequent claims. Save your insurance claims only for the big losses.

Strategy #10:
NEVER PAY OUT MORE IN PREMIUMS THAN YOU CAN COLLECT IN DAMAGES.

You pay so much extra for lower deductibles that, over the years, you could not collect in damages half of what you're paying in premiums. Lower deductibles waste dollars.

Remember, insurance is not free. Collecting on a claim from an insurance company is not a gift. The insurance company's cost of processing even the smallest claim is over $400 just for the administrative expenses and paperwork, and these costs are added to the premiums you pay for lower deductibles.

Strategy #11:
SUBSTITUTE A "FREE" CREDIT CARD FOR EXPENSIVE LOW INSURANCE DEDUCTIBLES.

For some the concern is, "What if I am responsible for a deductible or can't collect from the other driver, and don't have the extra money to fix my car?"

Your best "no cost" insurance is a no-annual-fee credit card (such as MasterCard) that you apply for separately and keep for emergencies only. It is to be for unusual one-time expenses only. With a $1,000 to $2,000 limit, you have the cash available, but — unlike insurance premiums — the credit card costs you nothing unless you actually use it!

Strategy #12:
READ THE FINE PRINT WHEN YOU TAKE ON A NEW CREDIT CARD OR CLUB, AND SAY "NO" TO ALL THE INSURANCE.

A number of credit cards and public clubs (such as auto clubs) offer various types of insurance plans as part of the "basic member service" — everything from accident and life insurance to trip interruption in the case of the travel clubs. Often, but not always, these coverages are elective. Sometimes the mere action of taking on the card or joining the club automatically "opts" you into the plan. After you pay the basic membership fee, you suddenly discover extra insurance charges on your first month's statement. Worse, such coverages are almost always overpriced because the club or card service is purchasing the insurance from a third party and then re-selling it to you. Read the fine print before you take on a new card or club, and be sure to expressly decline new coverages. Following the strategies in this book will give you all the coverage you really need.

HOW YOUR AUTOMOBILE INSURANCE
PREMIUMS ARE DETERMINED

Ever wonder how the insurance companies arrive at your premium? You may think the process involves determining the maximum amount you can afford to reasonably spend, and then doubling it! In fact, the actual process involves a number of different factors. In addition to how much and what kind of coverage you choose, there are five other variables relating to where you live, how you drive, and what kind of car you own — all these also affect the premiums you pay.

RATING TERRITORIES

Premiums are higher in cities where population density and traffic congestion are high, and lower in rural areas.

The company's accident experience in your area also determines your rates. Your premiums from company to company for the same city can vary as much as 50% because of different accident ratios for different companies.

DRIVER CLASSIFICATION

Age, sex, and marital status are all factors used in determining your insurance premiums. Those over 25, women, and married people have fewer accidents and the lowest rates. Males under 25 who are unmarried and the principal drivers of a car have the greatest statistical chance of accidents and, therefore, the highest rates.

DRIVING RECORD

Those responsible for accidents or who have been convicted of driving violations tend to have a greater chance for future accidents, and therefore, pay higher premiums. In most provinces points are assigned for moving violations. The more points you have, the higher your rates. Points remain on your driving record for two years, convictions remain on record for three years.

USE OF CAR

Those who drive to and from work have a greater chance for accidents than those who use a car for pleasure only. Premium categories are usually:

1. No commuting — lowest premium
2. Less than 10 miles to work — higher premium
3. More than 10 miles to work — higher premium
4. Business use — highest premium

TYPE OF CAR

Expensive cars cost more to repair and, therefore, cost more to insure.

Using the damageability rating charts at the end of this chapter will give you an inside look at how the insurance companies establish ratings.

Strategy #13:
CHECK INSURANCE RATES ON AN AUTOMOBILE BEFORE YOU BUY IT.

Because some cars are more expensive to replace or repair, insurance companies assign code numbers to each model. The higher the code number, the more expensive your car will be and the more expensive your collision and comprehensive premiums will be.

Such ratings are initially based on the sticker price and then raised or lowered depending on the average cost of parts and repairs on that particular model.

In Canada, there is no universal rating system. Each insurer issues its own codes for each car. However, since these codes are all based on the same underlying data, it is useful to know what the data is based on.

Generally, the insurers pool information among themselves about the average collision and personal injury claims made for each make and model. Certain cars will show above-average dollar claims and certain models will show below-average claims.

For example, for the 1990 model year, Chevy Chevette and Dodge Lancer showed claims very much below the norm relative to their sticker prices. On the other hand, the VW Jetta and Toyota Celica showed a claim history considerably above average.

The insurance premium for the car you insure will be based on data such as this. Insuring a Jetta or Celica anywhere in Canada will cost you slightly more than other cars in the same sticker class. (You can get your own copy by contacting your nearest office of the Vehicle Information Centre of Canada.) Clearly, the savings available from choosing a car known to have a "below average" claims history can be substantial.

AUTOMOBILES WITH THE BEST AND WORST CLAIMS EXPERIENCE

The table on pages 24 and 25 illustrates the insurance claim experience during a two-year period; however, based on information provided to the Vehicle Information Centre of Canada, the Givens Organization research staff has developed a simple rating system. Models have been rated from 1 to 5, 1 being a better-than-average rating and 5 being the worst claims experience.

An average rating has been calculated from three types of insurance coverages: collision, personal injury and comprehensive.[*] Insurance premiums are based on rates that average a vehicle model's record over a number of years in order to even out any distortions.

*Note: Insurance companies develop their own rating systems in Canada to determine what they will individually charge for your coverage. It will pay you to shop around.

STRATEGIES TO CUT YOUR AUTO INSURANCE PREMIUMS

Strategy #14:
SHOP AROUND TO SAVE 25% ON AUTO INSURANCE PREMIUMS.

Automobile insurance companies set premiums based on the amount of claims paid in each area. Auto insurance rates vary as much as 25% from company to company. According to an independent study, fewer than one in four drivers will get more than one quote before buying auto insurance. When your policy is up for renewal, get several quotes. Shop around. You will be amazed at the differences in prices.

Some of the companies that seem to have lower rates in many areas are Co-Operators, Dominion, Allstate, Liberty Mutual, Royal and Pilot. Many agents, to make shopping more difficult, will not quote over the phone, but don't let that stop you. Let your wheels do the walking.

Strategy #15:
DON'T TAKE EXTRA COVERAGES SUCH AS TOWING AND CAR RENTAL.

The premiums for extras on an auto policy cost you more money than you could ever collect. Towing and car rental costs between $20 and $80 extra per car per year, and yet, only a small percentage of

AUTOMOBILE DAMAGEABILITY RATING CHART

Acura

Integra	4.3

BMW

325	4.3

Buick

Century	2.0
Electra	2.7
LeSabre	
2 door	2.3
4 door	2.7
Regal	4.0
Skylark	3.0

Cadillac

Deville	3.3
Fleetwood	
Brougham	3.0

Chevrolet

Astro Wagon	1.7
Beretta	4.0
Camaro	4.7
Camaro Z28	4.7
Caprice	
4 door	1.3
Wagon	1.7
Cavalier	
2 door	3.7
4 door	2.7
Wagon	2.7
Celebrity	
2 door	2.3
4 door	2.7
Wagon	2.3
Chevette	
2 door	2.7
4 door	2.7
Corsica	2.7
Monte Carlo	3.3
Nova	3.0
Sprint	

2 door	3.7
4 door	3.3

Chevy/GMC

Blazer	
Jimmy 4WD	3.0
Jimmy S10 2WD	3.3
Jimmy T10 4WD	3.0
Suburban C/R 10	
Series	2.3

Chrysler

Daytona	4.0
Daytona Turbo	3.7
Dynasty	1.7
Fifth Avenue	1.7
Le Baron	
2 door	3.0
4 door	2.0
Le Baron GTS	2.3
New Yorker	2.3

Dodge

600	1.0
Aries	
2 door	2.3
4 door	1.7
Wagon	1.3
Caravan Wagon	1.7
Charger	3.7
Colt	
2 door	3.3
4 door	2.7
Lancer	2.0
Omni	2.3
Shadow	3.3

Ford

Aerostar Wagon	3.0
Bronco	2.7
Bronco II 4WD	3.0
Escort	

2 door	3.0
4 door	2.7
LTD Crown Victoria	1.7
Mustang GT/Cobra	5.0
Mustang L(X)	3.7
Mustang L9X)	
3DR/P	4.0
Taurus	
4 door	2.3
Wagon	2.3
Tempo	
2 door	2.7
4 door	2.7
Thunderbird	3.3

GMC

Safari Wagon	2.3

Honda

Accord	
2 door	3.0
4 door	3.0
Civic	
2 door	3.3
4 door	3.0
Wagon	1.3
Civic CRX	4.3
Prelude	3.7

Hyundai

Excel	
2 door	3.3
4 door	3.0
Pony	2.7
Stellar	3.7

Jaguar

XJ6	4.0

Jeep

Cherokee	
2WD	2.7
4WD	3.0

AUTOMOBILE DAMAGEABILITY RATING CHART

YJ Series	3.7

Lincoln

Town Car	2.7

Mazda

323	
2 door	2.7
4 door	3.0
626	
2 door	3.7
4 door	3.0
RX7	4.0

Mercury

Cougar	2.7
Grand Marquis	1.3
Sable	
4 door	2.7
Wagon	3.0
Topaz	
2 door	3.0
4 door	2.7
Tracer	
2 door	3.7
4 door	2.7

Nissan

Maxima	3.3
Multi 2WD	3.3
Pathfinder	4.7
Pulsar NX	4.3
Sentra	
2 door	3.0
4 door	3.3
Stanza	3.0

Oldsmobile

98 Regency	3.0
Calais	
2 door	3.0
4 door	2.7
Cutlass Ciera	

2 door	2.7
4 door	2.7
Cutlass Cruiser	
Wagon	2.0
Cutlass Supreme	
2 door	2.7
4 door	2.0
Delta 88 Custom	
Cruiser	3.3
Delta 88 Royale	
2 door	2.3
4 door	2.7
Firenza	3.0

Plymouth

Caravelle	2.0
Horizon	2.7
Reliant	
2 door	2.7
4 door	2.0
Wagon	2.3
Sundance	
2 door	3.0
4 door	3.0
Turismo	3.3
Voyager	1.7

Pontiac

6000	
2 door	2.3
4 door	2.7
Wagon	1.7
Acadian	
2 door	2.7
4 door	2.0
Bonneville	3.3
Firebird 6 Cyl	4.0
Firebird Trans Am	5.0
Firefly	
2 door	3.3
4 door	3.3
Grand Am	
2 door	3.0
4 door	3.3

Grand Prix	2.3
Sunbird	4.0
Sundance	3.0

Renault

Alliance	2.7

Suzuki

Forsa	3.7
Samurai	4.0

Toyota

4 Runner 4WD	3.3
Camry	
4 door	2.3
Wagon	1.7
Celica	3.7
Celica GTS	3.7
Corolla	2.7
Cressida	3.7
Supra	4.0
Tercel	
2 door	2.7
4 door	2.0
Wagon	2.3

Volkswagen

Fox	
2 door	3.0
4 door	3.3
Golf	
2 door	4.0
4 door	3.0
Jetta	3.7

Volvo

744	3.0

policyholders will ever file a claim on either. However, do insure your car phone, which is more expensive and highly visible.

Strategy #16:
DETERMINE HOW MUCH AN ACCIDENT OR A TICKET WILL RAISE YOUR PREMIUMS.

You'll be shocked at the different practices auto insurance companies have affecting policyholders who get ticketed or are involved in an accident. Some will raise your rates 25% after only one occurrence. Others will cancel your insurance altogether. Other companies give a light increase for one or two tickets, then add as much as 50% on the third. Choose a company that won't brand you a loser just because of one bad experience.

Strategy #17:
FIGHT THAT TICKET!

The hour or two spent appearing in court to fight that ticket could be an excellent investment. Contrary to popular belief, judges will listen to a reasonable explanation of your position and, if they like what they hear, may find you not guilty. Given the potential for premium hikes in the event of one or more convictions (Strategy #16), the savings could work out to a compensation for your time of several hundred dollars an hour!

Remember also that, if you should lose your case, you are legally entitled to an appeal provided you believe that injustice was done in some manner.

A gentleman in Toronto with a number of convictions on his record was stopped for speeding 40 kph above the limit. He decided that the ticket, which was based on a radar reading, was worth fighting. He spent weeks preparing his case by researching everything he could about radar. When the day of his trial came up, he discovered to his horror that the trial had taken place the previous day, and he had been found guilty in his absence. The fault was his — he had entered the wrong date in his diary. Nonetheless, he believed that he was still entitled to a fair hearing. He applied for an appeal solely on the grounds that, by his own error, he did not get his day in court. The appeal judge accepted this premise and granted him a new trial. What happened at the re-trial? When the new court date came up the crown prosecutor was unable to produce the arresting officer as a witness and the defendant was automatically found not guilty!

Strategy #18:

IF YOU HAVE MORE THAN ONE VEHICLE IN THE FAMILY, AND A DRIVER WITH AN UNUSUALLY HIGH PREMIUM, LIMIT THAT DRIVER TO "ONE CAR ONLY."

A driver with a poor driving record, a driver who has previously made an excessive number of insurance claims, and a teenage male driver all have one thing in common — high premiums. If you have more than one vehicle in your family, specify in the policy (or policies) that the problem driver is limited to one particular vehicle only, and you could chop a considerable amount off your total insurance bill.

Strategy #19:

ASK FOR ALL THE BASIC AUTOMOBILE INSURANCE DISCOUNTS.

There are discounts offered by auto insurance companies to those who fall into special groups. When buying auto insurance be certain to ask; the agent may not bring them up.

Discount	Amount Saved
Multi-car — More than one automobile insured by the same company.	5-15%
Driver Training — take a certified course.	5-35%
Anti-Theft Equipment Alarm — systems that disengage the ignition	5-20%
Senior Citizen	5-10%
House and car with same company	5-10%
Good Driver	5-20%

If you ask for all of the discounts to which you are entitled, your premiums may drop another 20%. It pays to ask.

REDESIGNING YOUR AUTOMOBILE INSURANCE POLICY

Use the form that follows to redesign your automobile policy for lower premiums. Part 1 gives you a synopsis of the coverages you need and don't need; Part 2 will help you analyze and redesign your auto policy. On this form, list the liability limits and coverages you have on each automobile that you now own, along with any changes you wish to make using these insurance strategies. If you have more than two automobiles, make a copy of the sheet. Contact your insurance agent and make all of the changes, noting the changes in your premiums. Also use copies of the form when getting auto insurance quotes. Many automobile premiums are stated on policies as six-month premiums. If you pay every six months you must double the premiums shown and add 4% to obtain the yearly figures.

REDESIGNING YOUR AUTOMOBILE INSURANCE POLICY PART 1

Coverages You Need

Liability
  Bodily Injury   Pays for damage to other people.
  Property Damage   Pays for damage to other people's property.
Comprehensive   Pays for damage to your car by fire, theft, or anything but collision.
Collision   Pays for damage to your car by collision with another car or object.
No-Fault (PIP)   Pays your medical and funeral expenses and work loss (Ontario, Maritimes, Yukon, & Quebec).

Coverages You Don't Need

Uninsured Motorists   Pays your accident and funeral expenses caused by a non-insured or under-insured driver. It's mandatory in most provinces, even though you don't need it.
Medical Payments   Pays your medical and funeral expenses.
Emergency Road Service   Pays for towing.
Car Rental Expense   Pays for a rental car if yours is damaged.
Death/Dismemberment   Pays for death or certain injuries.
Specialty Coverage   Pays for audio equipment, glass breakage, etc.

REDESIGNING YOUR AUTOMOBILE INSURANCE POLICY
PART 2

COVERAGES TO REORGANIZE

Coverage	Current Limits	Desired Limits	Current Premiums	New Premiums	NOTES
Bodily Injury Liability					Check for all possible discounts
Property Damage Liability					
Umbrella Liability					Optional for those needing high limits
Comprehensive Deductible					At least $500
Collision Deductible					At least $500

COVERAGES TO DROP

No-Fault				-0-	
Medical Payments				-0-	
Uninsured Motorists (PIP)				-0-	
Emergency Road Service				-0-	
Car Rental Expense				-0-	
Death/ Dismemberment				-0-	
Specialty Coverage				-0-	
Other				-0-	TOTAL AMOUNT SAVED:
TOTAL PREMIUMS	$			—$	=$

Note: In provinces that have no-fault insurance schemes, coverage for medical payments, uninsured motorists (PIP) and death/dismemberment are mandatory.

In some provinces, unnecessary coverages are unfortunately required. Check your provincial rules through your insurance agent or broker.

RENTAL CAR INSURANCE STRATEGIES

Strategy #20:
DECLINE ALL EXTRA COVERAGES
WHEN YOU RENT A CAR.

Another great insurance scheme has been created by the rental car companies. By advertising low daily or weekly rates, and adding on big unnecessary insurance premiums, the rental car companies create huge profits from the confusion and fear of their customers. Although extra insurance coverages are supposedly optional, the rental car company will do everything within its power to see that you end up buying them. All of these insurances are either unnecessary because you are already covered on other policies, or they are incredibly over-priced for the insurance you actually get.

Here are typical daily and weekly premiums:

	Daily	Weekly
1. Collision Damage Waiver (CDW)	$7.50	$52.50
2. Personal Accident Insurance (PAI)	3.00	21.00
3. Personal Effects Coverage (PEC)	1.25	8.75
4. Liability Insurance Supplement (LIS)	4.95	34.65
TOTAL	$16.70	$116.90

1. COLLISION DAMAGE WAIVER (CDW)

Year after year, rental car companies require that you become liable for more of the damage caused by a collision or rollover of a rented vehicle. Your deductible on damage to a rental car now ranges from $3,000 to the full value of the car. The rental car company will offer you CDW insurance for about $7.50 a day to cover the deductible.

Here is what they don't tell you. Even without the insurance, you may already be covered by the rental car company for fire and theft. Any damage deductible you pay will be reimbursed to you by your insurance company based on the limits in your own personal policy.

Strategy #21:

CHARGE A RENTAL CAR ON A CREDIT CARD THAT COVERS THE DEDUCTIBLE.

One of the new, valuable credit card services is automatic coverage of the rental car deductible when you charge the rental on your credit card. Many popular cards now include this service, so it's worth checking with your card issuer.

For example, the American Express Green Card will cover you to the full value of the rented car, subject to a $250 deductible, provided the vehicle is not rented for more than 31 days (trucks, vans, and exotics excluded). The American Express Gold Card offers the same deal except that the deductible is reduced to only $100. The corporate American Express Green Card will cover you to the full value with no deductible. If you should ever have cause to use these hidden services, be sure to report any accidents promptly to the card issuer using the appropriate toll-free number from the city you are in. If you delay reporting the accident more than 48 hours, you may lose all coverage.

2. PERSONAL ACCIDENT INSURANCE (PAI)

Personal Accident Insurance is nothing more than an expensive life insurance policy with medical payments. The policy states, "This coverage pays for death directly caused by an automobile accident independent of all other causes." Never take the insurance. You could be paying the equivalent of $1,000 per year for a $175,000 life insurance policy that covers you only a few minutes a day — while you are driving the rental car. The actual value of the insurance is less than $50 per year.

3. PERSONAL EFFECTS COVERAGE (PEC)

Personal Effects Coverage is insurance that covers loss or damage to your personal property in the rental car or hotel room while you are renting the car. Coverage is limited to $525 for you and your immediate family members. Again, an absolute waste of money. The exclusions — what they won't pay for — are almost comical:

teeth, contact lenses, furniture, currency, coins, tickets, documents, perishables, and mysterious disappearances. What in the world is left? Your own homeowner's policy already gives you the same coverage when you are away from home. Check with your insurance agent.

4. LIABILITY INSURANCE SUPPLEMENT (LIS)

When you rent a car, your automatic liability coverage for injury or death to others is the bare minimum required by the province. For an extra $4.95 a day, the liability coverage is increased to $1,000,000 or more. Your auto insurance policy may already cover you (up to its current limits).

You can pay as little as $100 a week to rent a car, and as much as $117 for additional unnecessary insurance coverages. The discount rental car companies in resort areas, such as Florida, are the most misleading in their advertising. By advertising rental rates as low as $99 a week, vacationers end up at the counter only to be threatened into accepting the "optional" insurance.

Rental agents are often paid bonuses for selling the extra insurance, and sales pitches are somewhere between aggressive and obnoxious. Some companies require a deposit of $750 if you don't take the CDW. You may end up taking the insurance just because you're afraid the deposit would put your VISA over the limit.

MOTORCYCLE INSURANCE

Strategy #22:
BUY A SEPARATE SIX- OR NINE-MONTH POLICY TO COVER MOTORCYCLES, MOPEDS, AND SNOWMOBILES.

Motorcycle insurance (including mopeds, snowmobiles, and other miscellaneous vehicles) is similar to auto insurance.

Most provinces requiring auto liability insurance also require motorcycle liability coverage. You should have liability coverage for your motorcycle. A car owner may insure a motorcycle with an endorsement to his auto policy. You are not covered for your motorcycle through your basic auto policy.

Motorcyclists can get coverages for bodily injury and property damage liability, medical payments (usually limited to $500), uninsured motorist coverage, and collision and physical damage coverage. Use the same strategies for your motorcycle as you would for your automobile. You probably will not need coverage for other passengers since they are covered by both the liability portion of your motorcycle policy and by their own hospitalization insurance.

Many insurance companies offer six-month and nine-month policies to motorcyclists and snowmobilers where the equipment is garaged for the winter or summer. Ask your agent; it may save you money.

HOMEOWNER'S INSURANCE

Strategy #23:

TAKE ONLY THE COVERAGES YOU NEED ON YOUR HOMEOWNER'S POLICY.

The risks you take when you own a home are called perils. These perils have been divided into 18 categories. The amount of premium you pay for a homeowner's policy is determined by the number of these perils you wish to cover. Almost all homeowner's policies cover:

- Your home,
- Other buildings on the property (such as detached garage),
- Your personal belongings (other than expensive items like jewellery and furs), and
- Living expenses for temporary relocation.

Additional coverages for such things as plumbing or electrical damage, or ice and snow, may add to the cost of the policy needlessly. Accept such coverages only after you determine if your particular situation justifies such extras.

The remaining coverages fall into six categories, and offer the most dubious value. There's little reason to add these endorsements to your policy:

1. Removal of debris.
2. Damaged property removal.
3. Fire department surcharges — up to $250.
4. Temporary repairs to prevent further damage to property.

5. Trees, shrubs, and plants — covered up to $500 or a maximum of 5% of the dwelling insurance.
6. Stolen credit cards — up to $500.

Strategy #24:
PURCHASE A PERSONAL ARTICLES "FLOATER" TO COVER EXPENSIVE PERSONAL ITEMS.

Your basic policy limits what you can collect for theft or damage of personal articles. Insure expensive jewellery, furs, and other personal property with a personal articles "floater." As your wealth increases and your personal assets increase, make certain your insurance protection is increased by this coverage.

Strategy #25:
BUY FLOOD OR EARTHQUAKE INSURANCE ONLY IF YOU ARE IN A GOVERNMENT-DESIGNATED FLOOD PLAIN OR EARTHQUAKE ZONE.

Flood and earthquake insurance should be purchased by those in designated potential disaster areas but not by others. To be eligible for flood insurance you must be in an area that practices land-use control measures, and in some cases your mortgage company will require the insurance. In some parts of the country earthquake insurance is too expensive to be practical. You can't afford to insure against every possible risk, so it pays to weigh the cost against the potential loss.

Strategy #26:
KEEP YOUR JEWELLERY INSIDE A VAULT.

Keep your valuables that you don't wear often in a safety deposit box, and you will be able to suspend the floater, generally, for the number of months that the items are locked up, resulting in even more savings.

Strategy #27:
VIDEOTAPE YOUR VALUABLES FOR INSURANCE RECORDS.

You can only collect for what you can prove you lost. The best way to provide an acceptable insurance record is to use your video camera to create a video record of furniture, knickknacks, artwork, clothes, stereo and video equipment (including model and serial numbers), musical instruments, and everything else of value. While you are taping, verbally record the value of the asset and where and when you bought it. Put the videotape in a safety deposit box along with receipts. Records won't help if they are lost along with the assets. If you don't have a video camera, use your slide or Polaroid camera and a tape recorder.

Strategy #28:
BUY REPLACEMENT-VALUE COVERAGE, NOT MARKET-VALUE COVERAGE, ON YOUR HOME AND CONTENTS.

Replacement-value coverage will pay whatever it costs to replace an asset that is lost, destroyed, or stolen. Market-value coverage will pay only the current value of the asset after age and wear and tear are deducted. If your five-year-old, $1,000 video player is stolen, the replacement-value coverage will pay you $1,000, but market-value coverage may net you only $200. Surprisingly, replacement-value coverage costs only slightly more per year.

Make sure your fire insurance is a replacement-cost policy, not a market-value policy. The value of your home may fluctuate with real estate market conditions, and a market-value policy may pay you less than the replacement cost. Ask for an automatic-appreciation clause in your policy that will raise your coverage limits each year without the necessity of checking with your agent.

Strategy #29:
IMPROVE YOUR HOUSE AND LOWER YOUR PREMIUMS.

Older houses tend to command higher premiums because of the likelihood of things going wrong. If you are doing extensive work on your home's structure — including such things as wiring and plumbing — check with your insurance agent or broker to see if the work you do will be recognized by the insurance company as reducing their risk and lowering your premiums. While the renovations are in progress, spend a few extra dollars and add an alarm system — most companies will reduce your bill 10% for this alone.

Strategy #30:
IF YOU ARE DOING BUSINESS OUT OF YOUR HOME, INVEST IN A SEPARATE BUSINESS POLICY.

For those who do business out of their homes, a separate business policy is insurance that offers excellent value. For example, if a customer slips on your sidewalk, that is a business risk. (If the postman slips on your sidewalk, that is a normal homeowner's risk.) Not only will your regular homeowner's policy be likely to exclude all business coverage, it is even possible for you to lose all the protection of your homeowner's plan if it turns out you were conducting business on the premises and did not get the proper coverage.

Strategy #31:
CARRY AS FIRE INSURANCE AT LEAST 80% OF THE REPLACEMENT COST OF YOUR HOME.

Fire insurance rates are set by considering location, distance from the nearest fire hydrant and fire station, the type of construction, and the age of the home. These are factors over which you have little control. You can, however, control the amount and kind of insurance you buy, which controls your premiums.

Carry enough insurance to cover at least 80%, but not necessarily 100%, of the replacement value of your home. You are automatically covered for up to 100% of a loss, as long as the policy is written for 80% or more of the value of your home. Never underinsure because if coverage is less than 80% of replacement cost and you have a loss, the policy will pay only a percentage of the loss. Never overinsure because you will be paying premium dollars on which you can never collect.

TENANT'S INSURANCE

Strategy #32:
**BUY A SPECIAL TENANT'S POLICY IF YOU RENT
A HOME OR AN APARTMENT.**

The typical tenant's policy is designed for those who rent an apartment or house or own a cooperative apartment. It insures household contents and personal belongings. Legally, tenants are responsible for the actual premises they rent to the extent that damage may be caused by factors under their care and control. For example, a tenant may cause damage to the apartment by leaving an iron on. A proper tenant's policy will offer inexpensive protection against this sort of liability and also insure your belongings whether stored in your rental unit or in any other part of the building in which you reside.

OWNER'S, LANDLORD'S, AND TENANT'S
LIABILITY INSURANCE (OLT)

Strategy #33:
**PROTECT YOUR RENTAL PROPERTIES WITH AN OWNER'S,
LANDLORD'S, AND TENANT'S POLICY (OLT).**

Insurance for landlords falls under the general category of public liability insurance. OLT policies cover the liability arising from the ownership and maintenance of a rental property. OLT policies are relatively inexpensive and can be added as a supplement to the fire insurance policy on a rental home or sometimes to your homeowner's insurance. They are good value for the money.

LOAN INSURANCE — CREDIT LIFE AND DISABILITY

Strategy #34:

SAY NO TO LOAN INSURANCE — CREDIT LIFE AND DISABILITY.

You can save $1,000 every time you borrow $10,000 for an automobile (or for any other purpose) by declining the credit life and disability insurance. Let's say you're buying a $10,000 automobile and financing it at the bank or credit union. The last question the loan officer will ask, right before he approves your application, is, "By the way, you do want the credit life and disability insurance, don't you?" You look up, caught off guard, and ask, "What's credit life?" "Well," he says, "credit life pays off your loan if you die, and disability insurance makes the loan payments if you can't work." It all sounds logical until you consider the cost. If you say yes to the insurance, you are overpaying by 800%! Sixty percent of the premiums go as a commission to the financial institution. That should tell you how much the insurance is really worth. Banks, credit unions, and finance companies can actually make more profit from loan insurance than from interest. How do I know? I am an owner of two banks in Florida in the United States.

What do most borrowers do? They look up at the loan officer and ask, "Do you really think I ought to take the insurance?" No loan officer has ever answered no, and millions of dollars of unnecessary insurance are sold in the process. The insurance is added to your monthly payments. If the credit life and disability premiums amount to $17 a month, you pay $810 on a 48-month loan, plus over $200 interest, which increases the cost of your automobile over 10%. Credit life insurance only pays the balance of the loan at the time the insured dies and is, therefore, expensive decreasing term insurance. If your car costs $12,000 and you die owing only one payment of $327, the insurance pays only $327. Your heirs get nothing from the policy; only the financial institution collects.

If you want a personal loan paid off if something happens to you, don't buy loan insurance, buy inexpensive yearly renewable-term life insurance. You will save 75% of the premiums.

MORTGAGE LIFE INSURANCE

Strategy #35:
REPLACE EXPENSIVE MORTGAGE LIFE INSURANCE WITH INEXPENSIVE TERM INSURANCE.

Mortgage insurance pays off your home mortgage if you die. The logic of mortgage insurance is sound. You want your family to be relieved of mortgage payments if you are not around. The problem is the high cost of the insurance compared to the risk. It is estimated that mortgage insurance companies actually pay out less than 30 cents in claims for every dollar they collect in premiums.

At age 54, $80,000 of mortgage life insurance can cost as much as $1,128 per year. At the same age, you can buy an $80,000 yearly renewable-term policy to accomplish the same thing for $200 per year, saving $900 a year. Mortgage insurance proceeds go directly to the mortgage company, but YRT proceeds go to your heirs. By correctly investing these proceeds, $80,000 in our example, the mortgage payments can be made until the home is paid for while completely preserving the principal.

DISABILITY INSURANCE

Strategy #36:
BUY DISABILITY INSURANCE ONLY IF YOU ARE IN POOR HEALTH OR ACCIDENT PRONE.

For people in reasonably good health, putting money in a good investment plan will pay far greater long-term rewards than dumping it into a disability insurance policy. Disability insurance promises to pay you cash if you become disabled and can't work. The concept is great, but once again, the costs far outweigh the potential benefits.

The restrictions and definitions of disability are so confining that few policyholders ever collect.

Should you decide you want disability insurance anyway, you can cut the high premiums by 50% by increasing the waiting period. The waiting period, similar to a deductible, is the amount of time you must be disabled and unable to work before the insurance takes effect. The usual waiting period is 90 days. By increasing the waiting period to six months or one year, the premiums drop as much as 50%, while still giving you protection against long-term disability.

You don't suddenly lose everything because you become temporarily unable to work. If you are injured on the job, the mandatory workmen's compensation insurance carried by your employer will pay you. Your employer may also have a disability plan as part of your company benefit package. Also, cancel or refuse the disability premium waiver on your life insurance and the credit disability insurance.

SPECIALTY INSURANCE

Strategy #37:
DON'T BUY SPECIALTY HEALTH AND LIFE INSURANCE POLICIES.

Avoid health and life insurance policies hyped on television and through the mail. The most popular versions are those that:

- Pick up where provincial health plans leave off,
- Promise low-cost life insurance to those age 55 to 75,
- Pay $50 a day, in addition to your hospitalization,
- Insure against one disease, such as cancer, or
- Provide coverage for special groups such as veterans.

The premiums are up to 400% too high for the potential pay-off, and the restrictions guarantee that few will collect. Many of the ads play on the fears rather than the good sense of retired people.

Chapter 4

BETTER LIFE INSURANCE FOR UP TO 60% LESS

Insurance — an ingenious modern game of chance in which the player is permitted to enjoy the comfortable conviction that he is beating the man who keeps the table.

Ambrose Bierce, *The Devil's Dictionary*, 1906

Objective: To cut the cost of your life insurance by up to 60% while increasing financial protection for your family.

Life insurance is a plan whereby you pay money to the company while you are alive and the company pays your chosen beneficiary when you are not. The longer you live, the more the insurance company profits. Life insurance is a must for anyone with family responsibilities and little personal wealth. Generally, however, it is misunderstood, oversold for underprotection, and vended through marketing gimmicks that offer little in the way of real value. Life insurance, literally, can also be detrimental to your wealth.

First, here are a few terms that you must understand in order to take control of your life insurance costs.

BENEFICIARY. The person(s) who receive the death benefit or face value of the policy.

DEATH BENEFIT. The dollar amount that will be paid to the beneficiary if the insured dies, also called the face value of the policy.

FEES AND COMMISSIONS. The amount the insurance company charges for administrative and selling expenses. Fees and commissions are added to premiums or are "hidden charges" included in the premium.

GRACE PERIOD. The extra period of time following the due date of a premium during which you have the opportunity to pay the premium to avoid cancellation of the policy.

GROUP INSURANCE. An insurance plan under which a number of employees or associates and their dependents are insured under a single policy, usually having lower premiums than an individual policy.

INCONTESTABLE CLAUSE. A provision that prevents an insurance company from challenging the coverage because of alleged misstatements by the insured after a stipulated period has passed.

INSURED. The person upon whose death the death benefit will be paid.

LIFE INSURANCE. A plan where you pay premiums to an insurance company while you are living and the company pays your chosen beneficiary when you expire.

OWNER. The person who pays the premiums. The owner can be the insured, the beneficiary, or even a third person.

POLICY TERM. The period during which the insurance is in force. The term can range from one year to an entire lifetime.

PREMIUM. The dollar amount you pay to the insurance company. Premiums can be paid in one lump sum (single premium), one cheque each year (annual premium), or periodically — by the half year, quarterly or monthly. Premiums can purchase insurance only, or with life insurance, they may be partially diverted into investments, prepaid policies, and retirement plans.

PREMIUM OFF-SET. After a certain number of years of premiums being paid in a whole life policy, the life insurance is considered fully paid up, and the death benefits and cash-surrender values increase.

RATE. The cost of a unit of insurance. A rate of $40 per $1,000 unit means that $400 buys you $10,000 of insurance.

RISK. A condition in which there is a possibility of loss; used to indicate the property insured or the peril insured against.

SETTLEMENT OPTIONS. One of the ways, other than immediate payment in a lump sum, in which the policyholder or beneficiary may choose to have the policy proceeds paid.

STOCK INSURANCE COMPANY. An insurance company owned by shareholders.

SURRENDER CHARGE. The amount of money the insurance company keeps if your policy is cancelled. Surrender charges apply only to policies with investment plans such as whole life and universal life, and can run into thousands of dollars.

UNDERWRITING. The process by which an insurance company determines whether or not and on what basis it will accept an application for insurance. An underwriter reviews all new and renewal applications to determine if the insurance company is willing to issue a policy.

UNIVERSAL LIFE. Term insurance coupled with an investment plan. The premiums are variable with the amount in excess of the insurance premiums and fees going into the investment plan.

Strategy #38:
IF YOU ARE SINGLE WITH NO DEPENDENTS, DON'T BUY LIFE INSURANCE.

About 30% of all the life insurance in force today is on the lives of single people with no family responsibilities. Who would get the insurance proceeds, the dog or goldfish? Life insurance should be used only to prevent a financial hardship that would be created if the insured dies. If you are single, invest your money for use while you are living.

Of a trillion dollars of life insurance in force, $300 billion is on the lives of single people with no dependents, a perfect illustration of how well salespeople are trained and how little we've learned about money and insurance. Since the chances of living through the years you are single, usually your 20s, are 985 out of 1,000, even a small burial policy, the salesperson's last sales pitch, is certainly a poor use of your money.

Strategy #39:
NEVER BUY LIFE INSURANCE ON CHILDREN.

The purpose of insurance is to protect against the loss of your financial assets. Although children may be an emotional asset, they certainly are not financial assets unless you have secured them high-paying jobs in television commercials.

Parents buy life insurance on children because they are told by a salesperson that it is the loving, responsible thing to do. Insurance on children is a life insurance salesperson's dream. The pitch goes something like this: "Because you love your children, you will want life insurance on them, won't you?" If your answer is no, then it sounds as if you don't love your kids. If you love your children, why would it help to collect large sums of money if they died? It wouldn't. Insurance belongs on the income-providing parent(s), not the children.

Another ridiculous salesperson's pitch is that if you insure a child while he or she is young, it guarantees the child's insurability later. There is a 99% chance that if a child reaches age eighteen, he or she will be insurable anyway.

Often whole life insurance is sold as a method of building enough cash value to pay for a college education for the child who is insured. A $50,000 life insurance policy on a one-year-old child could cost $250 per year and be worth $5,000 when the child reaches college age. A yearly investment of $250 correctly placed in a mutual fund family, can create a college fund of $40,000 in the same amount of time.

Insurance salespeople also claim that you should buy life insurance on children because you are "locking in" low rates on your policy. Here are three reasons not to fall for that sales pitch:

1. The truth is that you don't want to keep that policy long term anyway because insurance costs are declining as people live longer; your rates on your child's policy won't be adjusted downward as rates in general come down.
2. The yield on the insurance company's investments may increase, but the investment return on your policy probably will not be increased.

3. Insurance premiums are less per $1,000 today than they were 30 years ago, so today you can buy more protection for less premium than you are paying on old outdated policies bought by well-meaning parents.

There could be a rare exception if your child became a television or movie star or a professional athlete and you became disabled, making the child a breadwinner. In this circumstance, life insurance on the child might be prudent.

Strategy #40:
DETERMINE INSURANCE NEEDS FOR YOU AND YOUR SPOUSE BASED UPON WHO PROVIDES INCOME OR FAMILY SERVICE.

If your spouse is responsible for a significant amount of family income, he or she is a financial asset, and inexpensive term insurance makes sense until the kids are grown. If your spouse does not work, or intends to work only part-time, and you have no children, insurance is unnecessary. Life insurance on a non-income-producing spouse is meant to pay the replacement cost of the family services now provided, such as child care, cleaning, cooking, and chauffeuring.

Strategy #41:
SUBSTITUTE THE INCOME AND CAREER OF A SPOUSE FOR A LIFE INSURANCE POLICY.

Two-income families with no dependents, that is, if each spouse has roughly the same income, need little life insurance. Those that need life insurance protection the most are families with children or families with only one income. A good job or career represents far more substantial financial security than a life insurance policy. If you have no kids and a spouse with an established career, you need little if any life insurance. Referring to the Mortality Table on the next page, you will see that the chances of your spouse dying early are so small, you will be financially smarter to use the life insurance premiums you can save to build your investment program.

MORTALITY TABLE

This table shows you both the chance of dying at any age as well as the average life expectancy of a person at any age. At age 30, for instance, only 1.55 people out of 1000 will die that year.

Age	Deaths per 1,000	Expectation of Life (Years)	Age	Deaths per 1,000	Expectation of Life (Years)	Age	Deaths per 1,000	Expectation of Life (Years)
0	20.02	70.75	37	2.44	37.23	74	50.75	9.82
1	1.25	71.19	38	2.66	36.32	75	55.52	9.32
2	.86	70.28	39	2.90	35.42	76	60.60	8.84
3	.69	69.34	40	3.14	34.52	77	65.96	8.38
4	.57	68.39	41	3.41	33.63	78	71.53	7.93
5	.51	67.43	42	3.70	32.74	79	77.41	7.51
6	.46	66.46	43	4.04	31.86	80	83.94	7.10
7	.43	65.49	44	4.43	30.99	81	91.22	6.70
8	.39	64.52	45	4.84	30.12	82	98.92	6.32
9	.34	63.54	46	5.28	29.27	83	106.95	5.96
10	.31	62.57	47	5.74	28.42	84	115.48	5.62
11	.30	61.58	48	6.24	27.58	85	125.61	5.28
12	.35	60.60	49	6.78	26.75	86	137.48	4.97
13	.46	59.62	50	7.38	25.93	87	149.79	4.68
14	.63	58.65	51	8.04	25.12	88	161.58	4.42
15	.82	57.69	52	8.76	24.32	89	172.92	4.18
16	1.01	56.73	53	9.57	23.53	90	185.02	3.94
17	1.17	55.79	54	10.43	22.75	91	198.88	3.73
18	1.28	54.86	55	11.36	21.99	92	213.63	3.53
19	1.34	53.93	56	12.36	21.23	93	228.70	3.35
20	1.40	53.00	57	13.41	20.49	94	243.36	3.19
21	1.47	52.07	58	14.52	19.76	95	257.45	3.06
22	1.52	51.15	59	15.70	19.05	96	269.59	2.95
23	1.53	50.22	60	16.95	18.34	97	280.24	2.85
24	1.51	49.30	61	18.29	17.65	98	289.77	2.76
25	1.47	48.37	62	19.74	16.97	99	298.69	2.69
26	1.43	47.44	63	21.33	16.30	100	306.96	2.62
27	1.42	46.51	64	23.06	15.65	101	314.61	2.56
28	1.44	45.58	65	24.95	15.00	102	321.67	2.51
29	1.49	44.64	66	26.99	14.38	103	328.17	2.46
30	1.55	43.71	67	29.18	13.76	104	334.14	2.41
31	1.63	42.77	68	31.52	13.16	105	339.60	2.37
32	1.72	41.84	69	34.00	12.57	106	344.60	2.34
33	1.83	40.92	70	36.61	12.00	107	349.17	2.30
34	1.95	39.99	71	39.43	11.43	108	353.33	2.27
35	2.09	39.07	72	42.66	10.88	109	357.12	2.24
36	2.25	38.15	73	46.44	10.34			

Strategy #42:

BUY LIFE INSURANCE ON A WORKING SPOUSE OR A SPOUSE AT HOME IF YOU HAVE DEPENDENT CHILDREN.

A non-working spouse or one who works part-time can be a full-time nurse, chauffeur, teacher, cook, maid, and baby-sitter, which in today's world has tremendous monetary value. It is even difficult for a mother to significantly earn more take-home pay than the cost of clothes, commuting, taxes, and child care expenses, especially if there are two or more children involved. Inexpensive term life insurance on the spouse at home will provide the financial protection to run the household and raise the kids if the family were to become a one-parent household.

Many families must now have two incomes just to get by, even when there are dependent children. If the mother, in addition to working, takes care of the household, there is a need for life insurance protection on her if the husband's income alone could not cover the cost of child care.

COMPUTING HOW MUCH LIFE INSURANCE YOU NEED

Strategy #43:

BUY ENOUGH TERM INSURANCE THAT, IF INVESTED AT 12%, WOULD REPLACE YOUR CURRENT FAMILY INCOME.

The purpose of life insurance is to replace lost income if one or both spouses or parents are no longer living.

Refer to the Life Insurance Planning Chart that follows. Locate your approximate current family income in column A. In column B, you will find the 100% income figure required for your family to fund an investment program at 12% per year to pay your family the amount in column A. Later, I will teach you how to invest with a safe annual return of 15% and more. If your children are grown, or you have a financial hardship, you may reduce the amount of required insurance coverage in B to 50% of current income. The less responsibility you have, the less insurance you need.

The chart that follows shows the maximum insurance you will need to produce the same income your family now has, even if you are gone. Since the right term insurance is so inexpensive, a plan that replaces your income is a reasonable financial goal.

Strategy #44:

AS YOU GET OLDER, REPLACE LIFE INSURANCE WITH INCOME SOURCES.

As you get older, your responsibilities usually decrease and so does your need for life insurance. Your objective is to become self-insured, to build enough wealth that you have no need for life insurance.

During younger years, ages 20 to 50, couples usually have few assets and have children living at home, which creates greater financial responsibility. These are the years when adequate life insurance is most important in substituting for loss of potential income. As you grow older, your assets begin to substitute for the life insurance you need. Life insurance is just money, nothing more, and is a substitute for income that is lost in the event of the death of a spouse or parent.

Assets built over your lifetime that replace or reduce the need for life insurance are:

Guaranteed Investment Savings Accounts Certificates (GIC)
Treasury Bills, Notes, Bonds
Net real estate income
Stock dividends
Mutual Fund Shares
Spouse's job income
Old age security
Job related retirement programs
Employer-paid life insurance

The greater your non-job related income, the less life insurance you will need.

Life Insurance Planning Chart

Yearly premium cost for first 10 Years of amount of insurance shown in column B

Your or Spouse's Current Income (A)	Approximate Amount invested at 12% that would replace income 100% (B)	(C) Age 25	(D) Age 30	(E) Age 35	(F) Age 40	(G) Age 45	(H) Age 50	(I) Age 55	(J) Age 60
$20,000	170,000	203	203	212	288	390	567	839	1,247
25,000	210,000	239	239	250	344	470	689	1,025	1,529
30,000	250,000	250	250	263	375	513	750	1,125	1,675
35,000	300,000	290	290	305	440	605	890	1,340	2,000
40,000	350,000	330	330	348	505	698	1,030	1,555	2,325
45,000	375,000	350	350	369	538	744	1,100	1,663	2,488
50,000	420,000	386	386	407	596	827	1,226	1,856	2,780
60,000	500,000	450	450	475	700	975	1,450	2,200	3,300
70,000	600,000	530	530	560	830	1,160	1,730	2,630	3,950
80,000	675,000	590	590	624	928	1,299	1,940	2,953	4,438
90,000	750,000	650	650	688	1,025	1,438	2,150	3,275	4,925
100,000	850,000	730	730	773	1,155	1,623	2,430	3,705	5,575
125,000	1,000,000	850	850	900	1,350	1,900	2,850	4,350	6,550
150,000	1,250,000	1,050	1,050	1,113	1,675	2,363	3,550	5,425	8,175
175,000	1,500,000	1,250	1,250	1,325	2,000	2,825	4,250	6,500	9,800
200,000	1,750,000	1,450	1,450	1,538	2,325	3,288	4,950	7,575	11,425
300,000	2,500,000	2,050	2,050	2,175	3,300	4,675	7,050	10,800	16,300
400,000	3,400,000	2,770	2,770	2,940	4,470	6,340	9,570	14,670	22,150
500,000	4,200,000	3,410	3,410	3,620	5,510	7,820	11,810	18,110	27,350
750,000	6,250,000	5,050	5,050	5,363	8,175	11,613	17,550	26,925	40,675
1,000,000	8,400,000	6,770	6,770	7,190	10,970	15,590	23,570	36,170	54,650

All rates are guaranteed 10-year level term. Rates shown are for non-smoking male in good health. Female rates are equal or less

---

Strategy #45:

BUY ENOUGH LIFE INSURANCE TO MAINTAIN THE LIFE-STYLE OF THE SPOUSE WITH THE SMALLER INCOME.

If one spouse has a much higher income than the other, your strategy changes. If your income is $100,000 per year and your spouse's income is only $20,000 per year, your family lifestyle is probably far greater than the lower-paid spouse could afford alone. You will want to carry enough life insurance on the higher-paid spouse so that, if invested at 12%, the income would allow the lower-paid spouse to maintain the same lifestyle. There is no reason to couple the potential loss of a spouse with the potential loss of a home and investment accounts.

HOW TO AVOID COSTLY LIFE INSURANCE GIMMICKS

Strategy #46:

SELECT A COMPANY THAT SETS YOUR PREMIUM BASED ON YOUR "LAST AGE" RATHER THAN YOUR "NEAR AGE."

If you were born June 1, 1959, how old would you be on March 1, 1999? Though you may think, with some justification, that you are still only 39 years old, some companies calculate their premiums based on your closest next birthday rather than your last birthday. The savings available by being rated at your last birthday instead of your next one can easily add up to several hundred dollars a year.

Strategy #47:

DON'T BUY A WHOLE LIFE INSURANCE POLICY BECAUSE IT PAYS "DIVIDENDS."

Companies that sell life insurance are generally divided into two groups:

1. stock insurance companies
2. mutual insurance companies

Stock insurance companies are owned by shareholders and are run like any other private corporation. The stock is normally sold on the major stock exchanges. The profits these companies earn are returned to the shareholders as dividends.

Mutual insurance companies are technically owned by their policyholders. The objective of these companies, theoretically, is not to earn a profit, but to provide the lowest-priced insurance to their policyholders. Therefore, when a mutual insurance company has taken in more money during the year than it needs for expenses and paying claims, the company is supposed to return some of the excess money to policyholders as dividends. The insurance business doesn't work that way. It is important to note that the insurance companies call the returned money "dividends," but they are not considered dividends even by Revenue Canada and are not taxed as such. Dividends are defined by some provincial insurance departments as a return of overcharged premiums.

When a life insurance policy pays dividends, it is called participating; when it does not, it is called non-participating.

Participating policies pay dividends periodically. There are several options open to the insured when the dividends are paid:

1. The dividends can be returned to the insured in cash.
2. The dividends can be applied to future premiums.
3. The dividends may be used to buy so-called paid-up life insurance; however, the amount of paid-up insurance a dividend can buy is very small.

Most participating policyholders feel they are getting a great life insurance deal because the company pays "dividends." It seems like free money — but it is not. Based on our research into over 1,000 policies from North American stock and mutual insurance companies, we found that the premiums on the dividend-paying policies issued by mutual insurance companies were, on the average, higher by the amount of the dividends! In other words, you are paying too much, then getting your own money back as a dividend! What a scheme!

Strategy #48:
DON'T BUY "DOUBLE INDEMNITY" FOR ACCIDENTAL DEATH.

Instead, increase the base amount of your policy.

When you buy the double indemnity option, twice the face amount of the policy will be paid to the beneficiary, but only if the insured dies an accidental death within a specified period of time after the accident, usually 90 days.

The fact is, the cost per $1,000 for double indemnity is more expensive in some policies than the comparative cost (per $1,000) of basic yearly renewable term (YRT) insurance.

The basic YRT pays a death benefit for any type of death, not just accidental. Rather than spending money on double indemnity, increase your base policy to a higher death benefit for all causes.

Example: On a 35-year-old, non-smoking male, the base rate is about $.75 per $1,000 of YRT life insurance. Accidental death insurance is around $.90 per $1,000.

For the same total premium of $215 covering $100,000 of life insurance with an additional $100,000 accidental death benefit, you could instead own $220,000 of total life insurance protection. Example: The base rate is about $1.36 per $1,000 for a 10-year level term. The same company offers an accidental death benefit at $1 per $1,000, so $100,000 of natural death coverage plus $100,000 of accidental would cost $261 per year. For the same total premium of $261, you could instead own $173,500 of total life insurance protection.

In addition, chances of dying accidentally, instead of from other causes, are only about six out of 100. Those statistics are how the insurance company beats you with optional coverages.

Strategy #49:
NEVER BUY THE DISABILITY PREMIUM WAIVER.

The disability premium waiver (DPW) pays your life insurance premiums if you become totally disabled. The DPW is a form of expensive credit life insurance, one of the biggest financial ripoffs.

The cost of disability premium waiver can cost as much as 12% of the total premium for a life insurance policy.

DPW is not worth it. You must be totally disabled for six months or more to collect. After 24 months of total disability the definition of disability usually deteriorates from not being able to perform the duties of your occupation to not being able to perform the duties of any occupation.

Strategy #50:
DON'T BUY A LIFE INSURANCE POLICY SIMPLY BECAUSE YOU RECOGNIZE THE COMPANY NAME.

The tendency is often to believe that if you recognize the name of the company, somehow the insurance must be better. Name recognition in the insurance business comes mostly from the amount of money spent on advertising, money that is ultimately charged to policyholders as premiums. Because of the high overhead, term policies from the old-line, recognizable companies are usually much more expensive than from the companies you may not recognize. Choose based on lowest rates, not name recognition.

Strategy #51:
NEVER BUY WHOLE LIFE INSURANCE AS AN INVESTMENT.

Strip away all of the sales gimmicks and what you have left are only two basic types of life insurance policies: life insurance with a savings plan, and life insurance with no savings plan. Let's first look at those policies that combine insurance and saving.

WHOLE LIFE INSURANCE

Whole life is a plan where your money goes into a "hole," never to be seen again. Whole life has literally cheated millions out of billions since its inception. Whole life is not an investment at all. Creating cash value with an insurance company makes the insurance you are buying overpriced by 600%.

Whole life policies usually have level premiums (equal yearly instalments) and claim to build tax-deferred cash value. The cash value, which is built up by your premium payments, is minuscule compared to what you could create through proper investments.

EVALUATING CASH VALUE

At age 35, a father buys a whole life insurance policy under the
following terms:

$100,000	Death Benefit (face value)
$1,300	Yearly Premium
$35,400	Dividends after 20 years (paid in $26,000; return on investment equals 2.6% annually)

At age 55 he dies.

What his family could receive with term insurance ($250,000 @ $500/year) and balance invested at 15%:			**What his family receives with whole life insurance (permanent):**
$250,000	Death Benefit		$100,000
$118,000*	Dividends (on paid-up addition plan only)		$ 35,400
$368,000	**TOTAL**		$135,400

*$1,000 invested each year in a tax-deferred investment plan at 15% for 20 years would
accumulate to $117,810.

Whole life is therefore just a grossly overpriced term insurance policy
with a mediocre investment attached.

Recently, while I was on a radio show exposing the ills of the
whole life insurance industry, I received a call from an ex-whole life
salesman who related the following story.

"When I was young and less wise, I became a whole life salesman
for a major insurance company. My second month I sold a whole life
policy to a young couple in their early 20s with two small children.
The premiums were high, but the amount of insurance was only
$20,000 because the majority of the premium went to build the so-
called cash value. Three years later the husband, the insured, died in
an automobile accident, leaving the kids with no father and the family with no income.

"When the wife turned in the insurance claim she received $20,000
but, of course, not a dime of the cash value she had accumulated.
The money barely covered the funeral arrangements and a few
months' family expenses.

"I realized," he said, "that had I done what was good for the family instead of what was good for me and the insurance company, I would have sold the family a term policy. For the same exact premium, I could have sold the family almost $1,000,000 of life insurance with no artificial savings plan and the wife and children would have been taken care of financially for the next 20 years or more.

"This experience," he continued, "shook me emotionally so badly that I quit the life insurance business forever. I honestly felt because of my knowledge and their lack of it, that I had stripped this family of the protection and help they really needed."

Don't make the same mistake. Divide your life insurance from your investments and use your life insurance dollars to buy the maximum necessary protection for those you love and need to protect.

Strategy #52:
DON'T FALL FOR THE BIGGEST LIES ABOUT WHOLE LIFE INSURANCE.

"You can borrow the cash value at 5% to 8%."

What a benefit! The insurance company is charging you interest on your own money, which you overpaid in premiums, and then reduces your death benefit by the amount you borrow.

"Your policy will eventually be paid up."

In reality, a paid-up policy is created only by overpaying your premiums. The overpayment eventually pays your future premiums. Therefore, all paid-up policies are just prepaid policies.

"You'll be earning interest."

Whole life policies pay an average of only 1.3% interest. Worse yet, you never receive it. The interest earned is added to your cash value.

"Your insurance policy is a tax shelter."

You are told that whole life insurance enjoys some special tax status. For instance, you can borrow money from your insurance policy tax-free. You can borrow money from anywhere tax-free!

"If you buy life insurance when you're young, it will cost less."

It is true that yearly premiums are less when you are younger, but only because you will pay greater total premiums over a longer period of time. The only reason to buy life insurance when you are young is financial protection for your family, not saving money.

Strategy #53:
DON'T BUY LIFE INSURANCE TO AVOID THE THREAT OF BEING UNINSURABLE IN THE FUTURE.

Because a life insurance policy can be cancelled by the company only for non-payment of premiums, salesmen often use the threat of future uninsurability to get you to buy an outrageously priced policy.

The truth is that about 97% of all those who apply for life insurance are accepted and approximately 5% are charged extra because of poor health. All insurance is a bet, and in the case of insurability the odds are already overwhelmingly on your side. The question of future insurability is a scare tactic used by salesmen for the purpose of trying to sell you more insurance at an earlier age.

UNIVERSAL LIFE INSURANCE

Universal life is a term insurance policy coupled with an investment plan. The investment can pay a fixed interest rate or, in some cases, can be self-directed into mutual funds. The cost of insurance and fees and commissions are deducted from your premium, and only the balance goes into the investment. Universal life insurance makes a poor plan for many reasons:

1. You are not paid the 8% to 10% claimed by the company.
2. The fees and commissions are far too high and can increase during the period you are paying premiums.
3. There is a huge surrender charge if you change your mind.
4. The face amount is usually guaranteed for only 10 years and can cause you to have high premiums later.

A 45-year-old man buys a universal life policy combining a $100,000 death benefit with an investment promising a yearly return of 10% for 20 years. He pays $2,000 in premiums per year or $167 a month. He is paid the 10% only on the money that goes into the investment; that is, what is left from the $2,000 premiums after the fees, commissions, and, of course, the cost of the insurance itself, are deducted. In a typical universal life policy, the first-year fees and commissions alone can amount to $600. He loses 30% of his $2,000 to fees and commissions. Only about $1,100 the first year goes into the investment and earns 10%.

Let's say tomorrow afternoon you stroll into your bank and put your $2,000 into a certificate of deposit. "No problem," the new accounts officer tells you. "By the way, there is a $600 charge for opening the account." How quickly would you be out the door, into the parking lot, leaving only a trail of dust behind you? Losing the money to life insurance makes no more sense than losing money to the bank. The actual yearly investment return on most universal life policies is less than 6% for the first 10 years. Each year in a universal life policy, the cost of the insurance increases, further reducing the amount that goes into the investment, but you never see it happening because your premium remains the same. The high surrender charge penalty is the insurance company's method of making it impractical for you to change your mind and drop the policy. Those companies that charge the least in front-end fees usually have the biggest surrender charges.

EVALUATING UNIVERSAL LIFE INSURANCE PLANS: IS THERE A GOOD ONE?

The Charles J. Givens Organization has studied 200 universal life policies with the following results:

1. THE COST OF THE INSURANCE IN A UNIVERSAL LIFE PLAN

In the ideal universal life policy, the term insurance yearly premium would compare to the lowest-cost yearly renewable term (YRT). No plan we evaluated had really competitively priced term insurance.

2. NO FRONT-END COMMISSIONS

In the ideal policy, there would be no commission or front-end load on the amount of the premium going into the investment plan. The commission paid on the universal life insurance should be no more than the lowest commissions on a term policy. The lowest commission rates we could find were about 5%, the highest about 90%, and the average about 70% the first year. In all cases the commission applies to the entire premium, not just the insurance portion. Those with the lowest front-end commissions usually had the largest surrender charges.

3. SURRENDER CHARGES

The surrender charge is the money the insurance company keeps out of your investment should you change your mind and cancel the policy. The ideal surrender charge is zero; second best would be 5% the first year, declining to zero after the first five years. The surrender charges are highest during the first five years and run as much as 30% to 100% of your total cash value. Often the higher the up-front fees and commissions, the lower the surrender charges.

4. CHOICE OF INVESTMENTS

Other than the cost, the most important point to consider is where your money is invested. The ideal plan would give you a choice of no-load mutual funds. The poorest plan is one that invests your money at a fixed or fluctuating interest rate. Some plans do offer mutual funds as an option. As you can see, current universal life policies fail in all but the choice of investment category.

TERM INSURANCE — THE RIGHT INSURANCE

Strategy #54:
BUY ONLY TERM LIFE INSURANCE AND DEVOTE THE REST OF YOUR FINANCIAL PLAN TO PROSPEROUS LIVING.

Term insurance is pure insurance protection, no bells, whistles, fancy packaging or investments to buy. The premiums per $1,000 of insurance are therefore the lowest of any form of life insurance. If the insured dies within a given period of time, the company pays the agreed-upon sum of money to his/her beneficiary. Once a term policy is purchased, future insurability is guaranteed up to age 70, 90, or even 100 depending on the company that issues the policy.

You can look at term life insurance as if the insured bet the premiums paid on his/her policy against the possibility of collecting the amount of insurance over some period of time. If the insured dies, he or she wins the bet, so to speak, and the heirs collect the face value of the policy. If the insured lives, the insurance company wins by collecting premiums without paying off. Obviously, life insurance is one bet you always hope to lose.

As each of the terms for the insurance comes to an end, the insured will discover that the cost of the insurance for the next term will increase. Why? Because the insured is getting older. The mortality table (page 46) demonstrates an ever-increasing number of deaths per 1,000 as the sample population moves upward from age zero to 100. Since the risk of death is greater, the cost of the insurance is greater.

Term is the least expensive life insurance, often 50% to 60% less than the insurance-plus-investment policies such as whole life and universal life. Term insurance pays salesmen far less in commissions and, therefore, is seldom offered if you don't insist. Because insurance policies make poor investments, term insurance is the life-insurance choice of all knowledgeable insurance buyers.

Although most people falsely believe that term insurance cannot be bought as you get older, the truth is that both yearly renewable term and level term guarantee your insurability to age 90, and with some companies, to age 100.

Strategy #55:

CHOOSE THE RIGHT KIND OF TERM INSURANCE FOR YOUR SITUATION — YEARLY RENEWABLE TERM OR LEVEL PREMIUM TERM.

There are three different types of term insurance you should understand.

1. YEARLY RENEWABLE TERM (YRT)

You buy a policy for one year at the end of which time you receive a renewal notice for the next year's premium. The younger you are, the lower the rates begin, increasing each year by a few dollars. YRT is the least expensive and the best value of the three types of term insurance. The insurance is guaranteed renewable every year as long as you pay your premium. As you get older, your life expectancy decreases, so the premium increases. Regardless of age, YRT polices have, in the past, been the best insurance value.

2. DECREASING TERM

With decreasing term, your yearly premiums remain the same, but the amount of insurance decreases each year. Decreasing term is used for both mortgage insurance and credit life insurance and is usually overpriced by 400% or more when used for those purposes.

3. LEVEL PREMIUM TERM (LPT)

You choose a policy period, five, 10, or 20 years. Both your premium and the amount of the insurance remain constant. You are actually overpaying the premiums in the early years so they don't increase in later years — not a good strategy since the younger you are, the less assets and cash flow you usually have. If you cancel because you find a better deal, you lose all the overpayments, and therefore this kind of term insurance is a poor value for good money managers.

In the past couple of years, however, new LPT policies have been created that make them the best overall financial bargain.

There are at least three unique circumstances in which level premium term rates will always be lower than yearly renewable term:

Age Group — If the yearly rates in your age group for level term are lower over a five- to 10-year period than equivalent rates for yearly renewable term.

Over 50 — If you are older than 50 and believe that you will have a need for life insurance for at least 10 years. After age 53 the annual increase in YRT premiums becomes far greater than in prior years, making level term a better choice.

Medical Condition — If you have a pre-existing medical or weight problem or your blood and/or urine samples indicate high levels of cholesterol, triglycerides, nicotine, caffeine, or alcohol. These factors may reduce life expectancy, causing additional premiums to be charged. Level term will have lower average yearly premiums.

Strategy #56:
**BUY YEARLY RENEWABLE TERM INSURANCE IF YOU
HAVE A SHORT-TERM NEED FOR
INSURANCE COVERAGE.**

If you need a life insurance policy for less than five years, such as life insurance required to obtain a personal or business loan, yearly renewable term may be your best bet. YRT rates are often best for one- to five-year periods when the absolute least price is the main consideration.

Many insurance companies offer the first three years of YRT insurance at an exceptionally low rate, believing that once you buy, they've got you and you won't notice the exceptionally high premiums you'll pay in the future. You can use these early-year low rates to your advantage when your need for extra coverage is short term.

Strategy #57:
BUY YEARLY RENEWABLE TERM IF YOU ARE A SMOKER OR ARE OVERWEIGHT, BUT INTEND TO CHANGE YOUR HABITS.

Another reason to buy YRT instead of level term is that you are either a smoker or overweight, but intend to change these habits in the next three years. Rates for those who are overweight or who smoke are much higher for both yearly renewable term and level premium term policies. You can profit from short-term YRT insurance now and then qualify for low non-smoker or better health rates in a few years.

Strategy #58:
REPLACE YOUR EXISTING WHOLE LIFE AND UNIVERSAL LIFE INSURANCE POLICIES WITH TERM INSURANCE.

There are no valid financial reasons for buying or keeping whole life or universal life policies at any age. You are always better off with term insurance and investing the difference yourself. If your health has deteriorated and you are no longer insurable, you should keep your existing policy. Otherwise, drop the whole life and universal life after replacing with term; reinvest your cash value in mutual funds or other good investments.

Get together all existing life insurance policies you own, including those on children. First, buy the right amount of the right kind of term insurance you determined earlier. Second, cancel your existing whole life and universal life policies using my strategies. Third, transfer your cash value to a tax shelter.

Strategy #59:
BORROW AND REINVEST YOUR LIFE INSURANCE CASH VALUE.

A second alternative, if your health makes you uninsurable, is to borrow the cash value of your policy at 5% to 8% interest and reinvest at 12% to 20% using investment strategies in the investment section. Borrowing your cash value is also a tax-free transaction.

Under the current Canadian tax laws, the general rule is that interest paid on borrowed money is deductible if the money is used as investment capital with a reasonable expectation of profit. Investing the borrowed cash value of your life insurance in a profitable investment makes the interest tax deductible.

Strategy #60:
DON'T GIVE LIFE INSURANCE PROCEEDS TO YOUR HEIRS IN A LUMP SUM.

Never set up your life insurance policy to give the proceeds to your family or other heirs in a lump sum. The $100,000 to $500,000 of income all in one year with no income in future years just doesn't work. Set up your life insurance plan to have the proceeds invested so income will continuously and automatically be generated for an unlimited number of years or until yearly income is no longer necessary.

Only then can you be certain that the money will last until the kids are grown and your spouse is provided for. After the kids are grown, you can have the principal split among your family members. In eight out of 10 cases studied, lump sum insurance proceeds left to families were totally gone in one to five years through unintentional mismanagement or poor financial advice.

REORGANIZING YOUR TOTAL INSURANCE PLAN

A typical family of four can easily pay as much as $4,700 on the myriad apparently logical insurance options (see column A, following). By using the life and casualty insurance strategies in chapters 3 and 4, their insurance costs are cut to $1,550, a savings of $3,150 per year.

Using column C, write in your current insurance premiums. As you use the strategies in these chapters, enter your new reduced premiums in column D to determine your total savings.

	A	B	You C	D
Type of Insurance	Before	After	Before	After
Life Insurance on children	$200	$ 0		
Universal Life Insurance	1,500	0		
Term Life Insurance	0	300		
Credit Life Insurance on loans	200	0		
Automobile Insurance	1,100	600		
Specialty Insurance	200	0		
Mortgage Insurance	600	300		
Homeowners Insurance	300	200		
Rental Car Insurance (vacation)	100	0		
Umbrella Liability Insurance	0	150		
Disability Insurance	500	0		
Other				
TOTAL	$4,700	$1,550		

Chapter 5

GIVE YOURSELF CREDIT

'Tis against some Men's Principle to pay interest, and seems against others' interest to pay the Principal.

Benjamin Franklin, *Poor Richard's Almanac*, 1753

Objective: Get control of your credit bureau file and establish good credit habits.

The bank must have slipped because it issued me my first credit card just before Christmas in 1965. The timing couldn't have been more appropriate. As in other gift-buying seasons, I was flat broke. I immediately charged $300 for a magnificent Tyco "HO" gauge miniature railroad layout "in one thousand easy-for-a-child-to-assemble" pieces. Ever since my mother sold my prized Lionel train set to get money for food I had dreamed of the day when I would have sons of my own old enough to help me disguise my desire to re-create my youth.

The night before Christmas, I was in the attic until six in the morning putting together the Ping-Pong-table-sized train layout. Time was running out, along with my alertness and patience. The airplane glue, with its high concentration of acetone, put a smile on my face, but made me feel like I was putting all those little plastic pieces together with gloves on. No matter. The boys were elated; Dad was exhausted. It was my Christmas "biggy" and I had pulled it off. Pride lit up the room as chemical smoke poured from the tiny engine, puffing its way through plastic towns, switches, and pâpier-maché mountains.

By three o'clock in the afternoon, I was asleep on the couch and the train began a perilous journey. Waking to the sound of a hammer striking metal, I stumbled into the garage to see my son Chuck, still in his blue Christmas robe, carefully dismantling the expensive, heavily financed engine into a hundred pieces. Resisting the temptation to faint, and holding back the tears, I screamed, "Chuck, what are you doing?"

"Dad, this is so neat. I just want to see how it works."

How can you get angry with a curious four-year-old? The train was gone, like so many Christmas toys, in a few, short hours. But the payments continued through the following Christmas.

There seems to be no end to the young couples I meet who have managed, quite unintentionally, to create the same kind of credit problem, by charging when cash is short and hoping the money will be there when each payment comes due.

There are three uses of credit (listed here from worst to best):

WORST — to purchase perishables, such as meals, gas, groceries, airline tickets.

BETTER — to purchase depreciables, such as automobiles, furniture, clothes.

BEST — to purchase appreciables, such as mutual funds, a home, or other investments.

Charging perishables is the least desirable and most misused form of credit. Payments linger long after the goods or services are gone. One month after you charge a meal you pay for the potatoes, the next month the steak, and finally the dessert. While buying this month's food, you're paying for last month's feasts.

Depreciable purchases include goods and services that will never again be worth what you paid for them. A better use of credit, yes, but stacking up long-term payments will eventually bury you.

The best use of credit is borrowing money at a low rate and investing at a higher rate of return. Appreciables include a home with a mortgage, margined mutual fund shares, rental real estate, and a leveraged business or RRSP. Leverage is the use of borrowed money to make money — often called using OPM (other people's money).

Financial success requires practiced discipline, and there is no better place to practice than with credit management. There are a few simple, but powerful strategies that will allow you to get control of credit.

Strategy #61:
**PAY OFF CREDIT CARD PERISHABLE PURCHASES
EVERY MONTH.**

Pay the credit card purchases you make this month with a cheque next month when you receive the bill. Never wait until you think you have the money — that time may never come. If you charge $100 for gasoline and meals, pay $100. The high interest charged by most credit card issuers, combined with the manner of calculating such interest (many cards start the meter ticking from day of purchase, not date of statement) makes credit card consumable purchases one of the least attractive uses of credit.

Strategy #62:

DEDUCT A CREDIT CARD CHARGE IN YOUR CHEQUE REGISTER AS IF YOU HAD MADE THE PURCHASE WITH A CHEQUE.

Count the money gone — it is. Circle the credit card purchases as you enter them in your cheque register and deduct the amount from your bank balance. The total of the circled items represents the extra credit card payment you will make at the end of the month. No more end-of-the-month shock. Because you have already deducted your credit card purchases from your balance, you have the money in your chequing account to make your payment.

Strategy #63:

DEVELOP A POSITIVE CREDIT PROFILE WITH THE "BIG 8."

The "big 8" elements of a positive credit profile, in order of importance, are:

1. A positive up-to-date credit report
2. A home with a mortgage
3. An American Express card and/or Diner's Club card
4. A job you've held for a year or more
5. A current or paid-off bank loan
6. A MasterCard or VISA
7. A department store credit card
8. A telephone in your name

The more checks you have, the easier it is to borrow money.

You can survive in Canada if you have poor credit — or worse yet no credit — but poor credit is a definite handicap to wealth building. To develop a positive credit profile, qualify yourself in as many categories as you can based on the above chart. The more categories under which you qualify, the easier it is to get credit.

Here is a model of a credit-scoring process taken directly from the procedures book of a finance company that will let you score yourself.

FACTORS	POINTS	YOUR SCORE	FACTORS	POINTS	YOUR SCORE
			Monthly Loan & Credit Cd. Pymts		
Marital Status					
Married	1	___	Zero to $200.00	1	___
Not Married	0	___	Over $200.00	0	___
Age			*Credit History*		
21 to 25	0	___	Loan — most banks	2	___
26 to 64		___			
65 and over		___			
Monthly Income			*Residence*		
Up to $600	1	___	Rent Unfurnished	1	___
$600 to $800	2	___	Own without Mtge	4	___
$800 to $1,000		___	Own with Mtge	3	___
over $1,000	6	___	Any Other	0	___
In Addition			*Previous Residence*		
Phone in Your			0–5 years	0	___
Name	2	___	6 Years and Up	1	___
Chequing					
or Savings	2	___			
			TOTAL POINTS		___

Loan and mortgage applications are usually approved or rejected based on a point system. One to six points are assigned to each item in eight different categories. If the number of points you score overall exceeds a certain total determined by the lender, your loan is approved; if you score less than the required total, your loan will likely be rejected. About 15 points is the minimum score required to pass the credit test. The more you score, the better your chances of obtaining credit.

Bank loan officers will not confirm the use of any point system evaluation. However, since the main criterion for loan approval is your ability to pay, a higher score means you are more likely to get your loan.

STRATEGIES FOR CONTROLLING YOUR CREDIT BUREAU FILE

Strategy #64:
CHECK YOUR CREDIT BUREAU FILE ONCE A YEAR.

The provincial consumer reporting agency (credit bureau) is the first place your potential creditors and employers will check. A positive up-to-date credit file is your responsibility, not that of the credit bureau, and is something you create, not something that happens automatically.

My organization recently conducted a credit bureau accuracy study. To our surprise, we discovered that 24 out of 25 credit bureau reports contained incomplete or incorrect data. Wait until you see yours! One report showed a man married to his first wife, whom he hadn't seen in eight years, and working for a company that had been out of business for six years.

Every credit bureau, by law, must on request give you a complete, accurate report of everything in your file, including your credit history and a list of every potential creditor and employer who has been given information from your credit file during the past year. Knowing what others know about you is half the battle.

To obtain a credit report, you are required to identify yourself by completing a mail-in form, or appearing at the credit bureau. A sample request form appears on the right. There is no charge to inspect your file. Every major city in Canada has a credit bureau (there are over 150 in Canada). Look in the telephone book under "Credit Reporting Agencies" or "Credit Bureaus."

Credit reporting agencies do not evaluate your credit file, but make the information available to credit bureau members who may be banks, mortgage companies, department stores, or other issuers of credit.

There are several strategies that will help you control your credit file.

Credit Bureau of Greater Toronto

Subject: Request to review my personal credit history file pursuant to the provisions of the Consumer Reporting Act of Ontario.

Please Print

Surname:_____ Given Name:_____ Initial:_____

Spouse's Name:_____

Date of Birth:_____ Social Insurance #:_____

Present Address:_____

Former Address (if present address has changed in past two years):

_____

Present Employer:_____

Occupation:_____

Former Employer (if present employer has changed in past two

years):_____

Telephone Number: Business_____ Home_____

I certify that the above information is correct and that I am the person so identified. NOTE: It is an offence under the Ontario Consumer Reporting Act to procure or attempt to procure personal information under false pretences.

Please Sign

Date: _____   Signature: _____

(Office Use Only)

Identification Produced: Completed

Call Consumer		
Send Consumer Copy		
Call Amended		
Send Amended		
Make Card		
Revision		
Update File (not revision)		
Completed (file back)		

Strategy #65:
KNOW HOW TO "READ" A CREDIT REPORT.

Credit reports are easy to read once you get the hang of it, and most come with explicit instructions. If you still have trouble, the credit bureau is required by law to spend time with you at its office explaining your report.

The credit bureau uses a rating system with the letters "O," "R," or "I," followed by a number from 0 to 9. "O" is a 30- to 90-day open account. "R" represents "revolving accounts" such as credit cards and department store accounts, and "I" is used for "instalment credit," such as an automobile or furniture loan. R-1 is the best; R-9 usually means the debt is a bad debt, it has been placed for collection, or the party has skipped. Your goal, of course, is to get all of your accounts to R-1 or I-1 status. When you do, the credit world is yours. A few prompt payments will usually upgrade any account.

CREDIT REPORT CODES

The following codes are used on a standard credit report:

TYPE OF ACCOUNT

Open Account (30 days or 90 days)	O
Revolving or Option (open-end account)	R
Instalment (fixed number of payments)	I

CURRENT MANNER OF PAYMENT

Too new to rate; approved but not used	0
Pays account as agreed	1
Pays 30 to 60 days late, one payment late	2
Pays 60 to 90 days late, two payments late	3
Pays 90 to 120 days late, three payments late	4
Pays later than 120 days	5
Making payments under consolidation order	7
Repossession	8
Bad debt; placed for collection; skip	9

The "Type of Account" and "Current Manner of Payment" are shown together in the "Credit History" section of a credit report under present status; e.g., R1 means "revolving account, pays as agreed."

Strategy #66:

CORRECT ALL PERSONAL DATA ERRORS ON YOUR CREDIT FILE.

Included in your personal data are your address, social insurance number, employment history, income, and telephone. This part of a credit file is the easiest to correct, but often the most inaccurate. Since as many as 24 out of 25 credit files can contain errors, check even the most obvious of entries.

Strategy #67:

HAVE THE CREDIT BUREAU RE-VERIFY AND CORRECT ANY INCORRECT CREDIT DATA.

Your credit files may contain information about late payments that weren't late or bad accounts that are not yours. Request that the credit bureau re-verify the incorrect data. The credit bureau has an obligation to use its best efforts to check and correct the file. Check to be sure the corrected data is entered into your file.

Occasionally, your creditor's records are wrong and the re-verified data will remain incorrect. If so, you will begin to get the runaround. Contact the creditor yourself to correct the errors and furnish cancelled cheques or other necessary information supporting your position. If you are not able to resolve your disagreement, write to your provincial representative, who has the power to order a credit bureau to correct information in your file.

Strategy #68:

HAVE ALL MISSING POSITIVE CREDIT DATA ADDED TO YOUR CREDIT FILE.

You will be surprised when you see your credit file at how much data and how many accounts are missing. Although there is no law or rule that you are required to supply any negative credit data about yourself, you have the right by law and the duty to yourself to have all the positive data and accounts added to your file.

Supply the credit bureau in writing with a list of all charge accounts, credit cards, loans, and mortgages you have kept current. Include the account numbers. Include loans that have been paid off or accounts no longer in use.

Strategy #69:
ADD THE REST OF THE STORY TO YOUR CREDIT FILE.

You have the legal right to add your side of the story to your credit file; that is, why your payments were late, or that credit information in your file is incorrect and is being re-verified. Add what you feel to be important information — such as being unemployed during the period when the payments were late or that you moved and the bills went to the wrong address. One failure of the credit reporting system is that your file often shows how many times you have been 30, 60, or 90 days late in paying, but does not show how long ago. Add to your file the fact that all late payments were prior to a certain date, and why they were late and that payments are now current. Your side of the story can make a difference to your potential creditors and employers.

Strategy #70:
HAVE THE CREDIT BUREAU REMOVE ANY DEROGATORY INFORMATION OUTSIDE THE STATUTORY LIMITS.

Negative information, such as a bankruptcy or convictions for crimes, can remain in your credit file no longer than seven years (six years in Nova Scotia). You have the right by law to a credit file that does not contain information older than these statutory limits. The credit bureau must remove older data, but you must check to make certain it is done.

Strategy #71:

USE SMALL CLAIMS COURT TO RESOLVE CREDIT DISPUTES.

What if you follow these instructions but can't seem to get a creditor to supply correct information to the credit bureau? Take 'em to court — small claims court, that is. (Small claims court is known under different names in different provinces. If in doubt, contact any local office of your provincial court system.)

For a small filing fee and without a lawyer, you can, in most provinces, file a suit claiming damages from the incorrect information. You probably won't have to go to court since it would be far less expensive for the creditor to straighten out the error than to pay a lawyer to fight your claim. Name both the lender and the credit bureau in the suit.

STRATEGIES WHEN CREDIT IS TOUGH TO GET

Strategy #72:

IF YOU ARE REFUSED CREDIT, FIND OUT WHY.

If you are turned down for a loan or mortgage, you need to know why, and finding out is in your best interest. After you receive the notice stating denial of your loan, write the company that rejected you. The lender should tell you specifically why your application was denied. (In Canada, lenders have no legal obligation to tell you why they turned you down, however.) You should then upgrade your credit bureau file and your next credit application to increase your chances of being approved.

Strategy #73:

TO GET CREDIT AS A SMALL BUSINESS OWNER, INCORPORATE AND LIST YOURSELF AS AN EMPLOYEE.

If you've ever owned a business, you know that credit is tough to get until you can show substantial income, assets, and longevity.

Try this: list yourself as an employee of the company and not the owner, and then arrange to have your accountant verify your income. Yet another approach is to incorporate your business. For less than $500 in most provinces, you can incorporate your small business without a lawyer by contacting your provincial corporate ministry for the appropriate forms and instructions. (If you should fill out any form incorrectly, in most cases you will be sent a "deficiency notice" telling you specifically what you did wrong. Simply correct the error as indicated and re-submit.) Next, pay yourself a big salary and simultaneously deduct your expenses as employee business expenses, furnishing copies of your T4 forms (instead of your personal tax forms) to a prospective lender. Give the lender the phone number of your bookkeeper, accountant, or other involved persons in order to verify your employment and salary.

IF YOU WANT THE CREDIT, YOU MUST LEARN TO PLAY THE GAME! STRATEGIES TO REBUILD YOUR CREDIT

Strategy #74:
USE A CO-SIGNER TO HELP (RE)ESTABLISH YOUR CREDIT.

By getting parents or friends to co-sign on mortgages, bank loans, or credit cards, creditors will extend credit to you they might otherwise refuse. A positive payment record will eventually qualify you for credit on your own.

Strategy #75:
**OVERCOME POOR CREDIT WITH A SECURED
CREDIT CARD.**

If credit troubles are reflected in your file, create enough good credit to offset the poor credit. Establish new credit sources as quickly as you can, and keep ALL payments up to date. Bury the bad among the good.

The easiest way to establish or re-establish your credit is through a secured MasterCard or VISA card. Secured means that you have made a deposit equal to or greater than the amount of credit you want, from $1,000 to $3,500.

CIBC, for example, offers such a card (VISA) if the applicant is willing to put up twice the amount of credit requested in cash.

The National Bank offers a secured MasterCard on the same terms. If you opt for a secured Gold MasterCard from the National, however, you need only put up 150% (1.5 times) of the amount of credit sought. (The card fee itself is slightly higher, however.)

After you have made regular, timely payments for 12 months or so, the security requirement is dropped and your deposit returned to you. After you have made payments, have your account re-verified and your credit file updated by the credit bureau.

Strategy #76:

TO RE-HABILITATE CREDIT, BORROW THE BANK'S MONEY AND USE IT AS SECURITY FOR A LOAN.

A banker is a person who will loan you all the money you want as soon as you can prove you don't need it. Banks, however, love to make fully secured loans to almost anyone. Here is how you get a bank to participate in your credit-building plan. Look the loan officer straight in the eye and say, "Mr. Banker, I need your help. I'd like to borrow $3,500. But, before you check my credit, let me tell you that you won't like what you see. I would like you to put the $3,500 in a savings account here in your bank and you can put a hold on the money. You will have no risk since you have the money, and by making monthly payments, I can (re)establish my credit."

During one of the shakiest periods of my credit life, I used this credit re-habilitation strategy with great success. I had recently exited the corporate world and bought a franchise for $5,000 to market motivational programs. Having been a typical medium-income, no-cash-on-hand corporate exec, I had to borrow the $5,000 and sell some stock to raise the start-up capital. I sold my home and boat, and ventured off to Gainesville, Florida, where there was no competition. The remaining money went out far faster than sales came in. After two months in Gainesville, a week before Christmas, I was broke. MasterCard and Mobil had demanded their credit cards back. My burgundy Continental Mark III was suddenly repossessed because of late payments. A vacate notice from the apartment manager was stapled to the door — something about over-due rent.

No car, no credit cards, no credit, no rent money, no cash, no Christmas presents — no kidding! The next step was the one-stop source of instant credit no matter what your credit history — the pawn shop. With tears in her eyes, my wife, Bonnie, handed me our only pawnable asset — an $800 set of sterling silver flatware, a Christmas present from her parents the year before. The unconcerned pawnbroker and I played a tug-of-war between the measly $80 he originally offered and the $200 I thought I deserved. We finally called it quits at $125, $80 of which went for the kids' Christmas presents, and the other $45 for Christmas dinner.

The first "must" was a rental car — difficult to get without a credit card. I borrowed $40 from a friend and spent the afternoon talking about money with the operator of an independent car rental agency. After two hours I said, "By the way, my wife could use a car while I'm gone the next couple of days." When he asked for a credit card, I told him I didn't have one with me, but was prepared to put down a $40 cash deposit. I could hardly believe my eyes as he pulled out the rental contract with a smile on his face. That little car got me through the next three weeks, until I had the money to take it back.

During the next month, I managed to stall the landlord, feed the family on cereal and fast-food hamburgers, and finally get some regular income from my business. Still no credit, however. I went to a finance company and began: "Look, Sir, give me some help. Lend me $300, but don't give me the money. Stick the cheque in your bottom desk drawer so you have no risk. I'll make payments, and you can give me a good credit report when anyone calls."

"Highly irregular," he said.

"Highly irregular situation," I responded.

After fifteen minutes of all the reasons why not, he finally said, "Why not?" And I was on my way to credit recovery. Later the same day, I went back to his office to sign the papers. Out of habit, I guess, they actually gave me the cheque. I did not pose a single objection. I used the $300 to open a chequing account at a bank down the street and then promptly went over to the loan officer. I began with the "I need your help ..." story, and told him I was already a customer of the bank, handing him my chequing account $300 deposit slip on which the ink was still wet. He lent me $1,000, and put the money in a savings account. The next day, I wrote cheques for two payments from the $300 I had originally put in the bank chequing account, and gave them to the teller with payment coupons. I wrote another $50 cheque to the finance company.

Still I needed a car. A friend drove me to a Cadillac leasing agency in Orlando. Sal, the manager, explained that it was four o'clock and he couldn't run my application through the credit bureau until the next day. I pulled out my aces.

"Sal, I live in Gainesville," I said. "How about if I give you two excellent credit references — one bank and one finance company?" Sal checked and found that I was two payments ahead on each account. Neither bothered to tell him the loans were less than a week old. I drove out of the lot with a beautiful new blue metal-flake Sedan de Ville. Within another 30 days, I had $4,000 in the bank from my business, the rent paid, a new Cadillac, and much of my credit restored. The next month I went back to Sal and leased another brand-new Cadillac for my wife, Bonnie. Nothing is impossible.

The cost of this strategy to you is minimal. Although you are paying interest on the loan, the bank is paying you interest on your savings account. Don't take no for an answer. Keep reaffirming that you need the banker's help and will eventually become an excellent customer of the bank. Persistence always overcomes barriers. Once you find a bank that will make the loan, make two payments within the first 30 days. Go to a second bank and repeat the entire process. You can show the loan officer at the second bank the one good credit reference you now have at the first bank. Make two payments at the second bank as well. Now you have two excellent credit references. After 90 days use the money in your savings account to pay off the balance of the loan. Have the credit bureau check your bank loan accounts, which now show that your payments were made on time and the loans paid off early.

Strategy #77:
KNOW YOUR CREDIT "RIGHTS."

All provinces (except Alberta and New Brunswick) have special legislation that protects your right to know what lenders think of your credit. Here are the basic rights granted in Ontario's Consumer Reporting Act:

1. To obtain from a credit bureau a report of what's in your credit file.
2. To know who has inquired into your credit file — stores, banks, and employers.

3. To request re-verification by the credit bureau if information is incorrect.
4. To get missing data added to your file.
5. To have detrimental credit information, such as a bankruptcy, removed from your file after seven years. (In Nova Scotia after six years.)
6. To put your side of the story in your credit file.
7. To privacy of the information in your file from anyone other than legitimate members of the credit reporting agency.
8. To have your credit report transferred from one area in Canada to another any time you move.
9. To use Consumer Reporting Act administrators and/or small claims court to resolve any disputes with the credit bureau about incorrect, inaccurate information in your file.
10. To know exactly why you were refused credit. You must contact the institution refusing credit as soon as possible. Note that in Canada if your credit rating is "good" and you are refused credit, the company does not have to tell you why you were refused.
11. To remain silent about poor credit information that does not currently appear in your file.

Strategy #78:
WHEN BORROWING MONEY, NEVER TAKE
NO FOR AN ANSWER.

Because one store, bank, or mortgage company turns you down, that doesn't mean that everyone will. Make obtaining credit a game and say to yourself, "I will not be denied." I once saw a now successful young lady get turned down by five banks in two days for a $2,000 business loan. The sixth bank said yes. Where would she be today if she had given up after five banks?

Use your good credit to build your wealth. Work on overcoming the stigma of poor credit in the shortest time possible, but most of all, put your credit profile and credit power where it belongs — in your own hands.

Chapter 6

BORROWING BASICS —
MORTGAGE AND LOAN
STRATEGIES

*Live within your income even if you have to borrow money
to do it.*

Josh Billings, humorist

Objective: Cut the cost of borrowing money by 30% to 50%.

It has been said that you are worth what you owe. At least that's
what you're worth to those you owe. Borrowing money has become a
way of life for too many of us. In this chapter we will look at powerful strategies for borrowing money, new types of mortgages that can
save you thousands, when it pays to refinance your home, and how
to cut your interest by 30% by choosing the right term for your automobile and personal loans. None of these strategies requires extra
time or effort — only knowledge and knowing what to say.

PERSONAL CREDIT

Strategy #79:
**GET TO KNOW A LOAN OFFICER AT A BANK
FOR MORE FINANCIAL CLOUT.**

Think for a moment of the names of the bank loan officers you already know or have dealt with, if any.

Now is the time to begin cultivating a better relationship with those you already know, and take the opportunity to begin a new banking friendship.

If you have no current banking relationship in place, stop in at two or three neighbourhood branches and open a dialogue with a loan officer by asking about the bank's current terms on automobile loans — just to break the ice. As conversation openers, try asking the banker personal questions from this list:

- How long have you been with this bank?
- What got you interested in banking?
- What are your goals in the financial world?
- How many kids do you have?
- Where do you borrow money when you need it?
- Do you ever have good deals on bank repo cars?

Why go to all this trouble? For one thing, establishing a relationship with the key people at banks opens up a world of opportunity for you. Many bank officers have a discretionary loan limit — an amount of money they can loan out without seeking approval from higher up. Once a banker gets to know you a bit better, you may find it easier to tap into this credit line.

Another example of "financial clout" is your banker's ability to waive procedures for you when you need a favour. For example, many banks have a "rule" that you can cancel cheques only in person, and, even then, only with a written direction. That's fine, but what if you have a cheque you know has fallen into the wrong hands and you are hundreds of miles away from your bank?

Establishing a personal relationship with your banker will enable you to bypass these and other rules over time.

Strategy #80:
ALWAYS ASK TO HAVE ADD-ON INTEREST CONVERTED TO THE ANNUAL PERCENTAGE RATE (APR) FACTOR BEFORE AGREEING TO THE TERMS OF A LOAN.

If you borrow money to make a purchase of certain goods and services, how much will it cost you? Add-on interest is a method used by banks and finance companies to quote a low interest rate while actually ripping you off with a high interest rate. Federal and provincial legislation requires that lenders disclose the actual cost of borrowing.

Interest rates on these loans are calculated using two totally different methods:

1. Simple Interest Method: The method of computing interest that charges you interest only on your monthly principal balance.
2. Add-on Method: The more expensive method and the more common method. Your interest is not on the outstanding balance each month.

How much is the real interest charge? While you do not have the use of the entire amount of money that you borrowed for the number of months you borrowed it — since you are paying it back bit by bit — you are still paying interest on the entire amount you borrowed! Therefore, the true interest rate is much higher.

See the table below comparing the simple interest and add-on methods using a $1,000 loan for one year at 12% interest. In this example, the borrower thinks he is borrowing $1,000 and paying 12% interest for the use of the funds until the loan comes due. In fact, the lender has pre-calculated the interest at $120, then added this to the principal ($1,120), and then set up an equal payment schedule based on $1,120/12 or $93.33. However, much like a mortgage, each $93.33 payment is in effect a blend of principal and interest. Clearly, by the final payment due in the last month, the borrower is paying interest as if he still had access to the full $1,000 whereas, in fact, he has not had the full $1,000 in his hands since the first month. (He has been paying it back, little by little, ever since.)

Method	Interest Rate	Quoted Finances	Approximate APR
Simple Interest	12.0%	$66.20	12.0%
Add-On	12.0%	$120.00	21.5%

With add-on interest you would be paying 81% more in finance charges than you would be with simple interest!

When calculating the true cost of a loan, be sure to count in all financing and qualifying charges such as appraisal costs. For example, consider a $10,000 loan at 12% with a $235 qualifying fee and $200 in special charges. If you choose monthly payments and a two-year term, your payments (including the $435 which is now part of the loan) will be $491.21 for a total payback of $11,789. In this case, considering that the original loan was supposed to be $10,000, the interest rate is 16.33%, not 12%.

Strategy #81:

NEVER SIGN A LOAN AGREEMENT
CONTAINING THE RULE OF 78.

In most instalment loans you are allowed to pay the loan off prior to its maturity. Since the interest is normally prepaid, some loan agreements provide for a refund of interest based on the rule of 78. The rule, which is unfair to borrowers, is used to determine the portion of the total interest charges the lender receives when you pay off your loan early.

Example: You borrow $1,000 for 12 months paid back in equal instalments. If you pay it off in three months and the total finance charge is $80 (8%), the amount the lender will receive is determined below.

Add the numbers 1 through 12, the total is 78. (1 + 2 + 3 + 4 + 5 + 6 + 7 + 8 + 9 + 10 + 11 + 12 = 78)

Even if the loan is repaid after one month, the lender will receive 12/78 of the total interest.

If you pay it off after two months, the lender receives 23/78 (12 + 11 divided by 78).

In our example the loan is paid off after three months, so the lender gets 33/78 of the total interest (12 + 11 + 10 divided by 78).

This comes out to be $33.85 ([33 divided by 78] x $80). Instead of the 8% promised ($80 for $1,000 loan), you would be paying an interest rate of 13.54% — about 69% more than you expected to pay.

MORTGAGE LOANS

Strategy #82:

LIVE ALMOST FREE BY BUYING INSTEAD OF RENTING.

Before considering a mortgage, you must first decide if owning a home is better than renting. In all of my experience, I have found only two valid reasons for renting: (1) you live with your parents rent-free, or (2) you live in a rent-controlled apartment in a city like Toronto where you pay $500 a month for a place that would normally rent for $1,300.

The arguments for both sides are age-old. By renting you know your real costs in advance. There are no surprises, your premises are guaranteed by law to be well-maintained, and the security of your lease protects you from sudden shifts in the economy.

The homeowner, on the other hand, seems to be entering a market fraught with peril. He may just as easily pay too much as too little for the property. There may be hidden and costly repairs required after move-in. Tax rates tend to fluctuate with politics and the state of the economy. When you own a home, you are your own landlord. The responsibility of fixing problems as they happen is entirely your own. And, since a home is a depreciating asset, you can count on it to do just that — depreciate and wear over time, requiring ongoing maintenance and repair to look its best.

Still, over time, the long-term model favours the homeowner. In Canada one of the best tax breaks available is the tax-free capital gain on the sale of a home you have lived in. If you are planning to stay in the same place five or more years, you can almost always do better with your own home than with a rental unit. Even if the housing market is soft, and you sell your home for only slightly more than you paid, you will still have lived on your premises for only the cost of your financing which, in many cases, may be significantly below your equivalent rental costs. And you get access to a larger, higher-quality living space in the bargain.

For example, let's say you buy a $200,000 home.

Price of House	$200,000
Down Payment	−20,000
Mortgage Amount	$180,000
Mortgage Interest Rate	× 10%
1st Year Interest	$18,000
1st Year Property Tax	+2,000
1st Year Expenses	$20,000
Yearly Appreciation (8%)	+$16,000
Non-tax on Appreciation (29% Bracket)	$4,640
TOTAL	$20,640
Cost of Living in House	Zero

The first-year interest expense is $18,000 and property taxes are $2,000 for a total of $20,000, but your investment return from tax-free appreciation may be as high as $20,000 in that same year, making your investment "free." If you rent a $200,000 home for $1,400 per month, you lose $16,800 per year or $84,000 during the five-year period. Why? There is no tax-free appreciation.

FINDING THE RIGHT MORTGAGE

Borrowing mortgage money once was a simple matter of completing the paperwork and waiting to see if you qualified. Today, mortgage decisions include a dozen options. Whether you are buying or refinancing a home, the correct choice of a mortgage is as important as the right choice of the property itself. The last person who should make your decisions is the loan officer, whose motives and profit objectives may be in conflict with yours.

Understanding the following mortgage terms and strategies is a prerequisite for taking control of your mortgage situation:

Fixed-Rate Mortgage (FRM)

If the interest rate remains the same for the term of your mortgage, you have an FRM. Fixed-Rate Mortgages have been the standard since the 1920s. When interest rates began soaring in the early 80s, and mortgage companies became concerned about locking in low fixed interest rates, long-term, adjustable-rate mortgages were born, although FRMs for terms up to five years are still the norm in Canada.

Adjustable-Rate Mortgage (ARM)

The interest rate of an adjustable-rate mortgage (ARM) changes periodically based on either a contractual agreement or changes of an economic factor such as Treasury-bill rates. ARMs are also called variable-rate mortgages. There are two types of ARMs, differentiated by the effects of interest rate changes.

A. Adjustable payments — Monthly payments are adjusted up or down to reflect changes in the mortgage interest rate.
B. Adjustable term — The total number of monthly payments is increased or decreased to reflect changes in the mortgage interest rates but the amount of the monthly payments remains constant.

Amortized Mortgage

This is a mortgage with equal monthly payments. The interest portion of the monthly payment decreases and the principal portion of the payment increases with each succeeding month. Note that not all mortgages are amortized. Payments of interest-only mortgages are also available.

Negative Amortization

Negative amortization means that the principal balance is increasing because of monthly payments that are less than the accrued monthly interest. The unpaid interest is converted to principal and added to the mortgage balance. Negative amortization mortgages are currently not available in Canada.

Cap

The maximum percentage an ARM interest rate may increase over the term of the mortgage.

Strategy #83:

IF YOU ARE TURNED DOWN FOR A MORTGAGE, OR HAVE AN UNUSUAL MORTGAGE SITUATION, CONTACT A MORTGAGE BROKER.

Mortgage brokers are in the business of finding mortgage money quickly and they can often produce results when other lenders cannot. Note that they may charge more for this service in terms not only of the lending rate but also in terms of up-front charges or "points." Often, however, the advantages outweigh the disadvantages. One Canadian businessman told me of an instance where he was buying properties in the Toronto market at the bottom of the 1990-91 recession. He had put in an offer for $250,000 on a property that had listed for $425,000 just six months earlier. The seller needed cash right away and the buyer was forced to close in three days or lose the deal. The shrewd buyer obtained his financing from a mortgage broker — he paid slightly more for the mortgage in terms of fees and charges, but he more than made up for this by getting a good deal on the property in the first place. Doing the paperwork for a bank or trust company would have taken too long.

Mortgage brokers are listed in your local phone directory.

Strategy #84:

**LET THE VARIOUS MORTGAGE LENDERS COMPETE FOR
YOUR BUSINESS, AND CHOOSE THE ONE
WITH THE BEST TERMS.**

Recently in Canada private services have been developed to allow borrowers to be matched with suitable lenders. The service works much like a computer dating service — you fill out a questionnaire and your data is then matched to lenders who want your business. Two interesting features of the service are that the lenders who respond positively must accept your business, and the fees involved for the matchmaking are paid by the lender, not the borrower. Check your phone book to see if such a service is available in your area.

Strategy #85:

**AVOID SIGNING A MORTGAGE
AGREEMENT THAT CONTAINS A
PREPAYMENT PENALTY.**

Use this strategy any time you are obtaining a new home mortgage.

Before completing a mortgage application, ask if there is a prepayment penalty (which is normally three months' interest). If so, and if they won't remove it, look for a lender with better terms. When looking for a mortgage you have up to 50 choices of different companies, depending on the size of your city.

If you have already applied for a mortgage, read the mortgage application to determine if there is a prepayment penalty.

Ask to have the prepayment penalty changed or stricken from the agreement. You will most likely have to speak to someone higher up than the mortgage clerk with whom you are initially working. Mortgages are a competitive business, and many institutions will waive the prepayment penalty to get you to sign with them. You have clout. Don't hesitate to use it.

Strategy #86:

NEVER PAY OFF A LOW-INTEREST MORTGAGE BECAUSE THE BANK OFFERS YOU A DISCOUNT.

When mortgage interest rates get higher, banks and mortgage companies send letters to those who have low-interest mortgages, offering a discount of 5% to 25% for paying off their mortgage early. Anything your bank or mortgage company wants you to do is probably in their best interest, not in yours. If you have an 8% or less fixed-rate mortgage and the current mortgage rates are 12% or higher, the bank can make more money if you pay off your mortgage in a lump sum. They then loan the money again at a higher interest rate. The higher interest is so lucrative that the bank can afford to give you a big discount as an incentive. The bank will earn thousands of dollars of extra interest over the next 25 years by giving the money to someone else at a higher rate. If you receive the discount letter from your mortgage company, trash it. The discount of 10% to 20% is never enough to offset the amount of interest dollars you are saving with your low-rate mortgage.

In addition, Revenue Canada has a special rule known as debt forgiveness, which usually applies where the forgiven debt relates to your business or investments. For example, if your mortgage balance on your business property is $30,000 but your bank lets you pay it off for $25,000 cash, the $5,000 debt forgiveness will reduce your tax losses, if you have any, or the tax cost of your assets.

Strategy #87:

CREATE YOUR OWN "GROWING EQUITY MORTGAGE" TO PAY OFF YOUR HOME IN HALF THE TIME WITH PAYMENTS YOU CAN AFFORD.

Growing Equity Mortgage (GEM)

In the United States, there is an alternative for saving money on mortgages. Some mortgage-lending institutions are now offering a little-known special 30-year mortgage called a Growing Equity Mortgage (GEM).

With a GEM, the first year's payments are about the same as with a

30-year mortgage. Payments then go up each year, but the extra amount of the payment is applied only to the principal so that your mortgage is actually paid off in 15 years, saving thousands in interest payments. The GEM therefore becomes a 15-year mortgage with lower payments in the early years when you need them.

Since there are currently no GEMs in Canada (no pun intended), you can create your own by simply prepaying next month's principal from your amortization statement. Most Canadian lenders will permit up to 10% additional principal payments in a year — but check with your lender to see if any special procedures or forms are required for you to take advantage of this strategy.

Strategy #85:
CUT THE NUMBER OF YEARS YOU PAY FOR YOUR HOME IN HALF WITH EXTRA PRINCIPAL PAYMENTS.

By now you know that the amount of time your mortgage is outstanding can be as significant as the amount you borrowed in the first place. Your goal is to arrange your financial affairs to repay your debt as quickly as possible. One way of doing this is by refinancing your existing mortgage for a shorter period — but this could result in thousands of dollars in new closing costs. Here's another approach — you can pay off your mortgage in half the time without refinancing simply by making extra principal payments. (Check with your lender first — see Strategy #85.)

Here's how: on the first of the month (when you ordinarily write your regular mortgage cheque), write a second cheque for the principal-only portion of the next month's payment.

How does this strategy work in practice?

Below is a section of a typical amortization schedule showing the breakdown of payments and how they apply.

Principal Payment #	Payment	Principal	Interest	Balance
30	$490.06	41.34	448.72	48,910.15
31	$490.06	41.72 (a)	448.34	48,868.43
32	$490.06	42.10	447.96	48,826.33
33	$490.06	42.49 (b)	447.57	48,783.84

Notice how the principal increases slightly each month and the interest decreases by the same amount.

When you write a cheque for payment 30 of $490.06, write a second cheque for $41.72 representing the principal-only portion of payment number 31, (a). The following month, write a cheque for payment number 32 and a second cheque for $42.49, the principal portion of payment number 33, (b). Mathematically, you are moving down your amortization schedule two months at a time. Notice that you never pay interest on a payment whose principal is prepaid. Therefore, the interest on the principal-only payment is the amount you have saved.

Paying the exact amount equal to the next month's principal is not a requirement for this strategy, but a convenient way of keeping track of your mortgage balance, and makes it easier to verify your account later on.

There are three conditions under which you would not make extra principal payments: if your mortgage interest rate is 9% or less, if you plan to live in the home less than three years, or if the house is a rental property.

Never pay off low interest mortgages — those under 9%. Instead, use the extra money in a better investment. If you don't plan to live in the home more than three years, extra principal payments will have little effect. Cutting the interest on rental property is not as important as cash flow. You make the payments on your home, the tenants make the payments on your rental properties.

Strategy #89:
THE BIGGER YOUR MORTGAGE, THE BETTER YOUR INVESTMENT.

Your home is more than a place to live, it is one of the best investments you'll ever make. Although the real estate market may behave erratically in the short term, over the long haul it tends to outperform other investments, particularly bank interest. When you take into account the extremely favourable treatment that Revenue Canada offers homeowners, plus the fact that you are living in (and enjoying) your investment as you proceed, you end up with a strong case for buying as much house as you can afford — and then some.

There are three positive uses of a mortgage:

1. To increase the return on a real estate investment through the power of leverage.

Leverage is the use of other people's money (OPM), and a home mortgage is an easy method of putting OPM to work. Earning $10,000 in a savings account would require an investment of $50,000 for two years at 10%. And 25% to 50% of your interest would be lost to taxes. Buy a $100,000 home with $10,000 down payment, and if the home appreciates 5% per year you can earn the same $10,000 in two years with no taxes. Your investment return would be 50% per year instead of 10%.

2. To buy a home without paying cash.

Although "creative financing" shouldn't be taken to extremes — like most things, it is good in moderation, but dangerous if overdone — it is still possible to purchase a home without having cash or credit. (See Strategy #90.)

3. To free up real estate equity for higher return investments.

Many of us become nervous when we notice a few hundred dollars of cash sitting around the house. We realize, quite correctly, that the money is idle if it sits in a drawer, but it is working for you if it is in the bank earning interest. Strangely, not so many people realize the same thing is happening to the built-up equity in their homes.

Consider the case of the 75-year-old widow in Montreal living in a home with a market value of over $200,000. She and her husband originally paid $30,000 for the home in the 1950s. The house has been paid up for well over a decade. As far as the homeowner is concerned, she has a tax-free profit of over $170,000 locked in to the house. But is that $170,000 producing any income for her? Not at all!

To see how to "unlock" the equity trapped in your home, see Strategy #94.

Strategy #90:
USE THE "TRIPLE PUNCH" STRATEGY
TO BUY YOUR FIRST HOME.

Learning how to buy your first home is not at all difficult if you have a good financing strategy. The triple-punch strategy will let you purchase your first home even if you have no cash or credit.

STEP 1: FIND PROPERTIES WITH EXISTING NATIONAL HOUSING ACT (NHA) MORTGAGES.

NHA mortgages are assumable in many instances without much qualification. For example, consider an $80,000 home with a $45,000 NHA mortgage. You can take over that mortgage with only your signature. Now you have financed the first $45,000 of that property.

STEP 2: HAVE THE SELLERS GET AN EQUITY LOAN FOR THEIR DOWN PAYMENT.

If the sellers need a 20% down payment or $16,000 cash, and you have no cash or credit, ask the sellers to get an equity loan for $16,000. The sellers will get the cash that they need, and you simply assume the payments on the equity loan.

STEP 3: GIVE THE SELLERS A SINGLE PAYMENT NOTE FOR THE BALANCE.

The balance is the difference between the cost of the house ($80,000) and the financing amount ($45,000 original mortgage + $16,000 equity loan = $61,000) or $19,000. Have the sellers hold a seven-year, single payment note for the balance of $19,000 that you owe them with the right to prepay at any time. The collateral for the note can still be the home in the form of a third mortgage.
   The sellers should be willing to do this if:

1. the home is really worth the selling price, and
2. the sellers have not had good luck in finding a cash buyer.

A single payment note is an agreement to pay back in seven years the $19,000 in one payment with all accumulated interest. Within seven years, the house you bought for $80,000 may be worth $120,000–$140,000.

You now have two choices:

1. Refinance the home and continue to live in it.
2. Sell the home and pay off the original seller, then move into a nicer home.

Using these steps, you can quickly buy your first home with no money down.

Strategy #91:
SELL AND BUY A HOUSE WITHOUT GETTING THE TAX SQUEEZE.

With the high cost of houses in Canada, it is becoming more and more common to ask the seller to take back a second (or a third) mortgage. In this way the seller gets his price, and the buyer gets his house.

What happens, however, if you are selling a home and end up taking back a mortgage, only to have to take out a mortgage when you purchase your own new home? In this case, you are receiving the interest income from the mortgage you took back — which is taxable — and paying interest on the mortgage you took out, which is not tax deductible.

To avoid this tax squeeze:

1. Only take back a mortgage, when selling, if there is a premium built into your price to allow for the hidden costs of setting up (and disposing of) the mortgage.
2. Once the mortgage is set up, sell it for cash through the services of a mortgage broker. You will lose some of the value of the mortgage in the short run, but over the long term, there will be greater benefits to your cash flow and your overall tax planning strategy.

BUILDING WEALTH WITH SHORTER MORTGAGES

Strategy #92:

**GET A FIVE-YEAR MORTGAGE, BUT AMORTIZE IT FOR
15 YEARS INSTEAD OF 25.**

You can save tens of thousands in mortgage interest by putting the time value of money on your side. The mortgage company will automatically give you a 25-year amortization if you don't object. Why? Because 25-year amortizations make mortgage companies rich.

As we have seen, time costs money. For every $50,000 you borrow at 12% interest for 25 years, your principal and interest will be $526.61 a month. At the end of five years (60 payments), you will have paid $31,596.60, but reduced your principal by only $2,173.21.

Instead, get a 15-year amortization loan and your monthly payments go up only about 15%. But at the end of the same 60 payments, you will have paid a total of $36,004.80, of which $8,173.54 will have gone toward principal. This strategy can save you hundreds of thousands over your lifetime.

Strategy #93:

**REFINANCE YOUR HOME AT A LOWER INTEREST RATE
ANY TIME THE NEW INTEREST RATE IS AT LEAST
2% LESS THAN THE OLD INTEREST RATE.**

Knowing when to refinance is as important as choosing the right mortgage. Some believe you should never refinance; others will tell you to refinance anytime interest rates drop. Neither is correct.

You cannot save money by refinancing your home every time interest rates drop because of the additional closing costs (legal fees, appraisal fees, application fees, interest penalties, etc.). The chart below will show you the approximate number of months it takes for lower payments to make up for the 3% to 4% closing costs.

Difference in Interest Rate	Number of Months Required
2%	26 Months
3%	22 Months
4%	18 Months

If the difference between interest rates on your old and new mortgage is 2%, 26 months of lower payments will offset the closing costs; 22 months at 3% and only 18 months at 4%. The lower payments from that point on will save you thousands. There's a nuisance factor to consider, also. If interest rates have dropped only 2% and there are only a few months remaining on your five-year mortgage, it's probably not worth it for you to refinance.

To determine the actual number of months of reduced payments required to offset the new closing costs, divide the closing cost amount by the amount you will save each month with your lower payment.

It would not be wise to refinance a $40,000 mortgage at a 1% difference in interest rates. The amount saved each month would be only $30, and if the new closing costs were $1,000, it would take you 33 months or almost three years to catch up. You may sell your home before then. How long you intend to own your home, therefore, is also an important refinancing consideration.

Always ask if the closing costs of a loan or mortgage can be added to the loan amount. Use other people's money whenever possible.

Strategy #94:

BORROW YOUR HOME EQUITY FREE BY COMBINING AN EQUITY LOAN WITH A GOOD INVESTMENT PLAN.

Home equity is like money in a shoe box gathering dust in your closet. It may make you feel good, but it is not working for you. There are a dozen good emotional reasons for accumulating a large amount of equity in your home, but not one good financial reason.

My Hungarian relatives lived on the south side of Chicago in the United States in an area known as Cottage Grove. Most worked for the Pullman Railroad Car Company until retirement. They lived in three-storey row houses that they were somehow able to buy on their small salaries. To save money, they never took expensive vacations, or spent much on themselves. One of life's biggest events after marriage and children was paying off the mortgage and celebrating the event with a mortgage-burning party. In this ethnic neighbourhood where half the residents never learned English, a fire was built in the street in front of the debt-free property. With great fanfare, the proud owners threw their cancelled mortgage documents into the flames while the neighbours danced and sang in a joyous circle. Great party, but a losing financial strategy. They may have owned their homes, but that was all they owned.

Today millions of people are following the same dead-end path, living a financially austere life even though they have wealth that could be unlocked from the equity they have built up in their homes. Your home equity, if borrowed and reinvested, can be an excellent source of income. Using a combination of a low-interest home "equity loan" or mortgage and a good, safe investment plan that pays over 20% per year, you can borrow your home equity free — with enough income from the reinvested equity to both make your mortgage payments and improve your lifestyle. For every $50,000 of home equity, you can increase your income $8,000 per year for the rest of your life without depleting the principal.

If you have a low-interest first mortgage, the "equity loan" is the best alternative for freeing up your home equity. Unlike a regular mortgage, which gives you a fixed amount for a fixed term, the equity loan gives you a line of credit which you can "use as you choose."

Money in any amount (up to the value of the loan) can be borrowed or paid back at any time during the term of the loan, usually by writing a cheque against your loan account. You only pay interest on the money you borrow, and you stop paying interest on any portion that you pay back with no prepayment penalty.

Using the powerhouse combination of a low-interest home equity loan or mortgage, and a good safe investment plan that pays up to 20% per year, you can gain substantially. You will be able to make your mortgage payments and enjoy a happier lifestyle at the same time.

WHERE TO GET THEM

Equity loans are available from:

- Trust companies
- Savings and loan institutions
- Banks
- First and second mortgage companies
- Brokerage firms
- Mortgage brokers (independent mortgage sources)
- Credit unions

POINTS AND OTHER FEES

Shop around; the rates and terms vary from institution to institution. Expect to pay about $150 for a required appraisal, and an application fee of about $85. You may also be asked for "points". Points are simply extra charges for the financing — one point is equal to 1% of the total initially borrowed. Points are usually paid in cash at the time of closing or are added to the principal and financed with the total loan. If you add the points to your principal, be aware that your overall borrowing cost is affected — points will add two to three times their original amount when financed, which is the same as increasing the interest rate. For example, eight points on a 15-year mortgage amortization is the equivalent of 1% extra interest. Similarly, an 8 1/2% mortgage with four points is the same as a 9% mortgage with no points.

The maximum loan you can obtain is determined by a formula called the "appraisal lending value" — usually about 75% of the appraised value of your property, less any existing mortgage. If, for example, your home appraises for $110,000, the mortgage company's appraisal is 75%, and your first mortgage balance is $45,000, your maximum equity loan would be $37,500.

(Appraisal Lending Value) — Existing Mortgages = Maximum Loan
(75% × $110,000) — $45,000 = $37,500

HOW TO INVEST YOUR EQUITY LOAN MONEY

The next step is to formulate your investment plan. Your investments must provide a return great enough to make the payments on your loan and give you additional income. The chart below will give you suggested investment plans based on the amount of equity you have available. Modify the suggested plans to fit your specific investment needs: maximum growth, maximum income, or maximum tax shelter. Make your plan before you withdraw the money from your equity loan account.

BORROW YOUR HOME EQUITY FREE — INVESTMENT PLAN
Equity Loan 11% Interest 15-Year Amortization

Investment	Amt. Invested	Expected Income	Cash Income	Deferred Income		
Amt. Borrowed/Invested = $20,000; Yearly Interest = $2,200*						
Mutual Funds[1]	10,000	15%	1,500	—	Total Income	$4,500
Discount. Mtg[2]	10,000	30%	2,000	1,000	Interest pymts	−2,200
			3,500	1,000	Net Income	$2,300

Amt. Borrowed/Invested = $50,000; Yearly Interest = $5,500*						
Mutual Funds[1]	25,000	15%	3,750	—	Total Income	11,250
Discount. Mtg[2]	25,000	30%	5,000	2,500	Interest pymts	−5,500
			8,750	2,500	Net Income	$5,750

Amt. Borrowed/Invested = $100,000; Yearly Interest = $11,000*						
Mutual Funds[1]	50,000	15%	7,500	—	Total Income	22,500
Discount. Mtg[2]	50,000	30%	10,000	5,000	Interest pymts	−11,000
			17,500	5,000	Net Income	$11,500

* Only the interest portion of the monthly payments is shown since the principal portion of the mortgage payback is your money.

[1] Mutual Funds (See Investment Section)
   No commissions using no-load funds.
   Money Movement Strategy used to earn 15% to 20% per year average.
   All earnings can be either withdrawn to make mortgage payments or reinvested.

[2] Discounted Mortgages
   Mortgages purchased at 30% discount from face value.
   20% is current income from monthly interest received.
   10% income is generally deferred until mortgage matures.

Strategy #95:
NEVER USE MORTGAGE GRACE PERIODS.

Using mortgage grace periods can damage your credit profile. Even though you are not charged a late penalty until after the tenth of the month, paying after the first will be counted as late and could end up on your credit file. Let me share with you my own experience.

After I bought my first 40 rental homes, I found I could create a tremendous float by mailing the mortgage cheques so they would arrive at the mortgage company not by the first, but by the tenth of the month. The process also allowed me extra time to collect past-due rents to cover the mortgage payments. Using the grace period soon caught up with me. Even though all mortgage companies gave me until the tenth of the month before a late charge was assessed, payments after the first were counted as late and new mortgages became more difficult to obtain. My payments are now mailed to arrive by the first of the month.

Strategy #96:
CLAIM A DEDUCTION FOR YOUR HOME MORTGAGE INTEREST PAYMENTS.

Revenue Canada does not normally permit homeowners to deduct interest paid on mortgages taken out to purchase a home. However, interest paid on loans whose purpose is to earn investment income is generally deductible. For that reason, you can usually deduct mortgage interest paid on rental properties. To the extent that you generate equity in your home you can use the proceeds of a mortgage for investments, and that interest can become tax-deductible. If, for example, you were to receive a large sum of money, don't be so quick to invest it. Put it toward your home mortgage. If you decide to invest later, borrow money on your home. That way, when you file your tax return, you claim an interest deduction on the portion of your mortgage loan used for investments. Similarly, any large amount of savings you accumulate might be placed against your mortgage — to pay off non-deductible interest — and then you would re-finance to apply funds to a business activity which, in turn, could permit you to claim a deduction on the interest portion of the mortgage on your property. You have to play the game!

If, for example, you were to free up the equity in your home by re-financing for the purpose of generating investment income (see Strategy #94), the interest could be deductible.

PERSONAL FINANCE STRATEGIES

Strategy #97:
IF THE RETURN ON A POTENTIAL INVESTMENT IS LESS THAN THE INTEREST ON A LOAN, PAY CASH. IF THE RETURN IS MORE, BORROW TO BUY AND INVEST YOUR CASH.

Automobiles and other rapidly depreciating assets are certainly not investments, but you face the same financing decisions as with mortgages. Should you finance the automobile or other purchase, or pay cash? Of course, the question only applies to those who have the cash.

You must first understand an important financial measuring stick called "opportunity cost," or what I call "opportunity lost." If you pay cash, you automatically lose the opportunity to invest that cash. If you could borrow at 12% to buy an automobile, but instead pay cash, your opportunity cost is what you could have earned by investing that same amount of money, minus the 12% interest. If you could have earned up to 20% in no-load mutual funds (you'll learn how later), your opportunity cost would have been 8% (20% minus 12%). You would be losing an opportunity for earning an additional 8%. In this case, the greater profit would come from borrowing to buy the automobile and investing your dollars in the mutual fund. However, if a 9% bank certificate of deposit is the best investment you know of, you would be better off paying cash for the car. Paying cash instead of financing at 12% is like investing your money at 12% interest. Every financial decision has an opportunity cost, and computing your opportunity cost will show you the correct decision.

Strategy #98:
NEVER BUY OR FINANCE EXTENDED WARRANTIES.

Another rip-off, usually encountered when purchasing electronics, appliances, or automobiles, is repair insurance or extended warranties. The real purpose of an extended warranty is to add to the dealer's profit at your expense. The extended warranty will pay the cost of repairing the item you buy after the manufacturer's warranty runs out.

What happened to the good old days when manufacturers tried to get us to believe that their products were fail-proof? Audio and video equipment usually comes with a 90-day manufacturer's warranty; appliances, like washers, dryers, and microwaves usually have a year to break down at the manufacturer's expense; and automobiles are guaranteed from one to five years, depending on how difficult the car market is at the time. The extended warranty, created and sold by the retail store, not the manufacturer, kicks in only when the manufacturer's warranty expires.

There are a number of good reasons such extended warranties are a financial mistake.

1. If you finance the amount of the extended warranty, you will be paying interest on the cost of an agreement that won't be in effect for one to three years.
2. You pay for the warranty itself in advance even though it won't be in effect for one to three years.
3. By the time the warranty becomes effective, you may have sold, lost, or replaced the item on which you bought the warranty.
4. The warranty is a limited guarantee and does not cover normal wear and tear or rough handling — or, in the case of a video recorder or camera, dropping the equipment. These are in reality the major causes of defects.
5. The cost of the warranty is astronomical compared to the amount of money the dealer actually pays for the real repairs. Less than 20% of all the extended warranty monies collected by a dealer are paid out in repairs. The rest is profit.
6. Salesmen are normally paid a big commission for intimidating you into saying yes to extended warranties.

Why then do people fall for the extended warranty scheme so easily? Reason: Most people will mistakenly buy anything that seems to contribute to peace of mind or a sense of security with no idea of how to calculate value.

Strategy #99:
DOUBLE THE WARRANTY ON YOUR PURCHASES FOR FREE.

American Express automatically doubles the manufacturer's warranty for most items (except cars) purchased on the card (Blue, Gold, or Platinum) by cardholders. "Locking in" the double warranty usually requires notifying Amex by phone or mail following the purchase. Since there is no extra charge for this warranty, it is excellent value for the money.

The same coverage is available with most "gold" or "premium" cards issued in Canada.

> *Strategy #100:*
> ## FINANCE FURNITURE, STEREO EQUIPMENT, AND OTHER PERSONAL ASSETS NO LONGER THAN 24 MONTHS; AUTOMOBILES NO LONGER THAN 36 MONTHS.

In today's world of easy money, you become bombarded with opportunities to pay over time, rather than pay at this time. Choosing a shorter-term loan for hard goods, as with a mortgage, can save you thousands.

When it comes to borrowing, the only two questions Canadians have learned to ask are: "How much is my down payment?" and "What are my monthly payments?" The most important element of a loan, however, is your total payments; that's what eats into your lifetime wealth. "The longer the term, the lower the monthly payments" is a true statement, but the law of diminishing returns raises the total cost far beyond the benefit of lower payments. When you lengthen the term of a loan to reduce the payments, the total interest paid increases dramatically.

When you shorten the term, your monthly payments are slightly higher but two positive financial rewards are yours:

1. You pay less total interest; what you buy costs less.
2. A greater percentage of each payment is applied to the principal instead of interest.

Let me show you how this strategy works on an automobile or other personal loan. For example, you buy an automobile on which you obtain a $10,000 loan at 14%. You have a choice of terms ranging from 24 to 60 months.

EFFECT OF CHOICE OF TERMS

36-Month Loan Comparison

a Term	b Monthly Payment	c Total Paid	d Total Interest	e Interest Saved	f Increased Payment
24 Mos.	$480	$11,520	$1,520	—	—
36 Mos.	341	12,300	2,300	—	—
48 Mos.	273	13,100	3,100	$ 800	$ 68/mo.
60 Mos.	233	13,960	3,960	1,660	108/mo.

The chart shows the real cost of a loan for terms ranging from 24 to 60 months. Notice that by financing for 60 months instead of 24 months, you will pay $2,440 additional interest or 25% more for your car (column *d* $3,960 — $1,520).

Another way to use the chart is to compare a 36-month loan with a 60-month loan. If you get a 36-month loan instead of a 60-month loan you save a total of $1,660 and your payments are only $108 more per month (columns *e* & *f*). In addition, you stop making payments 24 months earlier. The lender always wins with 48- and 60-month loans. You win with 24- or 36-month loans. Use the chart to plan your next financed purchase.

Strategy #101:

MAKE EXTRA PRINCIPAL PAYMENTS TO CUT PERSONAL LOAN TERMS AND INTEREST 30% TO 50%.

Not only can you make extra principal payments on a mortgage, you can do the same thing with any high interest loan or to rid yourself quickly of 21% credit card interest. You can pay off a 48-month automobile or furniture loan in 24 months by making extra principal payments along with your regular payments. If you just financed $10,000 at 14% interest for 48-months, begin immediately including next month's principal payment along with this month's full payment. Look at the Automobile Loan Amortization Schedule below. Let's say you've made payment number one for $268.27, and you are ready to make payment number two.

AUTOMOBILE LOAN AMORTIZATION SCHEDULE

Month 1 through 5 of a $10,000, 14%, 48-month loan.

Payment #	Amount	Principal	Interest	Balance
1	$268.27	$159.94	$108.33	$9,840.06
2	$268.27	$161.67	$106.60	$9,678.39
3	$268.27	$163.42	$104.85	$9,514.97
4	$268.27	$165.19	$103.08	$9,349.78
5	$268.27	$166.98	$101.29	$9,182.80

The first month of the loan you pay $268.27.
   The second month you pay:

   cheque #1 — second month's regular payment of $268.27
   cheque #2 — third month's principal of $163.42
   Total = $431.69

   The third month you pay:

   cheque #3 — fourth month's regular payment of $268.27
   cheque #4 — fifth month's principal of $166.98
   Total = $435.25

The extra principal payments will pay off the loan in 24 months instead of 48 months.

If your lender requires you to pay in increments of full payment amounts, in our example, $268.27, make extra principal payments in that amount every other month.

Strategy #102:

**TO ELIMINATE HIGH-INTEREST CREDIT CARD DEBT, MAKE
EXTRA PRINCIPAL PAYMENTS EACH MONTH OF
$25 TO $100, PLUS THE MINIMUM PAYMENT, PLUS THE
AMOUNT OF YOUR PURCHASES.**

Using credit cards often feels like getting something for nothing, at least until the bill arrives. Credit card interest is often 21% or higher in Canada or 1¾% per month, and should be a primary target for the "extra principal payment" strategy.

You'll be surprised how quickly you can eliminate your credit card debt with only a few extra dollars each month. Since the monthly interest is computed on your principal balance, making extra principal payments will rapidly decrease your monthly interest and balance.

Let's say, for example, your MasterCard balance is $1,100, your required monthly payment is $60, and you purchased $110 this month. You must send in a cheque for $220 as follows:

New purchases amount	$110
Required monthly payment	+$ 60
Additional optional payment	+$ 50
TOTAL PAYMENT	$220
NEW BALANCE	$880

You'll pay off your balance in half the time. If you have to scrimp and save in some other area — do so. It's imperative that you come up with the extra money this month so you can pay the entire bill in half the time! Otherwise, the credit card debt will never be paid off, exactly what the credit card companies love to have happen.

Strategy #103:

REPLACE HIGH-INTEREST CREDIT CARDS
WITH LOW-INTEREST CREDIT CARDS.

For every thousand dollars of average balance, you would normally pay $210 per year at 21% interest. With an 18% card, you will pay only $180, saving you $30 per $1,000 of average balance, or 15%.

Can you find lower-interest cards? The answer is yes, but you may have to ask around. For example, when most cards were charging 21% to 22% in 1990, these cards were offering 17.75% to 18%:

- Bank of Montreal MasterCard "Gold"
- Canada Trust MasterCard "Supercard"
- National Bank MasterCard "Gold"

* In order to get a "gold" card you must have an income of $30,000 or more (exclusive of commission income). There are joint husband/wife accounts where the minimum income is $45,000. You must have steady employment and a good credit rating.

The fee for these cards is slightly higher than higher-interest cards and the cards are harder to qualify for than regular cards. Still, if you use your card on a regular basis, the lower interest rate will more than compensate for the higher fee and the inconvenience. (Fees range from $40 to $120 per year.)

Strategy #104:

AVOID THE "SPREAD" FOR PURCHASES MADE IN THE U.S.

With the advent of free trade, more and more Canadians are making purchases across the border, either in person or via mail or phone.

If these purchases are financed by a credit card issued on a Canadian bank or financial institution, each transaction will be converted into Canadian dollars as it is posted.

Banks are not foolish. They understand that, whatever they do, they want to make a profit. This thinking applies to the conversion rate the bank uses to determine what you really owe, in Canadian dollars, on your purchase.

In converting currencies, banks buy low and sell high. The difference between the buy and sell is usually about 5% at any given time — this is called the "spread."

UNDERSTANDING THE SPREAD

Consider, for example, that you are taking a trip to New York and you want to convert $1,000 for spending money on your trip. Assume that the bank conversion rate quoted that day is 1.13/1.18. This means that they will sell you U.S. currency at $1.18 Cdn, and buy U.S. currency from you at 1.13 Cdn to the U.S. dollar.

If you were, on the morning of your trip, to convert your $1,000 Cdn to U.S. funds at the 1.18 rate, you would get $848 U.S. If your trip was suddenly cancelled, and you wanted your Canadian funds back, you would then convert back at the rate of 1.13 Cdn to every U.S. dollar. You would get back $958.24. What happened to the other Canadian $41.76? That's the spread.

AVOIDING THE CREDIT CARD SPREAD

Every time you purchase an item in the United States on your Canadian credit card, you are paying the higher rate, and that includes some hidden profit for the credit card company.

To avoid this hidden "fee," set up a separate bank account in U.S. funds. These accounts are available at virtually all Canadian banks and financial institutions. They generally include both interest and chequing privileges, depending on the account chosen.

Once you have an account set up, your strategy is to avoid any subsequent transactions that involve a currency exchange. Settle your U.S. bills via cheque or money order drawn on your U.S. account. If you need cash for your U.S. trip, go to your bank and ask to withdraw U.S. funds from your own account. (There is no charge for this, but some banks will want 24 hours notice to prepare the cash.) If you receive any funds in U.S. denomination, do not convert them. Deposit them to your U.S. account directly. Finally, if you must have a credit card for your purchases in the United States, apply for a card issued by a U.S. bank in U.S. denomination, and settle the monthly statements with cheques drawn on your U.S. account.

Strategy #105:

GO FOR THE "GOLD" AND GET THOUSANDS OF DOLLARS OF COVERAGE FOR AN EXTRA $15 PER YEAR.

Initially, the gold or premium versions of the standard credit cards were of interest only for their snob appeal, but in the past few years, an extensive benefits package has given the cards exceptional value. (To obtain the showy cards, you do need to show income slightly higher than the level required for the basic cards.)

For example, for $50 a year, or an extra $15 over the basic card, the Bank of Montreal Gold card (minimum income $35,000, or $45,000 joint income) includes these extras:

- rental car Collision Damage Waiver (CDW)
- personal-accident insurance package when travelling
- accidental-death insurance package when travelling
- personal-effects insurance package when travelling
- 24-hour out-of-province/out-of-country medical when travelling (supplements provincial health plans)
- hotel convalescent package — cost of staying in a hotel if you get sick during a trip
- cash advance and travel documents replacement while travelling
- purchase insurance (theft) for 90 days after shopping
- "double the manufacturer's warranty" for most items purchased with the card

Banks vary in their credit requirements, but, generally, the cards are available to a family where the combined family income is in the $50,000 a year range which — according to Statistics Canada — includes the majority of Canadian households.

If you do not meet the requirements for the premium card but still want the card, some banks will permit you to "secure" a premium by leaving funds on deposit to cover the amount of your credit limit — see also Strategy #75.

Chapter 7

SEND YOUR KIDS TO UNIVERSITY OR COLLEGE (ALMOST) FREE

Experience keeps a dear school, but fools will learn in no other.

Benjamin Franklin, *Poor Richard's Almanac*, 1743

Objective: Combine a college loan with an investment that will cut the real cost of educating your children by 50% to 100%.

The traumas of raising children are no longer limited to diapers, grades, first dates, and first automobiles. The third-biggest expense you'll ever encounter, close behind income taxes and buying a home, is putting your kids through university. The cost of even the most modest four-year university education now exceeds $20,000 with room and board.

My parents began a university fund for me using U.S. Savings Bonds. By the time I was 13, there were several thousand dollars neatly tucked away for an education at M.I.T. Then, in 1953, my parents' business slipped past the point of no return. Their last attempt to save it was to withdraw the university funds and dump the money into the business. Less than a year later, they were bankrupt, and M.I.T. became a faded dream.

Years later, my father did scrape together $300 to enroll me in Millikin University in Decatur, Illinois, but my $27-a-week shoe salesman's job didn't provide enough money to keep the education going. Second semester, it was over. I was still paying off the balance of the first semester's tuition and the school would not let me enroll for another term without more money. Ironically, 25 years later, when

107

the university found out that I had become financially successful, they had no shame in asking me for contributions.

My experience is certainly not unusual. Many parents have traditionally found themselves unable or unprepared to finance university educations for their children. Either they intended to save money while the children were growing, or they were sold a life insurance policy that eventually failed to create enough cash value to pay for university. Most educational investment plans are doomed to the same failure. Because of inflation over any 20-year period, parents end up using their lifetime savings or going deeply in debt to finance the education that an 18-year savings plan would not support.

There is a simple plan that will allow you to educate your child, grandchild, or even yourself in any college or university in Canada — FREE!

Strategy #106:
BUY A HOME THAT WILL PAY YOUR EDUCATION LOAN.

About three months before your child begins university, buy a four-bedroom home, condo, or duplex with as big a mortgage as possible within a few miles of the university campus. Furnish your property in "early Salvation Army" and rent it to four students, with leases co-signed by their parents. Finance the entire education with the profit from the sale of the property when your child graduates.

Choose a property within a couple of miles of the campus, so that transportation for your resident students is not a problem. The property should have four bedrooms for two reasons: maximum rent while you own the property, and maximum value when you sell. The house should be in good condition, requiring only cosmetic, not major, surgery.

During the four-year term, your property should appreciate significantly because of the shortage of off-campus housing in almost every university campus area.

Now let's look at the details.

Strategy #107:
TURN YOUR PROPERTY INTO A MINI STUDENT DORM.

Furnish your property with used, inexpensive furniture from any salvage store. Another possibility is to shop the "contents" sales regularly placed in the classifieds by people in the process of moving. In the '90s, those in the job force will switch employment more frequently than in any decade previous — since the cost of moving large articles is often more than their value, you can catch some wonderful bargains by keeping an eye open.

Keep it simple. You will want a bed, desk, chair, chest of drawers, lamps, and a small bookcase for each bedroom, and basic furniture for the rest of the house. Let students supply their own linens and kitchen utensils. Don't be surprised if you can furnish the entire house for little more than $2,000!

Note also that depreciation write-offs may generally be claimed against rental income, along with other costs of the project. Most of the furniture you will purchase will be in the 20% class, meaning that you can, on a declining-balance basis, expense 20% of the cost each year you run the property (except the first year, during which the "half-year" depreciation rule would apply, and you could only expense 10% of the value.)

Strategy #108:
RENT YOUR PROPERTY BY THE BEDROOM ON A YEARLY LEASE TO INDIVIDUAL STUDENTS, CO-SIGNED BY PARENTS.

Renting the property to students is the easiest part of the strategy. Since most students would rather live off campus, there is always a housing shortage. Place ads under the "share" column of the school and local newspapers, as well as posting notices on the school bulletin board. Most university admissions or student housing offices keep a registry of available housing in which you will want to list your property.

Maximize your income by renting by the bedroom on separate leases. Check with others who own rental property in the area to determine the rent you should charge. You will find you can get $300 to $450 per student, per month, depending on the city, cost of properties in the area and the shortage of housing. The total rent of $1,200 to $1,800 per month will be more than adequate to offset the mortgage, taxes and maintenance costs, and give you extra money for university expenses.

Two caveats about renting to students: First, rent only on a full year's lease, not a lease that covers only nine months of the school year. Give each student the option to sublease if he or she will not attend summer school. Second, make certain that parents co-sign the lease. With a co-signer, you are protected from the problem of collecting for damage or unpaid rent.

Blank leases are usually available from any business stationery store in the province where you live. Some provinces maintain a system of rent control which places restrictions on the ability of the landlord to deal with his tenants as he wishes. Since these laws will affect your project, you should make a copy of this legislation for your records — you can usually find the appropriate documents at any public library.

Strategy #109:
MAKE YOUR SON OR DAUGHTER
THE PROPERTY MANAGER.

Pay your child a salary of about $100 a month, and let him or her handle the regular duties of a property manager, including:

- collecting rents,
- inspecting the property once a week for cleanliness and damage,
- renting the property when there is a vacancy,
- contracting any repair work that needs to be done,
- reporting to you on the financial and physical condition of your property.

The $1,200 per year you pay your child should be tax deductible, assuming the money is legitimately paid for property management. The deduction should save you $540 per year in personal taxes alone (assuming an effective 45% tax bracket) or more than $2,000 over the first four years. The salary you pay your child can then be used by him or her to pay for books, supplies, or food.

Strategy #110:

PLAN TO MAKE A PROFIT WHEN YOU SELL THE PROPERTY, BUT POSSIBLY RUN A SMALL LOSS INITIALLY.

Don't be surprised if the ongoing expenses of your project (utilities, repairs, taxes, property manager fees) cause you to show a small loss each year.

As many people in the rental property sector have discovered, there is no harm in running a loss initially as long as you expect to sell the property at a profit down the road.

Using this strategy, you are already ahead of the game in terms of your own personal tax savings if the property is just breaking even — or perhaps even running at a small loss.

With rental properties that generate a loss (where the deductible expenses exceed the rents collected) the amount of the loss can be used to further reduce your taxable income from other sources, and so add to your tax savings while you maintain control of the property.

The one exception, however, is a rule which states that capital cost allowance, or depreciation, taken on a building used as a rental property may not be used to create a loss by itself. For example, assume you have a building with rents of $4,000 in one year and allowable expenses of $3,200. The maximum capital cost you could deduct on behalf of the building would, under this special rule, be limited to $800.

Strategy #111:

USE THE PROFITS FROM YOUR INVESTMENT TO PAY OFF YOUR EDUCATION LOANS.

When your child graduates, the time has arrived to sell the property. With appreciation, the property should be worth considerably more at the end of four years, depending on the original price. Because of the demand for housing in university areas, the increase in value of your property may be substantial. The best and simplest way of selling the property for top dollar is to run the following advertisement in the school and city newspapers:

"Send your child to university free — call me for details!"

You'll receive a dozen calls the first day alone. Since you have the proof you can send your child to university free, you will have no problem selling the property to the parents of an incoming freshman.

Here's another tip: when you schedule appointments to show the house to prospective purchasers, schedule two or three at the same time. The presence of other buyers often inspires one to move quickly — don't be surprised if you have several families bidding up the price!

Strategy #112:

ASK THE GOVERNMENT FOR AN
INTEREST-FREE LOAN.

The Secretary of State's Office of the Canadian government maintains the Canada Student Loans Program — although it leaves the day-to-day administration of the program to the various provincial governments. All provinces (except Quebec) will have at least this one program to offer plus, depending on the province contacted, additional or supplemental programs of their own.

Regardless of which program you elect to pursue, the objective in all cases is to obtain an interest-free loan which, for the time your child is in university, you can use to fund your child's education.

In the case of the basic federal program, for example, the maximum amount to be made available to the student is determined after first looking at the costs of the tuition and the potential weekly contribution of the parents.

If the loan is approved, then the interest payments while the child is in school (and for a period of six months thereafter) are paid by the federal government to the lender of record. All payments on the principal are suspended during that time.

After the child is out of school for six months, arrangements have to be made with the program to repay the loan. Generally, this is done over a period of between four and nine years — with an especially favourable interest rate pre-set by the program.

Strategy #113:
DON'T OVERLOOK THE TUITION FEE TAX CREDIT.

Students are able to claim tax credits against their own tax liability of 17% of their tuition fees plus an "education credit" of $10.20 a month for each month the student is registered as full time and attending qualifying educational institutions. Generally, full-time attendance at post-secondary institutions with a minimum three-week, 10-hour-per-week program will qualify.

These tax credits must be used by the student against his or her own tax liability first, but the unused portion of the tax credit, to a combined maximum of $600, can be transferred to a parent, grandparent or spouse and used by him or her as a credit against his or her own tax liability. Tax Form T2202 must be completed to accomplish this tax credit transfer.

For a student with little or no income, this could amount to a combined federal and provincial tax savings of over $900.

Strategy #114:
GIVE INCOME OR GROWTH INVESTMENTS TO YOUR CHILDREN SO THAT THE TAX DUE IS AT THEIR LOWER RATES.

Typically, you may be paying tax at a high rate on your investments while your children are paying little or no tax. See Chapter 12.

Part II

TAX-REDUCING
STRATEGIES

Chapter 8

MAKING YOUR LIFE
LESS TAXING

People who complain about the tax system fall into two categories — men and women.

Barry Steiner, *Pay Less Tax Legally*, 1982

Objective: Cut your income taxes by 50%.

One of the greatest pleasures I get out of my organization is the fact that I have saved countless thousands of members fortunes in taxes over the years.

I am convinced that the reason we have been so successful is aggressive tax planning. Tax planning is like a business — your business. Like any business decisions, you must weigh the economic considerations of your actions. Decide which course of action will result in your best financial advantage and then make a calculated, businesslike decision to pursue the most rewarding outcome for your particular situation.

The great entrepreneurs of our time, Ford, Carnegie and Bronfman built empires because they were skilled at making business decisions. You can save thousands in taxes by doing the same thing.

The biggest lifetime expense you'll ever encounter is neither a home nor a college education, but income taxes. What we were never taught is that the amount of income tax you are liable for has little to do with your total income, and everything to do with your knowledge of tax strategies.

The importance of an effective tax plan cannot be overstated. One-third to one-half of all the wealth you will accumulate in your lifetime is dependent on your tax-reducing plan and not your income, investments, or retirement program. The best defence is still a good offence — a tax plan that uses the tax laws to decrease instead of increase your taxes.

Where do we begin? By learning to turn the money you spend into legitimate tax deductions. Up to 60% of your income each year can become tax sheltered by combining everyday expenses with tax deduction strategies. This book contains over 300 strategies you can logically and legally use to cut your taxes and improve your lifestyle.

At 19, I dropped out of Milliken University after one semester, far short of the $300 tuition necessary to remain enrolled. Needing money to help support my mother and brother, I went to work in a foundry dumping "slag" — molten metal waste from the furnaces. If you ever want a job that will motivate you to do something with your life, work in a foundry for a while. That same year I started a rock-and-roll band — "Chuck Givens and the Quintones" — and I soon was making more money playing music on weekends than I made working in the foundry all week. Then came my first shocking experience with the tax system. My record-keeping skills were almost nonexistent, but I put together what I had and headed for the tax preparer's office. After only five minutes, I left with an assurance I could pick up my completed tax return in a week. When I returned, I got the shock of my life.

"I've got some good news and some bad news," muttered the CA. "The good news is your tax return is completed. The bad news is you owe an extra $2,000."

At the tender age of 19, I had never seen $2,000 in one place at one time, and knew that I had absolutely no chance of putting that much money together any time in the foreseeable future. My mind played visions of police cars and prisons.

In self-defence, I set out to collect and scrutinize every publication the tax authorities would give away free. I was determined to learn something about a tax system that was about to put me under. During the next three months, I scoured the pages looking for tax relief. Constantly, it seemed, I came upon possible deductions the CA had never mentioned. At the end of the three months, right before my return was due, I completed a new tax form myself. Based on my calculations, I did not owe the extra $2,000, and was entitled to a refund of some of the taxes that had been withheld from my paycheques at my full-time job. I was sure I'd made a mistake.

Returning to the CA's office, I asked, "Where did I go wrong?"

"You're not wrong," he said, "you're absolutely right."

The shock must have registered on my face. "What do you mean?" I said. "You had me scared to death, owing $2,000 I don't have, and yet when I do my own return, I get money back."

With a look of disgust, he came halfway out of his chair. "Let me tell you something, son! I am a tax preparer, not your financial advisor. You are paying me to take your numbers and put them on the tax forms. If you don't know how to tell me about what you're doing, I have no reason or responsibility in taking the deductions."

The light went on; I got it! If I ever wanted to protect myself from overpaying income taxes, I must learn everything possible about the tax system. No one, not even a tax preparer or CA, was going to do it for me the way it needed to be done. That experience has probably saved me more in income taxes than most people will make in a lifetime.

I have spent the last 25 years learning everything possible about the tax system and how to maximize your spendable income by minimizing your taxes. The tax system is not your enemy, unless you don't understand it. Your objective is to work with the tax system from an ethical business perspective. In business, the objective is to increase profits by reducing expenses. In your personal life, your objective is to increase spendable income by reducing your taxes.

In fact, many Canadians seem to confuse the tax system with a well-known charity of which the motto is Pay Your Fair Share. Unlike that charity, the Canadian government is not beholden to the populace for handouts in order to survive. Quite the opposite, in fact. There are specific rules and regulations governing taxation, and your only obligation, as a taxpayer, is to meet those obligations while at the same time arranging your affairs to pay as little tax as possible.

Paying as little tax as legally possible is not only your right but your duty — to yourself. If the Canadian government finds itself "short" in a given fiscal period it will undoubtedly find a new and interesting way of balancing its budget. Witness, for example, the recent GST program. But if you find yourself "short" as you near retirement, you will find that, unlike the government, you cannot raise more money merely by asking for it. Plan for your own future, and be assured that the government will plan for its own also.

Strategy #115:
USE ONLY TAX AVOIDANCE STRATEGIES,
NEVER TAX EVASION.

Tax evasion is knowingly breaking tax laws — for example, by purposely not reporting your income, or claiming tax deductions for assets you don't own or expenditures that you never made.

Some people seem to think that tax evasion may bring you fame or fortune. But, like other areas where people knowingly break the law, stiff legal penalties and even jail are more likely to be the result.

Tax loopholes, another often-used tax technique, are grey, untested areas of the tax law that allow you to claim "default deductions" that Revenue Canada might have ruled against had it had the foresight to see the possibilities. Since a specific "no" does not exist, you create a loophole by saying "yes" to a shaky deduction. Loopholes are often sought after by desperate, high-income taxpayers who never took the time to plan. Some loopholes are used purely out of greed, others are taken because of the gambling instinct. There is only one "do" about loopholes, and that is "don't."

Our tax strategies, on the other hand, refer to the practice of legally reducing your tax liability through positive, legal uses of the tax laws. There are over 100 legal ways to reduce your taxes and improve your affairs with the strategies in this book.

Some, like opening an RRSP or starting a small business, are straightforward. Others are more sophisticated and perhaps lesser known, but overall just as effective. Your own personal objective is to cut your tax to the minimum to take every deduction the law allows. Tax strategies are the financial formulas that allow you to create tax deductions where you had none before.

YOUR TAX-REDUCING STRATEGY

One question I am asked over and over again: "Is paying less taxes really legal, patriotic, and moral?" By following the tax laws and regulations when you use tax strategies, you automatically pay your fair share, even if your share amounts to zero. Two neighbouring families, each with a $30,000 annual income and two children, could both be paying their fair share of income taxes, even if one family paid $5,000 and the other paid nothing at all. It's the way the system was designed.

We have a system that imposes taxes, not on your total income, but on a far smaller number known as your taxable income: your residual income after you subtract your exemptions, adjustments, credits, and deductions. Within the difference between total income and taxable income lie your opportunities for applying legal, powerful tax-reducing strategies.

During one of the best discussions on tax strategies in which I have ever participated, a lady caller said she thought reducing your taxes was cheating. Her feeling was that she wanted to pay taxes to help the homeless. This may come as a surprise to you, as it did to her, but very few of your tax dollars go to the homeless, or many other places you might prefer the money to go. By learning legal strategies for reducing her taxes, she could have given her tax savings directly to the homeless herself.

Another woman in the studio audience felt that paying more taxes was patriotic. The courts say that paying taxes has nothing to do with patriotism whether you pay a lot or none at all. The money goes into the economy whether paid to the government or used by you for a deductible purpose.

The question of the legality and morality of tax avoidance was resolved over 50 years ago by the House of Lords in the Duke of Westminster case:

> Every man is entitled if he can to order his affairs so that the tax attaching under the [Income Tax Act] is less than it otherwise would be.

This quotation should govern both your tax planning and your tax attitude. Rearranging your affairs to create deductions where you had none before is the secret to paying less taxes. All of the tax strategies you will learn can legally and easily reduce your taxes by thousands of dollars each year. Your job is to pick those strategies that best suit you and your family. Tax strategies should form one-third of your written financial plan.

How much time is required for tax planning? Reducing your taxes can be a do-it-at-home, do-it-yourself, do-it-in-your-spare-time project, requiring no more than a few minutes a week. What you will soon discover is that one hour spent learning and applying a legal tax strategy can typically save you $100 to $300 in taxes.

That's like earning $100 to $300 per hour in a tax-free job!

Canadian tax lawyers who reviewed the manuscript of *Wealth Without Risk* told me that there are a number of "anti-avoidance rules" in the Income Tax Act. In fact, one of these, the "General Anti-Avoidance Rule," gives Revenue Canada broad powers to attack tax-motivated transactions of many kinds. Your readers must be advised of this, they said, when it comes to so-called "aggressive" tax planning.

Strategy #116

LET ECONOMIC CONSIDERATIONS MOTIVATE YOUR DECISIONS. YOU'LL LOSE MONEY IN THE LONG RUN IF YOUR DECISIONS ARE PURELY TAX-MOTIVATED.

No one can guarantee that you won't ever be hit by an anti-avoidance rule of Revenue Canada. But is this really a risk?

Late in 1990, a Revenue Canada official stated that since the General Anti-Avoidance Rule (GAAR) became effective (September 1988), there were only 14 cases brought to the attention of Revenue Canada where the GAAR should apply. What's more, most of these cases involved either hypothetical situations submitted for review or multi-million-dollar "ruling requests." And what would happen if Revenue Canada successfully applied an anti-avoidance rule? You would probably have to pay the tax that you would have been liable to pay anyway, along with some interest on unpaid taxes.

As far as I'm concerned, paying the tax you would have had to pay is no risk at all. As for the interest, you will have the use of the money that would have gone to pay your taxes. Using my strategies, you may be able to make a far better return that will more than make up for any interest penalty.

My experience, and that of countless thousands of Charles J. Givens Organization members in the United States, is that aggressive tax planning has worked for us — and it can work for you.

Finally, I will tell you that I have taken a great deal of time and trouble to make certain that the strategies in this book are as accurate as possible. I have even gone to the expense of having the entire manuscript reviewed by a team of Canada's finest tax lawyers.

As you will see, the tax-related material in this book is intended to be a general summary of tax-planning opportunities that may be available. You should be aware that the advisability of any strategy will depend on your particular financial, tax and legal circumstances.

My organization has helped hundreds of thousands in their financial and tax planning. If you are not a member of the Givens Organization, I suggest you join. You should always consult professional advisors before implementing any strategy you are not clear about.

Strategy #117:
DETERMINE YOUR TAX "RATE" TO TRACK YOUR TAX SAVINGS.

Canada has a graduated tax system. That means the more you make, the more they take. Many taxpayers incorrectly believe that by earning more money they can end up with less money because they move into a higher tax bracket. Not so. The higher bracket percentage applies only to the additional income you earn and does not affect the amount of taxes you pay on the amount of money you were already earning. Never fall back on the excuse that you don't want to make more money because you will end up in a higher bracket. Instead, make all the money you can and reduce the taxes you pay by using Tax-Reducing Strategies.

The first step is to know your tax bracket. It's like assessing the damage — knowing the percentage of each dollar you earn that is lost forever. For example, if you are in the 28% bracket, you work from 9:00 a.m. to 11:30 a.m. each day for the government, and the rest of an eight-hour day for yourself.

Your *effective tax rate* (sometimes referred to as your average tax rate or your effective tax bracket) is the percentage of your total income you pay in taxes. If your total income is $40,000 per year and you pay a total of $10,000 in federal and provincial taxes, your effective tax rate is 25% ($10,000 divided by $40,000 equals 25%). In tax planning, knowing your effective tax rate will motivate you to create a good tax plan.

Your *marginal tax rate* is the percentage of taxes you pay on your top dollar of taxable income. It is also the percentage of tax you pay on one additional dollar of income, or conversely, the percentage you will save in taxes for each additional dollar of tax deductions you create.

The need to think "marginally" arises from the government practice of taxing you based on incremental additions to your income. In effect, the government wants larger and larger shares of your income as it grows. So they tax at a certain rate for the first chunk of your income, then take a slightly larger percentage of the next portion of your income, an even larger percentage of the next portion, and so on.

The chart that follows shows the marginal tax rates for the 1991 tax year. Your marginal tax rate is the percentage shown in the right-hand column of the schedule. These tax rates are federal only. Each province (other than Quebec) will extract a further amount of tax, based on a percentage of federal tax. (So you have to know your federal tax owing to determine the provincial tax bill.)

The amount of tax varies in each province, but typically ranges from 50% to 60% of the federal rate. You can ballpark your combined federal and provincial tax liability by multiplying the federal tax liability by 1.5 or 1.6 (depending on the applicable tax rate for your province). For example, if your province has a 51% tax rate, you multiply by 1.51. You can find your province's tax rate by looking at Schedule 1 of your T1 income tax return.

The province of Quebec, unique in the country, has a completely separate tax system, which requires the filing of a separate provincial tax return with different calculations and tax rates.

TAX RATE SCHEDULE
FEDERAL TAX RATES — 1991

TAXABLE INCOME	MARGINAL RATE ON ADDITIONAL TAXABLE INCOME
0 – $28,784	17%
$28,785 – $57,568	26%
$57,569 plus	29%

Note: The taxable income brackets shown above are partially indexed each year to account for inflation. Tax rates exclude federal and provincial surtaxes.

COMPUTING YOUR TAXES

As a result of the recent tax-reform changes, the calculation of your tax liability involves a number of new steps. Your first step is to calculate the total income you received during the tax year. Total income consists of employment income, pension income, income from other sources such as family allowance payments, unemployment insurance benefits, rental and investment income, and self-employment income including business, professional, and commissions.

The next step is to calculate your net income for tax purposes. There are a few deductions you may subtract from total income that will allow you to determine your net income. These deductions include contributions to a registered pension plan or to an RRSP, union or professional dues, child-care expenses, allowable business investment losses, moving expenses, alimony payments, investment-interest expenses, and employment expenses. From your net income you

Schedule 1 — Detailed Tax Calculation (see guide)

1990 Rates of Federal Income Tax

Taxable Income	Tax
$ 28,275 or less	17%
$ 28,275	$ 4,807 plus 26% on next $ 28,275
$ 56,550 or more	$ 12,158 plus 29% on remainder

Federal Income Tax — *Use the " 1990 Rates of Federal Income Tax" above.*

Taxable Income from line 400 on page 4 of your return

On the first		tax is
On remaining		tax at ____ % is

Total Federal income Tax on Taxable Income

Add: Tax Adjustments (please specify; see "Line 500" in guide)   **500**

Total

Subtract: Total Non-Refundable Tax Credits from line 350 on page 2 of your return   501

Federal Dividend Tax Credit: 13⅓% of Taxable amount of dividends from taxable Canadian corporations (line 120 on page 1 of your return).   502

Minimum Tax Carry-over (see "Line 504" in guide)   504

Total of above credits

Basic Federal Tax 506

Subtract: Federal Foreign Tax Credit — make separate calculation for each foreign country. ⊙

(a) Income Tax or Profits Tax paid to a foreign country   507

(b) Net Foreign Income † 508 / Net Income ††   X ("Basic Federal Tax" plus any Dividend Tax Credit) =

†   Net foreign income must be reduced by any foreign income exempt under a tax treaty (line 256).

††   Net income (line 236) (or if you filed a form T581 election, use line 7 of that form - if negative, enter zero) less any capital losses of other years allowed (line 253), employee home relocation loan deduction (line 248), stock option and shares deductions (line 249), capital gains deduction (line 254) and any foreign income exempt under a tax treaty (line 256).

Deduct (a) or (b) above, whichever is less 509

Federal Tax (please enter this amount on line 406 on page 4 of your return) 406

Federal Individual Surtax (see "Line 419" in guide)

Basic Federal Tax (line 506)

Subtract: Federal Forward Averaging Tax Credit (attach form T581)

Amount (A)

Add: 1. Amount (A)   x 5%

     2. Amount (A)   minus $15,000.00 x 3%

Individual Surtax (add lines 1 and 2 above)   510

Subtract: Additional Federal Foreign Tax Credit from Part II of form T2209   511

Sub Total   517

Subtract: Additional Investment Tax Credit from Section II of form T2038   518

Federal Individual Surtax (please enter this amount on line 419 on page 4 of your return)   419

Ontario Income Tax

Use form TIC (ONT.) TC to calculate your Ontario Income Tax then calculate your taxable income by subtracting allowable deductions as specified in your Revenue Canada tax guides.

There are a number of tax credits for which you may qualify that reduce your federal tax bill on a dollar-for-dollar basis. Most of these tax credits (actually referred to as "non-refundable tax credits") used to be known as personal exemptions. These tax credits include the basic personal amount, age amount, married amount, amounts for dependent children, and so on.

Finally, provincial taxes are a percentage of your basic federal taxes. (In addition, federal and provincial surtaxes may apply.)

There is a major difference between a tax deduction and a tax credit. Deductions reduce your taxable income by your tax rate percentage, but credits actually reduce your tax bill dollar-for-dollar. If you are in the 26% marginal tax bracket, $1 of tax deductions will reduce your tax bill by $.26 (26% × 1.00), but $1 of tax credits reduces your tax bill by one full dollar. Tax credits are, therefore, in this example about four times as powerful as deductions in reducing the amount of taxes you owe.

The bottom line is this: the more deductions and tax credits you create, the less you pay in taxes.

DETERMINING YOUR INCOME TAX*

The following chart will help you estimate this year's taxable income, as well as your tax liability.

Part I — CALCULATION OF INCOME

I. INCLUDE:

Employment Income	$ _____
Pension Income (including Old Age Security, Canada and Quebec Pension Plan benefits)	_____
Taxable Family Allowance Payments	_____
Unemployment Insurance Benefits	_____
Taxable Amount of Dividends from Taxable Canadian Corporations	_____
Interest and Other Investment Income	_____
Rental Payments	_____
Taxable Portion of Capital Gains (before capital gains exemption)	_____

Alimony and Separation Allowance Income	_____
Annuity Income	_____
Business or Professional Income	_____
Farming and Fishing Income	_____
Royalty Income	_____
Total Income Before Deductions	$ _____ (A)

*Note: This chart has been simplified for your convenience in estimating your taxable income and taxes. Your actual taxes may differ, for example, if you have foreign income or if you fall under the social benefit repayment rules — around $50,000 annual income. The chart also ignores such items as federal and provincial surtaxes, as well as GST, child tax and other federal and provincial tax credits.

II. DO NOT INCLUDE:

Tax-free Insurance Proceeds	$ _____
Gifts	_____
Inheritances	_____
Total	$ _____

PART II - DEDUCTIONS THAT REDUCE TOTAL INCOME

Pension Plan Contributions	_____
RRSP Contributions	_____
Union, Professional and Like Dues	_____
Child-Care Expenses	_____
Moving Expenses	_____
Tax-Deductible Alimony and Separation Allowances	_____
Carrying Charges for Investments	_____
Other	_____
Deductions from Total Income	_____ (B)
Net income for tax purposes (A minus B)	_____

PART III - DEDUCTIONS IN COMPUTING TAXABLE INCOME

Stock Option and Share Deductions	_____
Losses Carried Over from Other Years	_____
Capital Gains Exemption	_____
Other	_____

Total Deductions in Computing
  Taxable Income   _____ (C)

Taxable Income (A – B – C)   _____ (D)

PART IV - COMPUTE FEDERAL TAXES

Multiply Federal Tax Rates (from
Tax Rate Schedule, Page 124) times
Taxable Income(D) _____ + _____ %× _____ (D) = _____ $(E)

                Dollar Amount   Fed. Tax Rate   Taxable Income   Federal Taxes

Example 1: If your taxable income is $27,000, your Federal Taxes
           would be:
                0 + 17% × 27,000, = $4,590

Example 2: If your taxable income is $58,000, your Federal Taxes
           would be:
              $12,377 + 29% × ($58,000 – $57,569) = $12,502

Note: The effective federal tax rates for the above examples are
17% and 21.6% respectively. For tax bracket see the tax table on page
124.

PART V — APPLY FEDERAL TAX CREDITS*

Basic Personal Amount $ _____

Age Amount $ _____

Married Amount $ _____

Amounts for Dependent Children
  ($ ____ per child)   _____

Additional Personal Amounts   _____

Credits for Canada or Quebec
  Pension Plan Contributions and
  Unemployment Insurance Premiums   _____

Pension Income Tax Credit   _____

Disability Tax Credits   _____

Tuition and Education Tax Credits   _____

Medical Expense Tax Credits   _____

Charitable Donation Tax Credits[†]   _____

Total Non-Refundable Tax Credits   _____

Dividend Tax Credit (16⅔%
   of Dividends from Taxable Canadian
   Corporations)   _____
Total credits (Add all of the above)   _____ (F)
Basic Federal Tax (E - F)   _____ (G)

*Note: The actual value of non-refundable tax credits at the federal level is generally 17% of the
   amounts on page two of your T1 tax return, except for charitable donations in excess of
   $250. Charitable donations are tax credits at the rate of 17% of the first $250, 29% of
   amounts over $250.

Total Non-Refundable Tax Credits   _____
Dividend Tax Credit (16⅔%
   of Dividends from Taxable Canadian
   Corporations)   _____
Total credits (Add all of the above)   _____ (F)
Basic Federal Tax (E - F)   _____ (G)

VI — COMPUTE PROVINCIAL TAX

Multiply provincial tax
   rate times Basic   _____ % × _____ = _____
Federal tax (G)   Provincial Tax   Basic Federal   Provincial
                              Tax   Tax Due

†Note: The above calculations are not applicable to the Quebec tax system.

PART VII — COMPUTE TOTAL TAX

Basic Federal Tax   _____
+ Provincial Tax Due   _____
Total Tax Due for the year   _____

Strategy #118:
PAY INSTALMENTS AND OTHER TAXES ON TIME
TO AVOID BIG PENALTIES.

Interest penalties on unpaid taxes are one of Revenue Canada's most
lucrative sources of income. Over the years, countless millions of dollars have come into the tax coffers as a result of taxpayers' sloppiness
in keeping up to date on tax payments.

Revenue Canada is entitled to charge interest on unpaid taxes and delinquent instalments. The interest rate is set quarterly based on the average 90-day government of Canada T-bill rate during the first month of the preceding calendar quarter, plus an additional charge of 2%. Next to credit card interest, sitting on your tax payments past the due date can be one of the most expensive drains on your funds.

If more than one-quarter of your total income is not subject to withholding at source, and your federal tax for the current and previous year is more than $1,000, you are required to make quarterly tax-instalment payments using your personalized T7D form where you bank, or if you do not have a personalized form, use the remittance form in the appropriate Revenue Canada Instalment Guide. Otherwise, the interest penalties mentioned above will apply. Additional interest charges may apply for late or delinquent instalments. Generally, to the extent that interest payable exceeds $1,000, a 50% interest surcharge will apply.

You can base your required tax instalment payments on the actual tax you paid for the preceding year or an estimate of the tax for the current year, whichever is less. However, if you base your instalment payments on your estimate of the tax for the current year and it is too low, the interest penalties will still apply.

THE CHARLES J. GIVENS TAX-REDUCING STRATEGIES — HOW THEY CAN WORK FOR YOU

The following example illustrates how tax-reducing strategies can make a huge difference to your personal fortune.

Figure 8.1 shows the tax return of an individual who does not take advantage of the Charles J. Givens tax-planning strategies. As you will see, the individual ends up having $49,256 in taxable income (see line 260), with tax credits of only $1,184 (line 338).

Figure 8.2 shows the same individual's tax return, using several Charles J. Givens' tax strategies, which you will learn in forthcoming chapters. As you can see, the taxpayer has slashed his taxable income to $26,789. In addition, his tax credits have nearly doubled to $2,078.

How much in real dollars does the tax plan save?

Without the Charles J. Givens tax-reducing strategies, the individual's total payable tax would be more than $13,800 (see line 435). Using the tax-reducing strategies, the individual will slash his taxes by over $10,400 and reduce his tax bill to $3,400! If this process is repeated every year for 25 years, with the tax savings invested at 10% (after tax), the difference could accumulate to more than $1,000,000 simply by using the Charles J. Givens tax-reducing strategies!

FIGURE 8.1 / Without Charles J. Givens Strategies

Please do not use this area	▐◆▌	Revenue Canada Taxation	Revenu Canada Impôt	**T1 GENERAL 1990**

Federal and Ontario
Individual Income Tax Return
Step 1 - Identification ─────────────────────── Complete the following ───────

Usual First Name and Initial   Surname, Family or Last Name (Please print)

Your Social Insurance Number

Present Address (Please Print) *Number, Street and Apt. No., or P.O. No. or R.R. No.*

Your Spouse's Social Insurance Number

City

On December 31, 1990, you were: Married ☐1 Widow(er) ☐2 Divorced ☐3 Separated ☐4 Single ☐5

Name of Spouse

Province or Territory   *Postal Code*

Address of Spouse: same as mine ☐ or

Your Date of Birth   Day   Month   Year

Have you filed an Income Tax Return before?   YES ☐   NO ☐
If "YES", please indicate for what year: 19 ☐

Your Province or Territory of Residence on December 31, 1990, was:

Name on last return: same as above ☐ or

If you were self-employed in 1990, please state province or territory of self-employment:

Address on last return: same as above ☐ or

If you became or ceased to be a resident of Canada in 1990, give:
Day   Month   Day   Month
Date of Entry ☐☐ or Departure ☐☐

Type of work or occupation in 1990

Name of present employer

If taxpayer is deceased, please give date of death: Day   Month   Year

Step 2 - Calculation of Total Income

Please do not use this area

Employment Income Employment income before deductions from Box (14) or Box (C) on all T4 slips (attach copy 2 of T4 slips)	101	45386 00	⊙
Commissions from Box (42) or Box (P) on all T4 slips, included in above total **102**			
Other employment income including tips and gratuities, etc.	104		⊙
Pension Income Old Age Security pension (from Box (18) or Box (F) on T4A(OAS))	113		⊙
Canada or Quebec Pension Plan benefits (attach copy 2 of T4A(P) slip)	114		⊙
Other pensions or superannuation (attach copy 3 of T4A slips)	115		⊙
Family allowance payments (attach copy of TFA1 slip)	118		⊙
Unemployment Insurance benefits (attach copy 2 of T4U slip)	119		⊙
Income from Other Sources Taxable amount of dividends from taxable Canadian corporations (attach completed Schedule 5)	120	2354 00	⊙
Interest and other investment income (attach completed Schedule 5)	121	1516 00	⊙
Partnership income: limited or non-active partners only (attach completed Schedule 5) Net 122			⊙
Rental income Gross **160** Net 126			⊙
Taxable capital gains (attach completed Schedule 3)	127	3500 00	⊙
Alimony or separation allowance income	128		⊙
Registered retirement savings plan income (attach T4RSP slips)	129		⊙
Other income (please specify: see line 130 in guide)	130		⊙
Self-Employment Income Business income Gross **162** Net 135			⊙
Professional income Gross **164** Net 137			⊙
Commission income Gross **166** Net 139			⊙
Farming income Gross **168** Net 141			⊙
Fishing income Gross **170** Net 143			⊙
Total Income (add lines 101 to 143 inclusive - please enter this amount on line 200 on page 2) **150**		52756 00 ◆	52756 00

PLEASE DO NOT USE THIS AREA		
605		600

Step 3 - Calculation of Taxable Income

	Total Income (from line 150 on page 1) **200**		52756 00
Registered pension plan contributions	**207**	⊙	
Registered retirement savings plan contributions (attach receipts)	**208**	⊙	
Annual union, professional or like dues (attach receipts)	**212**	⊙	
Child care expenses (attach form T778)	**214**	⊙	
Attendant care expenses (attach form T929)	**215**	⊙	
Allowable business investment losses	**217**	⊙	
Moving expenses (attach form T1-M)	**219**	⊙	
Alimony or separation allowance paid	**220**	⊙	
Carrying charges and interest expenses (attach completed Schedule 5)	**221**	⊙	
Exploration and development expenses (attach completed Schedule 5)	**224**	⊙	
Other employment expenses (attach form T2200 or TL2)	**229**	⊙	
Other deductions (please specify; see line 232 in guide)	**232**	⊙	
Add lines 207 to 232 inclusive **233**	NIL	▶	NIL

Net income before adjustments (subtract line 233 from line 200) **234** — 52756 00

Social benefits repayment: if you reported income at line 113, 118 and/or 119 see line 235 in guide • ⊙ **235**

Net Income (subtract line 235 from line 234) **236** 52756 00

Accumulated forward averaging amount withdrawal (attach form T581) **237**

(add lines 236 and 237) **239** 52756 00

Employee home relocation loan deduction (from T4 slip)	**248**	⊙	
Stock option and shares deductions	**249**	⊙	
Limited partnership losses of other years	**251**	⊙	
Non-capital losses of other years	**252**	⊙	
Net capital losses of other years (1972 to 1989)	**253**	⊙	
Capital gains deduction (attach form T657)	**254**	3500 00 ⊙	
Northern residents deductions (attach form T2222)	**255**	⊙	
Additional deductions (as specified at line 256 in guide)	**256**	⊙	
Add lines 248 to 256 inclusive **257**	3500 00	▶	3500 00

Taxable Income (subtract line 257 from line 239 and proceed to Step 4 below) **260** 49256 00

Step 4 - Calculation of Total Non-Refundable Tax Credits

Basic personal amount	Claim $6,169.00 **300**	6169 00	
Age amount, if you were born in 1925 or earlier	Claim $3,327.00 **301**		
Married amount (see line 303 in guide)	**303**	⊙	
Amounts for dependent children (see line 304 in guide)	**304**	798 00 ⊙	
Additional personal amounts (attach completed Schedule 6)	**305**	⊙	
Canada or Quebec Pension Plan contributions			
Contributions through employment from Box (16) or Box (D) on all T4 slips (maximum $574.20)	**308**	• ⊙	
Contribution payable on self-employment earnings (from page 3)	**310**	•	
Unemployment Insurance premiums from Box (18) or Box (E) on all T4 slips (maximum $748.80)	**312**	• ⊙	
Pension income amount (maximum $1,000, see line 314 in guide)	**314**	⊙	
Disability amount for self (claim $3,327.00)	**316**	⊙	
Disability amount for dependant other than spouse	**318**	⊙	
Tuition fees for self (attach form T2202A or receipts)	**320**	⊙	
Education amount for self (attach form T2202 or T2202A)	**322**	⊙	
Tuition fees and education amount transferred from child (attach form T2202 or T2202A)	**324**	⊙	
Amounts transferred from spouse (attach completed Schedule 2)	**326**	⊙	
Medical expenses (attach receipts and complete Schedule 4)	**330** 504 00	⊙	
Subtract: 3% of line 236 above or $1,542 whichever is less	1542 00		
Allowable portion of medical expenses	NIL ▶ **332**	NIL	
Add lines 300 to 326 inclusive and line 332 (IF THIS AMOUNT EXCEEDS THE AMOUNT AT LINE 260, SEE "LINE 335" IN GUIDE) **335**	6967 00		

NON-REFUNDABLE TAX CREDITS: 17% of line 335 or see Table A instructions **338** 1184 00

Charitable donations (attach receipts)	**340**	⊙	
Gifts to Canada or a province (attach receipts)	**342**	⊙	
Total Donations (see line 347 in guide)	**344**	Credit claimed **347**	

Total Non-Refundable Tax Credits (add lines 338 and 347 and proceed to Step 5 on page 4) **350** 1184 00

Taxable Income from line 260 on page 2	400	49256 00

─────── **TABLE METHOD ONLY** ───────

Federal Income Tax (look up amount from line 400 in Table A)	401	
Enter: Total non-refundable tax credits from line 350 on page 2	402	

Federal Tax (line 401 minus line 402; if negative, enter zero or from line 406 on Schedule 1) 406			8764 00
Federal political contribution tax credit Total contributions **409**		⊙	
Allowable tax credit (from calculation at line 410 in guide)	410	•	
Investment tax credit (attach form T2038 (IND))	412	•	
Labour-Sponsored Funds tax credit (attach receipts)	414	•	
Total of above credits 416		▶	NIL
Federal tax before federal individual surtax (line 406 minus line 416: if negative, enter zero) 417			8764 00
Federal individual surtax (look up amount from line 406 in Table B or from line 419 on Schedule 1)	419		438 00

Net Federal Tax (add lines 417 and 419) 420		9202 00

Ontario tax (see line 423 in guide)	423	4645 00
Canada Pension Plan contribution payable on self-employment earnings from page 3	431	
Repayment of Social Benefits (from calculation at line 235 in guide)	432	
Repayment of child tax credit overpayment from Schedule 7, Part B	434	•

Total Payable (add lines 420 to 434 inclusive) 435		13847 00 •

─ **Please do not use this area** ─

683		
684		

Total income tax deducted from all information slips	437	12360 00	• ⊙
Federal Credits			
Child tax credit			
(attach Schedule 7, complete Parts A and B)	444		•
Federal sales tax credit			
(attach Schedule 7, complete Parts A and C)	446		•
Canada Pension Plan overpayment	448		•
Unemployment Insurance overpayment	450		•
Refund of investment tax credit			
(attach form T2038 (IND))	454		•
Part XII.2 tax credit (attach T3 slip)	456		• ⊙
Provincial Credits			
Ontario tax credits	464		•
Other Credits			
Tax paid by instalments	476		• ⊙
Forward averaging tax credit (attach form T581)	478		•

Total Credits (add lines 437 to 478 inclusive) 482	▶	12360 00

Subtract line 482 from line 435 and enter
the difference in applicable space below.   1487 00

A difference of less than $1.00 is neither charged nor refunded.

I hereby certify that the information given in this return and in any documents attached is true, correct and complete in every respect and fully discloses my income from all sources.

Please sign here

	Area code			Date
Telephone				

It is a serious offence to make a false return.

Privacy Act Personal Information Bank number RCT/P-PU-005

Refund **484**	▼	•
Balance Due **485**		1487 00 •

Amount Enclosed	1487 00 ●

Please attach cheque or money order **payable to the Receiver General. Do not mail cash.** Payment is due not later than April 30, 1991.

469

┌ **Language of correspondence — Langue de correspondance** ─

Please indicate below the language of your choice for subsequent correspondence and returns.	Veuillez indiquer plus bas dans quelle langue vous désirez recevoir toute correspondance subséquente et vos prochaines déclarations de revenus.

1. English ☐ Anglaise
2. French ☐ Française

490

If you paid to have your return prepared, please check box ➡ ☐

Form authorized and prescribed by order of the Minister of National Revenue for purposes of Part I: Part I.1 and Part I.2 of the Income Tax Act, Part I of the Canada Pension Plan and Part VIII of the Unemployment Insurance Act.

FIGURE 8.2 / With Charles J. Givens Strategies

Please do not use this area	🍁	Revenue Canada Taxation	Revenu Canada Impôt		T1 GENERAL 1990

Federal and Ontario
Individual Income Tax Return

Step 1 - Identification

Complete the following

Usual First Name and Initial   Surname, Family or Last Name (Please print)

Your Social Insurance Number

Present Address (Please Print) *Number, Street and Apt. No., or P.O. No. or R.R. No.*

Your Spouse's Social Insurance Number

City

On December 31, 1990, you were: — Married Widow(er) Divorced Separated Single 1☐ 2☐ 3☐ 4☐ 5☐

Name of Spouse

Province or Territory   *Postal Code*

Address of Spouse: same as mine ☐ or

	Day	Month	Year

Your Date of Birth

Have you filed an Income Tax Return before?   YES ☐ NO ☐
If "YES", please indicate for what year: 19 ☐☐

Your Province or Territory of Residence on December 31, 1990, was:

Name on last return: same as above ☐ or

If you were self-employed in 1990, please state province or territory of self-employment:

Address on last return: same as above ☐ or

If you became or ceased to be a resident of Canada in 1990, give:

	Day	Month		Day	Month

Type of work or occupation in 1990

Date of Entry ☐☐ ☐☐ or Departure ☐☐ ☐☐

Name of present employer

If taxpayer is deceased, please give date of death: Day Month Year

Step 2 - Calculation of Total Income

Please do not use this area

Employment Income	Employment income before deductions from Box (14) or Box (C) on all T4 slips (attach copy 2 of T4 slips)	**101**	45386 00 ⊙
	Commissions from Box (42) or Box (P) on all T4 slips, included in above total **102**		
	Other employment income including tips and gratuities, etc.	**104**	⊙
Pension Income	Old Age Security pension (from Box (18) or Box (F) on T4A(OAS))	**113**	⊙
	Canada or Quebec Pension Plan benefits (attach copy 2 of T4A(P) slip)	**114**	⊙
	Other pensions or superannuation (attach copy 3 of T4A slips)	**115**	⊙
	Family allowance payments (attach copy of TFA1 slip)	**118**	⊙
	Unemployment Insurance benefits (attach copy 2 of T4U slip)	**119**	⊙
Income from Other Sources	Taxable amount of dividends from taxable Canadian corporations (attach completed Schedule 5)	**120**	2354 00 ⊙
	Interest and other investment income (attach completed Schedule 5)	**121**	1516 00 ⊙
	Partnership income: limited or non-active partners only (attach completed Schedule 5) Net **122**		⊙
	Rental income Gross **160** Net **126**		⊙
	Taxable capital gains (attach completed Schedule 3)	**127**	3500 00
	Alimony or separation allowance income	**128**	⊙
	Registered retirement savings plan income (attach T4RSP slips)	**129**	⊙
	Other income (please specify; see line 130 in guide)	**130**	⊙
Self-Employment Income	Business income Gross **162** 7258 00 Net **135**		(8591 00) ⊙
	Professional income Gross **164** Net **137**		⊙
	Commission income Gross **166** Net **139**		⊙
	Farming income Gross **168** Net **141**		⊙
	Fishing income Gross **170** Net **143**		⊙
Total Income (add lines 101 to 143 inclusive - please enter this amount on line 200 on page 2) **150**		44165 00 ►	44165 00

PLEASE DO NOT USE THIS AREA						
605				**600**		

	Total Income (from line 150 on page 1) 200			44165 00
Registered pension plan contributions	207		⊙	
Registered retirement savings plan contributions (attach receipts)	208	7359 00	⊙	
Annual union, professional or like dues (attach receipts)	212		⊙	
Child care expenses (attach form T778)	214		⊙	
Attendant care expenses (attach form T929)	215		⊙	
Allowable business investment losses	217		⊙	
Moving expenses (attach form T1-M)	219	1435 00	⊙	
Alimony or separation allowance paid	220		⊙	
Carrying charges and interest expenses (attach completed Schedule 5)	221	2332 00	⊙	
Exploration and development expenses (attach completed Schedule 5)	224		⊙	
Other employment expenses (attach form T2200 or TL2)	229		⊙	
Other deductions (please specify; see line 232 in guide)	232		⊙	
Add lines 207 to 232 inclusive 233		11126 00 ◆		11126 00

Net income before adjustments (subtract line 233 from line 200) 234 — 33039 00

Social benefits repayment: if you reported income at line 113,
118 and/or 119 see line 235 in guide — 235 — • ⊙

Net Income (subtract line 235 from line 234) 236 — 33039 00

Accumulated forward averaging amount withdrawal (attach form T581) 237

(add lines 236 and 237) 239 — 33039 00

Employee home relocation loan deduction (from T4 slip)	248	2750 00	⊙	
Stock option and shares deductions	249		⊙	
Limited partnership losses of other years	251		⊙	
Non-capital losses of other years	252		⊙	
Net capital losses of other years (1972 to 1989)	253		⊙	
Capital gains deduction (attach form T657)	254	3500 00	⊙	
Northern residents deductions (attach form T2222)	255		⊙	
Additional deductions (as specified at line 256 in guide)	256		⊙	
Add lines 248 to 256 inclusive 257		6250 ◆		6250 00

Taxable Income (subtract line 257 from line 239 and proceed to Step 4 below) 260 — 26789 00

Step 4 - Calculation of Total Non-Refundable Tax Credits

Basic personal amount	Claim $6,169.00 300	6169 00		
Age amount, if you were born in 1925 or earlier	Claim $3,327.00 301			
Married amount (see line 303 in guide)	303		⊙	
Amounts for dependent children (see line 304 in guide)	304	399 00	⊙	
Additional personal amounts (attach completed Schedule 6)	305	5141 00	⊙	
Canada or Quebec Pension Plan contributions				
Contributions through employment from Box (16) or Box (D) on all T4 slips (maximum $574.20)	308		• ⊙	
Contribution payable on self-employment earnings (from page 3)	310		•	
Unemployment Insurance premiums from Box (18) or Box (E) on all T4 slips (maximum $748.80)	312		• ⊙	
Pension income amount (maximum $1,000, see line 314 in guide)	314		⊙	
Disability amount for self (claim $3,327.00)	316		⊙	
Disability amount for dependant other than spouse	318		⊙	
Tuition fees for self (attach form T2202A or receipts)	320		⊙	
Education amount for self (attach form T2202 or T2202A)	322		⊙	
Tuition fees and education amount transferred from child (attach form T2202 or T2202A)	324		⊙	
Amounts transferred from spouse (attach completed Schedule 2)	326		⊙	
Medical expenses (attach receipts and complete Schedule 4) 330	1504 00		⊙	
Subtract: 3% of line 236 above or $1,542 whichever is less	991 00			
Allowable portion of medical expenses	513 00 ◆ 332	513 00		
Add lines 300 to 326 inclusive and line 332 (IF THIS AMOUNT EXCEEDS THE AMOUNT AT LINE 260, SEE "LINE 335" IN GUIDE) 335		12222 00		

NON-REFUNDABLE TAX CREDITS: 17% of line 335 or see Table A instructions 338 — 2078 00

Charitable donations (attach receipts)	340	⊙	
Gifts to Canada or a province (attach receipts)	342	⊙	
Total Donations (see line 347 in guide)	344	**Credit claimed** 347	

Total Non-Refundable Tax Credits (add lines 338 and 347 and proceed to Step 5 on page 4) 350 — 2078 00

Taxable Income from line 260 on page 2 **400** | 26789 | 00

TABLE METHOD ONLY

Federal Income Tax (look up amount from line 400 in Table A)	**401**	4553 | 00
Enter: Total non-refundable tax credits from line 350 on page 2	**402**	2078 | 00

Federal Tax (line 401 minus line 402: if negative, enter zero or from line 406 on Schedule 1)	**406**		2475 | 00
Federal political contribution tax credit Total contributions **409**		⊙	
Allowable tax credit (from calculation at line 410 in guide)	**410**	•	
Investment tax credit (attach form T2038 (IND))	**412**	•	
Labour-Sponsored Funds tax credit (attach receipts)	**414**	•	
Total of above credits **416**		►	NIL
Federal tax before federal individual surtax (line 406 minus line 416: if negative, enter zero)	**417**		2475 | 00
Federal individual surtax (look up amount from line 406 in Table B **or** from line 419 on Schedule 1)	**419**		124 | 00

Net Federal Tax (add lines 417 and 419)	**420**	2599 | 00

Ontario tax (see line 423 in guide)	**423**	1311 | 80	
Canada Pension Plan contribution payable on self-employment earnings from page 3	**431**		
Repayment of Social Benefits (from calculation at line 235 in guide)	**432**		
Repayment of child tax credit overpayment from Schedule 7, Part B	**434**		•

Total Payable (add lines 420 to 434 inclusive)	**435**	3910 | 80 •

— Please do not use this area —

683 [ ]

684 [ ]

Total income tax deducted from all information slips	**437**	12360 | 00	• ⊙
Federal Credits			
Child tax credit			
(attach Schedule 7, complete Parts A and B)	**444**		•
Federal sales tax credit			
(attach Schedule 7, complete Parts A and C)	**445**		•
Canada Pension Plan overpayment	**448**		•
Unemployment Insurance overpayment	**450**		•
Refund of investment tax credit			
(attach form T2038 (IND))	**454**		•
Part XII.2 tax credit (attach T3 slip)	**456**		• ⊙
Provincial Credits			
Ontario tax credits	**464**		
Other Credits			
Tax paid by instalments	**476**		• ⊙
Forward averaging tax credit (attach form T581)	**478**		•

Total Credits (add lines 437 to 478 inclusive)	**482**	12360 | 00 ►	12360 | 00

Subtract line 482 from line 435 and enter the difference in applicable space below.

A difference of less than $1.00 is neither charged nor refunded.

| | | 8450 \| 00 |

I hereby certify that the information given in this return and in any documents attached is true, correct and complete in every respect and fully discloses my income from all sources.

Please sign here

Telephone | Area code | | Date

It is a serious offence to make a false return.

Privacy Act Personal Information Bank number RCT/P-PU-005

Refund **484** | 8450 | 00 •   Balance Due **485** | 8450 | 00 •

Amount Enclosed | | •

Please attach cheque or money order **payable to the Receiver General. Do not mail cash.** Payment is due not later than April 30, 1991.

469

— Language of correspondence — Langue de correspondance —

Please indicate below the language of your choice for subsequent correspondence and returns.

Veuillez indiquer plus bas dans quelle langue vous désirez recevoir toute correspondance subséquente et vos prochaines déclarations de revenus.

1. English ☐ Anglaise
2. French ☐ Française

490

If you paid to have your return prepared, please check box ➡ [ ]

Form authorized and prescribed by order of the Minister of National Revenue for purposes of Part I, Part I.1 and Part I.2 of the Income Tax Act, Part I of the Canada Pension Plan and Part VIII of the Unemployment Insurance Act.

Chapter 9

TAX-RETURN FILING STRATEGIES

Take it off, take it all off!

Gypsy Rose Lee, entertainer/author, 1936

Objective: Reduce your taxes and chances of an audit at the same time.

Although I have from time to time met people who truly feel that they have an obligation to fund the tax system with as much of their own money as possible — a minority to be sure — I have never met anyone who truly welcomed a tax audit.

The reasons are pretty straightforward. First, a tax audit will consume large amounts of your time and energy while you root around trying to find documents and receipts which may not be quite where you thought they would be. This time is unpaid time. To put that another way, it is time spent helping the government determine if they took their proper share of what you earned before, but it is definitely not time spent helping earn anything now.

Second, we now understand that, for the most part, the government is hesitant to waste its own time checking returns unless it genuinely feels that it will turn up extra revenue from the visit. As such, it is clear from the moment the audit notice reaches you that you and the government are going to disagree on a number of issues — the main one, of course, being that they say you owe more money, and you say you don't.

Since no one enjoys entering a situation predicated on conflict, not to mention a situation which wastes time and has a potential financial cost, it is clear that the audit process is not something to be relished.

In fact, the four-letter word that keeps most people from becoming better "tax strategists" is *fear*. Most fear in life comes from lack of knowledge, seldom from any real threat. In the case of Revenue Canada, fear is usually founded in fantasy, not fact — fear of an audit, fear of embarrassment, fear of harassment, and worse yet, fear of jail. Unless you are an outright tax cheater, you have nothing to worry about. To succeed financially you must have the confidence to use tax strategies. Confidence and courage come from knowledge of how the tax system really works, and how to use the system in your favour.

Here is the good news. The government simply lacks the resources to audit everyone. Your objective therefore is to not only reduce the tax that you owe but to reduce your likelihood of an audit at the same time.

Strategy #119:
CHOOSE AN AGGRESSIVE TAX PREPARER OR NONE AT ALL.

Whether or not you use a tax preparer is strictly a matter of choice. With the complexity of the Canadian tax laws, more and more people will probably look for help.

A good tax preparer is an aggressive tax preparer. Many tax laws and rules are written to intimidate tax preparers into becoming unnecessarily meek, mild, and conservative. If your tax preparer is full of warnings, such as, "I wouldn't take that deduction, it might send up a red flag," and is short on explanations, the money you are paying for so-called tax advice pales beside the money you are unnecessarily paying in taxes.

This is not to say, however, that you should always choose the tax preparer who promises you the least amount of taxes to pay. There are a few tax preparers who cross the line between tax avoidance and tax evasion by claiming non-existent tax deductions, or even suppressing income. Avoid these people like the plague! Instead, find an aggressive preparer who is able to work within the tax laws to allow you to pay the least amount of taxes.

The most effective way to choose a tax preparer is to interview several with one key question: "How much did you pay in taxes last year?" If the answer is a higher percentage of income taxes than you are paying, or a hedge like "None of your business!" you are dealing with a tax loser, not an effective tax preparer. If a tax expert can't help himself pay less tax, how can you expect that he will be able to help you? Another approach is to quiz your friends until you find one who is near the zero tax bracket. Use his or her tax preparer. But even if you use a tax preparer, you must still learn to communicate effectively about taxes.

Strategy #120:
PREPARE YOUR OWN RETURN AT LEAST ONCE.

One question I am often asked at my workshops is, "Should I prepare my own return?" The answer is yes — completely once, and partially each year. Without understanding how deductions and credits affect your return, you will never have the confidence or develop the knowledge to reduce your taxes. In addition, you should know that no tax preparer knows it all. If you truly want to reduce your taxes, you must become something of an expert about tax affairs on your own. The best way to begin is by doing your own return.

Pencil in your income and deductions — even if you intend to take your papers to a tax preparer. This process will discipline you into becoming a better record keeper as well as create a checklist for possible deductions and needed records.

By becoming your own tax expert, you will be in a position to tell your tax preparer what approaches to use in preparing your return. You will also be able to review your tax preparer's calculations to make certain that illegal shortcuts have not been taken or items have not been overlooked that may result in your having to pay more tax than necessary. There are hidden traps in the way that your tax preparer may take deductions. Tax preparers may, for instance, choose alternatives for automobile, interest, or investment deductions that save preparation time but give you far less in deductions. You must be in a position to tell your preparer what forms and formulas to use if you want to pay less in taxes.

Strategy #121:
WHEN IN DOUBT, DEDUCT IT.

Most taxpayers think they are doing themselves a favour by being ultraconservative in taking deductions. Nothing could be further from the truth. If you are tax-deduction "shy," not only do you end up spending thousands of dollars in unnecessary taxes, you don't even reduce your chances for audit. Most audits are done at random and have little to do with whether you take all of your allowable deductions or only a few.

If you want to reach your financial goals, you must adopt the winning tax strategy: When in doubt, deduct it. Take everything the law allows. Follow the rules, but deduct all grey areas in your favour. Deducting grey areas does not constitute tax evasion: grey areas are simply areas of ambiguity and uncertainty about what the tax laws really mean.

Remember, also, that most tax returns are not audited by Revenue Canada. This means that when it comes to deducting grey areas, odds are that you will be allowed the deduction with no hassle.

In fact, even if Revenue Canada examines your return, you will still have a good chance of winning your point. You will be surprised, as you learn more about taxes, at how much of the Income Tax Act is ambiguous. Tax laws are passed by politicians who have little or no experience in tax matters. Simple record keeping and tax strategies will always have you prepared to win your point.

Strategy #122:
NEVER FILE YOUR RETURN LATE.

The tax-filing deadline for personal tax returns is usually April 30. If you file your return late, stiff penalties apply. You must pay a late-filing penalty equal to 5% of the unpaid balance of the taxes as of April 30, plus 1% of the unpaid balance for each full month (to a maximum of 12 months) that the return is late. Even stiffer penalties can apply if you file late more than once in any four-year period.

If you do not have the money to pay your taxes, filing your return on time will enable you to avoid the late-filing penalty of 5%. In this case, try attaching a series of post-dated cheques to your return. Revenue Canada will not count a post-dated cheque as a payment on time, but if the last day for paying penalty-free taxes arrives and you still don't have the money, a post-dated cheque or series of cheques should get you off the hook as far as timely filing. Circle the date or include a note about the cheque(s) so someone will notice your intent. Your notice of Assessment will not take into account the cheques that are still post-dated when the notice is prepared. The cheques will be credited to your account when they become payable and you will receive an acknowledgement from Revenue Canada. However, you will still be charged interest from April 30 until the account is paid in full.

If, on the other hand, your return will be filed late (for whatever reason) and you have the money to pay the taxes, you should estimate your taxes and pay them to Revenue Canada in order to minimize your late-filing fee.

Strategy #123:
AVOID TRIPPING OFF THE REVENUE CANADA COMPUTER.

Revenue Canada relies largely on computer analysis to pick up irregularities in income tax returns. You should avoid filing your return in such a way that the computer will choose your return for further scrutiny. One obvious example is math errors. A significant number of math errors in your return will guarantee closer scrutiny of your documents, scrutiny that might lead in a direction you would rather not take. Similarly, unusually high amounts in any one category are likely to trip the computer as well. Say, for example, that you have a valid deduction for moving expenses — a deduction that meets all the guidelines Revenue Canada has issued relating to moving for purposes of changing employment. If, as it happens, you moved from Newfoundland to Victoria, it is likely that your moving expenses — even if you hired a reasonably priced moving company — will be higher than the norm. It follows that sending in your return with this deduction, even though the deduction is 100% correct, is more likely to bring additional attention to your documents, and increase the chance of an audit.

Strategy #124:
INCLUDE AN EXPLANATION WHEN YOU FILE.

If you have business, professional, or commission income and your expenses-to-income ratio shifts upward dramatically, the computer may flag your return. Likewise, if you show several years of small business losses, you could also trip off the computers. Don't avoid taking deductions out of fear. If you include an explanation of why the change occurred you may reduce your chance of audit on these items.

Strategy #125:
AVOID THE NO-TAX HONOUR ROLL
BY PAYING A MINIMUM TAX.

Although in the United States the zero tax bracket is an enviable position in which to be and doesn't raise eyebrows (I paid no income tax legally for 20 years), in Canada the zero tax bracket is to be avoided.

If you have a high income, be careful of aggressive tax strategies that would result in your claiming so many deductions and credits that you pay absolutely no taxes. Most tax advisors I've spoken with believe that somewhere in Ottawa, there is a list of such people. People on this list may be in for some special attention by Revenue Canada, even though what they are doing is perfectly legal.

As a result, if you're thinking of investing in a tax shelter or using other aggressive strategies that will leave you in a zero bracket, back off a bit and pay at least $200 in taxes. On the other hand, if you legally qualify for the deductions, don't pass up more than that amount.

Strategy #126:
SEND YOUR OWN "REMINDER NOTICE"
TO REVENUE CANADA.

The bigger the refund you claim, the longer you may have to wait to get your cheque from Revenue Canada. If, by mid-summer, you're still waiting, call or write your District Taxation Office to see where your money is. Your letter may speed up the processing of your return. It is your money you never owed in the first place; don't hesitate to ask where it is.

Strategy #127:
APPLY FOR A REDUCTION OF
AT-SOURCE DEDUCTIONS.

If you anticipate claiming a refund due to deductions such as alimony and separation payments, RRSP contributions, and most important, a good tax plan, apply to have the source deductions (withholding tax) on your paycheque reduced. Subsection 153 (1.1) of the Income Tax Act gives you the right. This rule allows Revenue Canada to reduce your source deductions if you would otherwise suffer "undue hardship." Although undue hardship sounds fairly extreme, most tax offices are fairly easy on you when it comes to allowing a reduction.

To get the ball rolling on a withholding tax reduction, call the payroll division of your District Taxation Office and tell them that you want to apply for a reduction of source deductions pursuant to subsection 153 (1.1) of the Income Tax Act. The office will then send you a form that asks you to substantiate the deductions on which you base your claim.

In Canada, many so-called "tax shelters" are sold not merely on the intrinsic value of the underlying investment — which is how they should be sold — but, rather, on the promise by the promoter to reduce your at-source payroll deductions. In effect, the cost of the investment then seems to be coming from the government instead of you. Don't be fooled! You can set up your own "tax shelter" — such as a self-directed RRSP — choosing investments you like, without any onerous management charges and, using this strategy, arrange to get the same payroll break that fast-talking salesman promises! (For more information on self-directed RRSPs, see Chapter 13.)

Using this strategy, you can get the use of your money now, instead of waiting for a refund.

Remember, a refund is the return of your own money, without interest or even a thank-you letter, that you never owed in the first place.

Strategy #128:

WRITE YOUR DISTRICT TAX OFFICE IF YOU'VE MISSED A TAX DEDUCTION.

In many instances, perhaps as a result of your new-found tax knowledge, you will find that you've missed a tax write-off, or otherwise made a mistake in filing one or more of your tax returns.

Amending your tax return is easier if you have not yet received your Notice of Assessment for this year. In fact, you don't even have to file a new tax return. All you have to do is send a letter to the District Taxation Office where you file your return outlining the change you wish to make. Include any necessary supporting documentation.

If you wish to make a change after you have received your Notice of Assessment or filed your return, send the information to the tax office where the return is stored (a call to your District Taxation Office will find you the address). If the matter has not been settled within 90 days after you have received your Notice of Assessment, you should file a Notice of Objection (Form T400A) in order to protect your claim.

Technically, Revenue Canada is not legally bound to accept adjustments if more than 90 days have passed since you received your Notice of Assessment. However, if as long as three years have not gone by since the date of your notice, Revenue Canada will usually allow adjustments for errors and omissions.

Strategy #129:

PREPARE YOUR TAX RETURN "ELECTRONICALLY."

There a number of tax-preparation software packages available for less than $75. These programs are compatible with all IBM-type systems currently in use. They simplify the tax-preparation process by doing all the math automatically as you enter data.

Usually the program will also contain a "self-check" mode which pre-audits your return to make sure that the correct schedules are included. This in itself is worth the price of the program — the less reason Revenue Canada has to go over your return, the less likely you are to be audited. By taking advantage of these features, you are not only saving time but reducing your chances of an audit as well.

Strategy #130:
GET YOUR REFUND QUICKLY BY SENDING IN YOUR RETURN "ELECTRONICALLY."

Revenue Canada is in the process of phasing in a program that allows taxpayers using tax-preparation software to send in their returns electronically using a common computer modem. Electronic transmission of your return assures you the fastest possible turnaround time for refund processing, and minimizes the likelihood of error caused by human mishandling or misfiling. If you are owed a sizable refund, this is the way to make sure that the money is in your hands as soon as possible.

Strategy #131:
"ORGANIZE" YOUR TAX RETURN TO SPEED PROCESSING.

If you are sending in your return via hard copy (by mail) there is a preferred order in which the forms making up the return should be stapled together. If you do not follow this order, your return will have to be manually rearranged. This extra step significantly increases the odds of errors and delays. To streamline the processing time that Revenue Canada will take with your return, follow this simple rule:

Attach all forms, schedules, and enclosures, top edges together, to the top left of page 3 of your return in the proper sequence (ignoring forms or schedules not applicable to your return). The code number of the form appears on top of the form itself.

Strategy #132:
IF YOU ARE SELF-EMPLOYED, MAKE YOUR INSTALMENTS ON TIME.

Self-employed taxpayers, who do not have deductions taken off at source, are required to remit quarterly instalments on the 15th of March, June, September, and December of the current tax year. Each such instalment should be one-quarter of the estimated tax for the present year, or one-quarter of the tax actually paid the previous year, whichever number is lower. Any over-payment can be claimed back in the regular April 30th filing the following year.

Sometimes self-employed taxpayers will ignore the instalments, feeling that paying arrears and interest may be a better deal. It isn't. The current interest is based on the previous quarter's 90-day T-bill rate plus 2%. In addition, extra penalties may apply. Essentially, this is based on 50% of either your interest charges for the year in excess of $1,000, or your interest charges for the year on one-quarter of your proper investment requirements, if this is more than $1,000. And this interest is not deductible!

Strategy #133:
EARN "CONTRA-INTEREST" TO OFFSET LATE
OR DEFICIENT INSTALMENTS.

If your instalments have been late or deficient, it is possible to earn offsetting or "contra-interest" if you accelerate or increase your instalments later in the year over your normal requirements.

To the extent that you do this, you will earn "interest," which will offset late or deficient interest charges.

If you are in the 45% bracket and earn "contra-interest" at 12%, this is equivalent to earning interest on a fully taxable investment at a rate of nearly 22%.

Chapter 10

WINNING
THE TAX AUDIT

You pays your money and you takes your chances.

Punch, 1846

Objective: Gain the upper hand in a tax audit.

Isn't it strange how the possibility of an audit makes you feel guilty even when you're not?

An audit is nothing more than your opportunity to prove to the government that you are a good record keeper. If you're not, your first audit can go a long way in motivating you to become one. Fear of being audited comes from a lack of knowledge, not from any real threat.

The first time I was audited was 1963. The item in question: a $35 education deduction for a night-school course in English Literature. I felt it helped me improve my job skill, which was writing excuse letters to irate customers who had not received their orders. The auditor, a very pleasant lady indeed, said, "English Composition, yes; English Literature, no. No deduction." Since the rest of the return passed, I reluctantly acquiesced and paid the $1.17 in extra taxes. It must have cost the government $500 in time and correspondence to collect my money!

Your best defence in an audit is a good offence. Be civil, knowledgeable, and assertive. Remember, knowledge eliminates both fear AND bigger tax bills! The more you learn about how to report your income and deductions correctly, the less your chances for audit.

Strategy #134:
DON'T REACT TO AN AUDIT AS MORE THAN IT REALLY IS.

A tax audit is simply a review of your tax return to determine its accuracy and completeness. It is not an accusation that you have done something wrong. Knowledge of audit objectives and procedures gives you the same level of power and clout that most taxpayers attribute only to Revenue Canada. Knowledge can reduce an audit to the impartial review it is supposed to be.

In Canada, most tax advisors estimate that less than 5% of personal returns filed by taxpayers are subject to full-scale audits. More frequently, however, a taxpayer will only be asked for additional information about specific items claimed on a tax return. An information request is not a full-scale audit. Furnish only the information requested for the item under review to ensure that the question does not lead to a wider audit of your tax return.

At the other end of the review spectrum is a visit from the Special Investigations branch of Revenue Canada, known as SI. A visit from SI means that Revenue Canada is seriously considering filing tax evasion or similar charges. Under these circumstances, run, don't walk, to the phone to contact a tax lawyer.

The primary reason SI gets involved is when someone is suspected of trying to hide income from potential taxes, in other words intentionally cheating or trying to defraud the government. SI usually does not deal with the legitimate deductions you claim or think you are due unless they think you are knowingly taking big deductions for things you don't own or never did.

Strategy #135:
DON'T LET THE AUDIT DRAG ON.

The longer an audit goes on, the greater the chance that the tax auditor may discover deficiencies in your return.

Allow the auditor access to your tax records on your premises, but do your best to discourage the auditor from making copies or taking the records away. If a tax auditor has possession of your books and records or copies of them, the tax auditor has unlimited time to review them.

Note also that you are responsible for your own records and, should something be innocently lost or misplaced, you may not be able to win your audit argument without supporting documents.

Strategy #136:
LEARN HOW TO BEHAVE IN AN AUDIT.

It is important to mind your manners when you're being audited. But contrary to what many people believe, you can be aggressive and well-mannered at the same time when negotiating with Revenue Canada. Here are some rules to follow:

- Say little; smile a lot. Never volunteer information.
- If you feel strongly about your position, let the auditor know. Often the auditor will let the point go in your favour.
- Provide as much documentation in your favour as possible for each point in an audit.
- Don't give up, even if you don't have all the documentation.
- Don't make too many concessions.
- Don't be rushed unless you feel hurrying will work in your favour.
- Don't complain about the tax system; the auditor pays taxes, too.
- Don't try to tape-record the conversation.
- Act with confidence that you're right. You probably are.
- Tax auditors are not well paid. If a tax auditor sees you driving a Mercedes or wearing a Rolex, he or she will not be sympathetic. Take off your fancy jewellery and wear your most conservative clothes.
- Give the auditor adequate space and other facilities to carry out the audit.
- Be courteous to the auditor and avoid being abrasive or argumentative.
- Don't present your receipts in a brown paper bag. The auditor will assume that, if you're that disorganized, there must be errors on your tax return somewhere.

Strategy #137:
MAKE WRITTEN SUBMISSIONS BEFORE A REASSESSMENT.

If Revenue Canada proposes to reassess you additional taxes, you will probably be given the opportunity to make written submissions to state your case prior to the reassessment being finalized. Your written statement will often bring favourable results as it may force the tax auditor to reconsider his or her position. Make sure that you have marshalled proper technical support for your position from a publication, from a tax advisor or from the information in this book.

Strategy #138:
FILE A NOTICE OF OBJECTION.

If you are unsuccessful in talking Revenue Canada out of reassessing your return, you have 90 days from the date of notice of reassessment to file a Notice of Objection (Form T400A, available from your District Taxation Office.)

Note: Proposals have recently been made to simplify the Notice of Objection procedure, and extend the time frame for filing a Notice of Objection.

There is no charge for filing the notice, and it guarantees an independent review of your case by an Appeals Officer of Revenue Canada. Be sure to state the technical basis for your objection. Simply saying that you have been hard done by, or that the tax rules are unfair, will not help you with the tax department.

Strategy #139:
TAKE THEM TO COURT!

If you have been assessed for more taxes, or you have been unsuccessful in talking Revenue Canada out of reassessing your return, you are entitled to appeal to the Tax Court of Canada to settle your tax dispute. Under new court rules, if the taxes in question are less that $7,000, you can appeal under a streamlined procedure that relaxes the legal rules of evidence and you can represent yourself or even be represented by a non-lawyer. You present your side of the argument; Revenue Canada presents its side. Your case will be heard by an impartial judge.

Strategy #140:
APPLY THE LIMITATIONS PERIOD TO AN AUDIT.

Once you file your tax return, Revenue Canada has a limited time to challenge it. In fact, as long as there hasn't been a serious misrepresentation, there is normally a reassessment limitation period of three years from the date of your Notice of Assessment or Reassessment. However, if you have made a misrepresentation that is attributable to neglect, carelessness, or wilful default, or you have committed any fraud, there is no limitation period.

If the limitation period has expired, you cannot be reassessed no matter how badly Revenue Canada may wish to try to collect from you.

Chapter 11

INVESTMENT-RELATED TAX-REDUCING STRATEGIES

Because our tax system discriminates between different types of investments, the way in which an investment is taxed can make a critical difference on the amount of taxes you pay.

David Louis, tax lawyer/author

Objective: Reduce taxes by choosing the most tax-effective investments.

Contrary to popular opinion, there are still a significant number of tax "breaks" built into the Canadian model. One of the best is a tax-free lifetime capital gains limit of $100,000.

This extraordinary break allows each individual to accumulate $100,000 of capital gains in a lifetime without tax. (Ordinarily, about 75% of any capital gain can be taken into income and taxed at the appropriate marginal rate.) In the case of a husband and wife, the benefit can be doubled — each spouse may accumulate $100,000 of tax-free capital gains in his or her lifetime. And this benefit is in addition to the tax-free gain on the sale of a residential home.

What is a capital gain? Well, there are some fine points in the definition that bear watching but, generally, a capital gain is the profit you make on the sale of an isolated "thing," as distinct from the interest you make on debt instruments (savings bonds, for example) or the profit you make in the ordinary course of your business. For example, bond interest, savings interest, wages, and the profits of your upholstery business for the year are all ordinary taxable income. The profit on the sale of IBM stock, the profit on the sale of shares of your business, the sale of a valuable antique, the sale of your summer cottage — all these can be eligible for capital-gains status.

A "grey area" comes in when Revenue Canada looks at the profit on the sale of a thing and decides that you are in the business of selling things of that sort on a regular basis. For example, a real estate speculator might have trouble convincing Revenue Canada that the profit on the sale of the cottage in Muskoka is a capital gain. Since he is in that business, the government may argue the sale is ordinary business income.

Other major tax benefits to watch for:

1. Capital gains instead of pure business income.

Even when the $100,000 lifetime limit is exhausted, capital gains are still preferred to ordinary income since only a portion (75%) is actually treated as taxable.

2. Dividends from Canadian corporations.

To encourage Canadians to invest in domestic companies, dividends from most Canadian companies are given a more favourable treatment than dividends from foreign businesses.

Strategy #141:
CHOOSE INVESTMENTS THAT QUALIFY FOR THE
DIVIDEND TAX CREDIT OR CAPITAL-GAINS EXEMPTION.

When making investment decisions, take into account the fact that capital gains and Canadian dividends are taxable at lower-than-normal rates.

Dividends from taxable Canadian corporations are taxable under the Gross-Up and Credit System. You may claim a dividend tax credit equal to 16⅔ of the actual dividend you receive. As a result, the effective tax rate per dollar of dividends is a maximum of about 30% (the exact amount depends on the province), as opposed to the 45%-plus rate that applies to fully taxable investment income. This tax break means that $1 of dividend income is worth as much to you as $1.25 or more of fully taxable income.

Preferential treatment is afforded capital gains as well. Until the end of 1989, only two-thirds of a capital gain was taxable. Beginning in 1990, three-quarters of a capital gain is subject to tax, the remainder is tax free. This means that the maximum effective tax rate per dollar of capital gains is about 35%.

Of course, if a capital gain is eligible for the $100,000 capital-gains exemption, there will usually be no tax at all! (In the case of qualified farm property or small-business corporation shares, the tax-exempt limit can be as high as $500,000.)

Note: Occasionally, the tax-free portion of capital gains could be subject to the so-called "minimum tax on the wealthy."

Strategy #142:
IF INVESTMENT LOSSES WILL REDUCE YOUR CAPITAL-GAINS EXEMPTION, DECLARE INTEREST INCOME FROM PRE-1989 INVESTMENTS AS EARNED NOW RATHER THAN WHEN ACTUALLY RECEIVED.

After 1987, capital gains, for which you are otherwise eligible, must be reduced by (post-1987) "investment losses," a generic term that takes into account cumulative deductions you may have claimed in the past without corresponding offsetting investment income.

For example, you claim a deduction for interest used to acquire a particular investment, but the investment itself does not yield income in that same taxation year. The position of the government is that they are being generous by allowing you to deduct investment-oriented interest expenses in the first place — allowing you both interest deductions, without offsetting taxable income, and capital-gains exemptions at the same time is just too nice a deal.

To make the new rules work, you are required to keep track of your investment losses from year to year whether or not you claim capital-gains exemptions in that year. The higher your cumulative investment-related losses, the less able you are to claim capital-gains relief — even if you've never claimed a capital-gains exemption previously.

For interest-bearing investments (including debt instruments) entered into before 1990, you have the option of waiting until interest is actually received before you are required to declare it as income up to a maximum of three years. For more recent purchases, a one-year deferral may be available. So, if you earn interest this year that you won't receive until next year, but have investment losses this year, a good strategy may be to declare the income now if it will increase your exemption. By increasing your investment income, your tax exemption will increase.

Strategy #143:
DEFER TAX ON DEFERRED-INTEREST INCOME WITH THE THREE-YEAR RULE.

When interest is deferred, it means you pay or receive the interest months or even years later. If you purchased an interest-bearing investment before 1990, you can defer the tax on the interest for up to three years if your interest payments are deferred, rather than actually paid within the year. The longer the interest payments are deferred, the longer your tax deferral can be. However, the maximum is the end of the third year following the year in which you bought the investment.

If the interest you earn is deferred to a subsequent year, you usually should not claim the income until you have to, unless for some reason you are in a lower tax bracket the year the interest is earned than you will be the year the interest is received, or if investment losses would reduce your capital-gains exemption (Strategy #142).

The following are examples of deferred-interest investments:

- Compound-interest Canada Savings Bonds.
- Special Guaranteed Investment Certificates (GICs).
- Stripped bonds (often referred to as stripped coupons).

Strategy #144:
TIME THE SALE OF INVESTMENTS SUBJECT TO CAPITAL GAINS TAX TO AVOID LOSING CAPITAL GAINS EXEMPTIONS.

Another way to cope with the investment-loss rules is to time your capital gains so they fall in a year when you do not have cumulative investment losses. For example, if you anticipate having a lot of investment-related deductions next year that will throw you into a cumulative investment-loss position, consider selling the successful investment this year, declare your capital gain, and enjoy the tax holiday.

Strategy #145:

TO CREATE AN INTEREST DEDUCTION, PAY CASH FOR PERSONAL PURCHASES AND BORROW TO INVEST.

When you borrow money to use for business or investment purposes, the general rule is that interest on the loans is tax deductible. (There are exceptions, such as when you borrow money to buy vacant land.) The security for your loan doesn't matter. If you borrow money to buy a car for personal (non-business) use, or by making credit-card purchases, the interest is not deductible.

You can plan your financial affairs to take advantage of the tax benefits of this rule. For example, if you are making both personal and investment purchases, and you have to borrow for one or the other, borrow to purchase the investments and pay cash for the personal assets. This strategy will allow you to claim an interest deduction on your tax return.

For example, let's say you have $10,000 in an investment such as Canada Savings Bonds or your bank account and you are going to buy a car. You could take out a loan to buy the car, but the interest would not be deductible unless, of course, you use the car in your business.

Your strategy? Take the money out of your investments to pay for the car. Later on, borrow money, using the car as collateral, to invest in mutual funds (for example), which will earn a higher rate of return than the interest rate you are paying for the loan on the car.

Your interest on the new loan should be deductible, returning to you in your refund cheque up to one out of two dollars you spent on the interest payments. Keep the money you borrow to invest in a separate bank account until it's invested so that you can trace the borrowed investment capital throughout the transaction.

Strategy #146:

DON'T LET CO-MINGLED FUNDS DISALLOW AN INVESTMENT-INTEREST DEDUCTION.

Co-mingling means that you put money from two sources in the same bank account — such as combining your payroll cheque with money you borrowed to invest. One way to easily lose a legitimate interest deduction on money borrowed to invest is to put the borrowed money into your regular bank account! You will then have difficulty proving that the borrowed dollars were actually used in the investment.

Instead, put the borrowed money in a separate account before investing or use the lending institution's cheque to directly purchase your investment.

Strategy #147:

ITEMIZE AND DEDUCT INVESTMENT AND SMALL-BUSINESS-RELATED EXPENSES.

Take full advantage of tax rules that allow you to deduct money you spend for investment purposes. For example, if you have a preparer do your income tax return, part of the charge may really pertain to your investments. If so, claim a deduction for this part of the charge. Ask your preparer to separate the charges for personal tax preparation from the portion representing investment or small business and send you separate bills.

Strategy #148:

DEDUCT INVESTMENT-RELATED INTEREST, BANK FEES AND BROKERAGE CHARGES.

Review bank and other financial records for investment-related charges, including interest on margin accounts and special bank fees.

These are generally deductible in the year you spend the money. If you paid a special brokerage or placement fee to obtain an investment-related loan, the fee is deductible over five years at 20% per year. Deduct investment-related interest and other carrying charges on form T1, Schedule 5, part IV.

Note that the actual brokerage fee paid for the acquisition of capital property (stocks, options) is not deductible by itself in the year of acquisition but, rather, is added to the cost base of the property for purposes of determining the capital profit (or loss) at time of disposition.

Strategy #149:

USE THE POTENTIALLY DEDUCTIBLE INVESTMENT EXPENSES LIST TO FIND MISSED DEDUCTIONS.

POTENTIALLY DEDUCTIBLE INVESTMENT EXPENSES LIST

Check those items that do or could apply to you and enter the amounts for last year and what you anticipate for this year.

	LAST YEAR	THIS YEAR
Accounting Fees	$ _____	_____
Tax Preparation Fees	_____	_____
Investment Counsel Fees	_____	_____
Brokerage Fees (deducted when you sell your investments)	_____	_____
Cost of collecting interest and dividends and other investment income.	_____	_____
RRSP administration costs (if billed separately)	_____	_____
Legal costs to collect investment income	_____	_____
Safety deposit box rental	_____	_____
Fees paid to a bookkeeper who keeps your investment records	_____	_____
Business portion of trips incurred to look after investments	_____	_____
Total Investment Expenses	$ _____	_____

Strategy #150:

USE THE REGISTERED EDUCATION SAVINGS PLAN (RESP), BUT ONLY IN CONJUNCTION WITH YOUR OVERALL INVESTMENT PLAN.

At first glance the Canadian RESP program may look like the best way to set aside scholarship money.

Registered Education Savings Plans (RESPs) work this way: Your contributions to an RESP, although not tax deductible, are invested in a special trust account in which earnings accumulate tax free until they are distributed to children, grandchildren or other family members in the form of post-secondary educational assistance payments.

You may invest as much as $31,500 per child, though total annual contributions are limited to $1,500 per beneficiary and contributions for a particular beneficiary may be made only over a maximum 21-year period. Each plan must collapse on or before the last day of the twenty-fifth year following the year the plan is entered into.

Most RESPs allow you to withdraw your contributions at any time, which is as it should be since it's your money and you've already paid taxes on it. However, the earnings and any capital appreciation remain in the plan until your designated beneficiary starts at the university and begins withdrawing needed education funds. If no beneficiary makes it to the university level, most, but not all, plans now contain special bail-out features that effectively allow you to access your investment earnings.

Some plans will permit you to redesignate a beneficiary if the original beneficiary decides that high school is enough. Others will permit you to donate the accumulated earnings to a university scholarship fund so that some student will benefit from your plan earnings.

Finally, self-administered RESPs are now available. You can actually choose the investments you want to make, such as mutual funds, and move your money from one investment to another, including foreign securities.

Are RESPs a good idea? In some ways, yes. When distribution finally occurs, the income earned from the investment is taxed at the recipient's tax rate, which is usually lower than yours.

However, unlike the RRSP, the RESP does not give you a break on funds that you set aside. In effect, you are filling your RESP with tax-paid money (although the compound interest and other earnings are tax-free while in the plan, and then taxed in the hands of the student when the plan is collapsed).

Consider this alternative. First, focus your financial energies to take advantage of the $100,000 tax-free lifetime capital gains provision, one of the only major benefits available from Revenue Canada in this era of Tax Reform.

Next, using the Money Movement Strategy (Chapter 23), build your wealth sufficiently to provide for your children or grandchildren directly. If you must choose between an RESP plan and an investment plan of the type explained in Chapter 23, choose the latter.

On the other hand, if you are confident that one or more of your children will use the RESP savings to attend an educational institution, the RESP plan should be considered.

Chapter 12

FAMILY TIES

Second-hand diamonds are better than no diamonds at all.

Mark Twain

Objective: Reduce taxes by shifting assets between family members and turning family expenses into tax deductions.

A family is like a business, and great dividends accrue to all family members when the business aspects of a family are recognized. Both business and family rely on income. Business income is derived primarily from the sale of products and services; family income is derived from a lifetime of personal services to your own or someone else's company. Both families and businesses have expenses including housing, transportation, utilities, insurance, storage, payroll (including family allowances and spending money), vacations, negotiations, purchase and sale of assets, communication, praise, discipline and, of course, taxes. By applying good business principles to the daily operation of a family, money-making and tax-saving strategies can put thousands of extra dollars into the family coffers.

Strategy #151:
SPLIT CAPITAL GAINS WITH OTHER FAMILY MEMBERS TO TAKE ADVANTAGE OF EXTRA EXEMPTIONS.

In Canada, all individuals, including every member of your family, are entitled to a lifetime capital-gains exemption. The current exemption is for $100,000 of capital gains with an additional exemption of $400,000 for capital gains resulting from qualified farm property or qualified small-business corporation shares. If you have used up your personal exemption, or for any other reason no longer have your exemption, you may transfer some of your investment capital to a child or grandchild who may then be entitled to claim a personal capital-gains exemption on any capital gain from future appreciation, on a later sale of the investment. But, if the investment produces income in the meantime, that income will be taxed in your hands, unless the child or grandchild is 18 or over in the year.

If, for example, you've used up your capital-gains exemption and you are in the 40% combined federal and provincial tax bracket, every $100,000 of capital gains you can successfully shift to another family member can potentially save your family as much as $30,000 in taxes. Under current laws, capital gains on property transferred or loaned to a child or grandchild are usually taxed at his or her lower rates. Where the property has already appreciated in the hands of the donor, the donor will almost always be considered to have sold the property at a fair market value, which may trigger some immediate capital gains liability. Generally, the most effective use of this strategy is to purchase a potentially high-yield capital property in the name of the child initially.

EXAMPLE	YOU	YOUR CHILD
(a) You keep all of the capital gain	$200,000	
Less capital-gain exemption	100,000	
	$100,000	
× amount of gain that is taxable after 1989	¾	
Taxable capital gain	$ 75,000	
× your tax bracket	.40	
Added taxes you pay	$ 30,000	
(b) You shift capital gains in excess of your exemption	$100,000	$100,000
Less personal capital-gains exemptions	$100,000	$100,000
Taxable capital gains	0	0

Example:

You purchased $20,000 of shares in a qualified small business several years ago that are today worth twice that amount — $40,000. It looks like this company could grow tremendously during the next few years, when your child will begin college. You decide to transfer the shares to your child. Revenue Canada considers that you have realized a capital gain of $20,000. If you do not use your capital gains exemption, you will have to pay taxes on the gain.

For the same reason, you should consider transferring any vacation home or cottage to your children at the earliest opportunity — see also Strategy #159.

TRUSTS

If you are uncomfortable with the idea of placing assets in the name of your child or grandchild — after all, they may spend your hard-won gains on fast cars and fashionable clothes, rather than on education as you intend — you can retain control of the assets by establishing a trust.

A trust is an arrangement that permits you (or someone you designate as "trustee") to hold assets for the benefit of others, called "beneficiaries." With the help of a good lawyer, you can establish a trust at any time, or you can direct in your will that one be established upon your death.

For tax purposes, trusts are considered to be individuals and are taxed just as you would be. Trusts created on death are taxed at the individual's tax rate. All other trusts, however, including the one you establish for your child or grandchild while you are living, are automatically taxed at the highest tax rate — which could be in excess of 45%, depending on the province.

When the trust distributes income (including capital-gains, in this instance) to your child, it may be possible to have that income taxed at your child's rate. It may also be possible for the trust to retain the income generated while the child himself is taxed "as if" the income were received — which means, using this technique, the trust could earn a fair amount of income without paying any taxes.

The trustees are required to file the tax returns. Seek competent legal and tax assistance if you think a trust might be appropriate for you.

SPOUSAL STRATEGIES

Capital-gains splitting is not available if you give investments, or money intended to buy investments, directly to your spouse. However, if you sell the investment to your spouse at "fair market value," and report any gain on your own tax return, you can effectively transfer future gains to your spouse. (If your spouse doesn't have the cash to buy the investment from you, you may take a promissory note for an amount equal to the "fair market value" of the investment. But your spouse must pay you interest at least equal to Revenue Canada's "prescribed rate" at the time of the purchase, and this interest payment must be made within 30 days after the end of each year. If this is not done, any income or capital gains on a future sale of the investment by the spouse will be attributed back to you — see also Strategy #155.)

Strategy #152:
USE INCOME SPLITTING TO PAY TAXES AT ANOTHER FAMILY MEMBER'S LOWER RATE.

Note: Income and capital gains are two entirely different concepts in Canadian tax law. See Chapter 11.

Income splitting means rearranging your financial affairs so that the income is taxed to a lower-bracket family member. The Canadian tax system is progressive, that is, lower income earners pay taxes at a lower rate and as your income increases you pay a marginally higher rate of taxes. For example, for 1991, while the marginal tax rate varies between provinces, in round numbers you would generally have paid out in taxes:

27% on taxable income up to $27,800
41% on taxable income from $27,800 to $55,600
45% on taxable income over $55,600

If one income earner in the family makes $80,000 taxable income, taxes would be about $30,000. However, if $27,800 of that taxable income were shifted to a non-income-earning spouse, the taxes would become about $7,500 for one and $17,500 for the other — a total of about $25,000, saving the family approximately $5,000 in taxes. Each $100 shifted from the higher 45% bracket to the lower 27% bracket will save $18 in taxes.

The Income Tax Act has been modified in recent years to prevent certain forms of income splitting. However, there may still be some opportunities available. For example, income generated from property transferred to a child aged 18 or over in the year is not generally attributed back to the transferer. For these types of opportunities to work, you will need to carefully document transactions and maintain separate bank accounts for members of the family involved in the income splitting so that funds may be accounted for properly. Also, you should bear in mind that any assets transferred become the property of the family member. You should no longer be able to access these assets or their income at will. Using this strategy, you could be able to save hundreds or even thousands per year per family member — in addition to tax savings from capital gains splitting (Strategy #151).

Note that even where the attribution rules do apply — the income in the hands of the family member is taxed as if you still had it — the "income on the income" is not attributed. If your child reinvests the income so produced, however, then future income generated by the reinvestment would be taxed at the child's or grandchild's lower rate, thus accomplishing some income splitting — see also Strategy #157.

One simple, but effective, way to split income with a lower-in-come-tax-bracket spouse is for the higher-income-tax-bracket spouse to pay all of the daily living expenses, leaving the lower-income-earning spouse the opportunity to invest more funds to be taxed at a lower bracket. For example, assume you make $60,000 per year and your spouse earns $10,000 that he or she usually spends on groceries, laundry, clothing, and other "essentials" of life. Using the 10% Solution (Chapter 21), you and your spouse save $6,000 and $1,000, respectively. Any income you receive from your investment is taxed at 45%, your spouse's at 27%. Let's assume you are both earning 15% on your investments. You will pay $405 in taxes; your spouse will pay $40.50.

If instead you pay the daily living expenses and your spouse invests $7,000 for the family, the earnings would be the same but the taxes would be only $283.50 at the lower-tax-bracket rate, saving your family $162 in taxes.

Another possible way to split income is to establish a small business and pay your spouse and children a reasonable salary for their services. (See Chapter 18; also Strategy #160.)

Strategy 153:
**LET FAMILY ALLOWANCE FUNDS
(THE "BABY BONUS") ACCUMULATE FOR
YOUR CHILD WITH MINIMAL TAX.**

Although the amount of your family allowance cheque is, generally, income to the higher wage earner in the family, compounded interest over subsequent years — if the cheques are deposited to an account in the specific name of the child — is not attributed back to the parent. This is, therefore, a valid technique for income splitting.

At $35 per month, for example, with an average 10% interest rate, this could amount to over $20,000 at the end of 18 years.

Strategy #154:
SPLIT CANADIAN PENSION-PLAN
PAYMENTS BETWEEN SPOUSES
TO SAVE TAXES.

Recently, Canada Pension Plan (CPP) rules were changed to permit spouses to share their CPP retirement pension payments, enabling them to save taxes when one spouse is in a higher income tax bracket than the other. Your marginal tax bracket is determined by the amount of income you receive during the year. Each $100 that can be shifted from the highest tax bracket to the lowest will save your family approximately $18 in taxes, assuming provincial income tax of about 50% and ignoring surtaxes.

How it works: Both spouses must be 60 or older and both must agree to split the pension payments. When you apply for CPP benefits through your local Health and Welfare Canada office (benefits don't come automatically), you and your spouse may indicate that you wish up to 50% of your personal CPP benefits to go to the other spouse. Health and Welfare Canada will determine the split based on the length of marriage and the amount of pension credits earned by both spouses during the period divided by two. The proportion of each spouse's benefits going to the other is the same.

For example, suppose that you and your spouse meet the age requirements and your entitlements are $500 and $200, respectively. Upon application, you both agree to share 50% of your CPP pension payment. You would give up $250 of your benefit to receive $100 of your spouse's benefit. You would each receive $350 per month. Basically, this represents a transfer of $150 per month. If from a higher-bracket to a lower-bracket taxpayer, the tax savings from this example would result in $27-per-month savings, or an additional $324 per year, again assuming provincial income tax of about 50% and ignoring surtaxes.

> ### Strategy #155:
> ### "SWAP ASSETS" BETWEEN SPOUSES TO TAKE
> ### ADVANTAGE OF INCOME SPLITTING.

Attribution tax rules are particularly designed to restrict you from splitting income with your spouse. There are specific rules in the Income Tax Act designed to prevent you from taking advantage of lower marginal tax brackets to reduce your family's total tax bill.

For example, you cannot ask your employer to pay you half of your wages and the other half to your spouse. If, for instance, you were being paid $70,000 a year, you would be in the 45% tax bracket. If instead you and your spouse were each paid $27,800 (same total family income), you would both be in the 27% tax bracket.

The Income Tax Act has rules restricting this type of practice.

Similar rules affect income-producing investments. Suppose you earn $60,000 per year and your spouse earns $15,000, so that your effective tax rate would be approximately 45% and your spouse's would be 27%. Now assume you own some bonds that are paying interest at $2,500 per year. You will be taxed $1,125 on that income. If you could give or lend those bonds to your spouse, the tax would be only $675, saving you $450.

The Income Tax Act attribution rules prevent you from such savings, however, by attributing the income from the bond back to the person — you — who transferred or lent the bond to your spouse. The attribution rules, in fact, attribute back to you any income or loss from the asset as well as any capital gain or loss when the bond is eventually sold.

A fair-market-value "swap" or exchange can usually avoid the attribution rules and allow the income splitting to work for you.

Say that you have shares which are selling at $19 a share, giving you a fair market value asset of $19,000. You paid $10,000 for the shares. You may either sell the shares to your spouse for $19,000 cash, or swap for something of equal value your spouse owns. (You must declare the $9,000 capital gain and pay taxes on it, unless you have and use some of your capital-gains exemption.) Where does your spouse get $19,000 on an annual income of $15,000? Good question!

The best alternative is to "swap" for something of value that your spouse owns and was purchased with his or her own money — preferably an asset that is not producing income, since you are already in the 45% tax bracket.

What kind of assets might your spouse possibly own that could be used to acquire the stock from you? Some possible assets might include:

- jewellery (which you may have given your spouse over the years)
- a car
- other stocks (non-income-producing)
- house or other real estate
- antiques
- coin or stamp collection
- boat

You must document the transfer, just as you would a transfer of property or stock to a stranger. The share ownership should also be changed by notifying the brokerage holding the shares, if it is a public corporation, or if you are holding them, by notifying the registrar or transfer agent of the corporation of the change. (You can find the address in the annual reports you receive from the corporation or in any library.) If it is a private corporation, share-transfer formalities should be observed.

Swaps are a viable strategy to consider when there is a sizeable difference in tax status between husband and wife, but one word of caution — there may be unexpected problems in the event of marriage breakdown or separation.

An example of an appropriate transfer of ownership of shares document follows:

SHARE PURCHASE AGREEMENT

A share purchase agreement is used to sell or purchase shares between individuals rather than a direct purchase from the corporation. It would particularly be used if you were selling shares in the corporation. Not only does this form specify the number of shares and the amount to be paid, it also makes provisions for any warranties or representations regarding the corporation that may be appropriate in the transaction, although these would vary in an arm's-length transaction and be more detailed.

INSERTION KEY

1. Date
2. Month
3. Year
4. Seller's Name
5. Purchaser's Name
6. Corporation Name
7. Province of Incorporation
8. Number
9. Location
10. Date
11. Time
12. Province
13. Province
14. City
15. Province
16. Witnesses' Signatures
17. Seller's Signature
18. Purchaser's Signature
19. Amount
20. Amount
21. Amount
22. Asset Name
23. Fair Market Value of Asset

SHARE PURCHASE AGREEMENT

THIS AGREEMENT made the ___ (1)____ day of _____(2)___, 199_(3) _

BETWEEN:

_____(4)_____
(hereinafter called the "Seller")
OF THE FIRST PART
- and -
_____(5)_____
(hereinafter called the "Purchaser")
OF THE SECOND PART

WHEREAS the Seller is the owner of ___(8)___ common shares in the capital stock of ___(6)____ LIMITED (the "Corporation") a corporation incorporated in the Province of ___(7)___;

AND WHEREAS the Purchaser wishes to acquire and the Seller has agreed to sell the said shares in the capital stock of the Corporation to the Purchaser (the "Purchased Shares");

NOW THEREFORE THIS AGREEMENT WITNESSETH that in consideration of the mutual covenants and agreements hereinafter contained the parties hereto covenant and agree as follows:

Section 1 - PURCHASED SHARES AND PURCHASE PRICE

1.01 Subject to the terms and conditions hereof the Seller hereby sells, assigns and transfers to the Purchaser the Purchased Shares for a purchase price as set out in Exhibit "A" hereto (the "Purchase Price")

1.02 The Purchaser shall pay the Purchase Price in accordance with Exhibit "A";

Section 2 - REPRESENTATIONS AND WARRANTIES OF THE SELLER

The Seller represents and warrants to the Purchaser and acknowledges that the Purchaser is relying upon such representations and warranties in connection with the purchase by the Purchaser of the Purchased Shares that:

2.01 The Corporation is a corporation duly organized and validly existing under the laws of the Province of ___(12)___, as the case may be, and has the corporate power and authority to carry on its business as it is now being conducted.

2.02 The Purchased Shares are owned by the Seller as beneficial owner of record with good and marketable title thereto, free and clear of all mortgages, liens, charges, security interest, adverse claims, pledges, encumbrances and demands whatsoever.

2.03 No person, firm or corporation has any agreement or option or any right or privilege (whether by law, pre-emptive or contractual) capable of becoming an agreement or option for the purchase from the Seller of any of the Purchased Shares.

2.04 The Seller is a resident of Canada within the meaning of the Income Tax Act of Canada.

Section 3 - COVENANTS OF THE SELLER

The Seller covenants and agrees with the Purchaser that on or before the Closing Date he will do or will cause to be done the following:

3.01 To deliver to the Purchaser on Closing:

a) A signed transfer form:

b) A share Certificate representing the Purchased Shares duly endorsed on the reverse side thereof with signature guaranteed by a chartered bank or trust company;

Section 4 - REPRESENTATIONS AND WARRANTIES OF SELLER AND PURCHASER

4.01 Seller and Purchaser hereby represent and warrant that there has been no act or omission by the Seller, Purchaser or the Corporation which would give rise to any valid claim against any of the parties hereto for a brokerage commission, finder's fee, or other payment in connection with the transactions contemplated hereby.

Section 5 - SURVIVAL OF COVENANTS, REPRESENTATIONS AND WARRANTIES OF SELLER AND PURCHASER

5.01 The covenants, representations and warranties of the parties contained in this Agreement shall survive the Closing and shall continue in full force and effect indefinitely for the benefit of the relevant party.

Section 6 - CLOSING

6.01 The Closing shall take place at __ (9)___ on ___(10)___ at ___(11)___ or at such other time and place as the parties hereto may agree upon.

Section 7 - GENERAL

7.01 The parties hereto agree to do and perform such acts and execute such documents as may be required from time to time to give effect to this Agreement and every part thereof.

7.02 This Agreement shall enure to the benefit of and be binding upon the parties hereto and their respective heirs, executors, administrators, successors and assigns.

7.03 This Agreement (including the Exhibit hereto and any written amendments hereof executed by the parties) constitutes the entire Agreement and supersedes all prior agreements and understandings, oral and written, between the parties hereto with respect to the subject matter hereof.

7.04 The section and other headings contained in this Agreement are for reference purposes only and shall not affect the meaning or interpretation of this Agreement.

7.05 This Agreement, and the transaction contemplated hereby, shall be governed by, construed and enforced in accordance with the laws of the Province of ___(13)___. The parties herein agree to submit to the personal jurisdiction and venue of a court of subject matter jurisdiction located in ___(14)___ in the Province of ___(15)___.

7.06   In the event that litigation results from or arises out of this Agreement or the performance thereof, the parties agree to reimburse the prevailing party's reasonable solicitor's fees, court costs, and all other expenses, whether or not taxable by the court as costs, in addition to any other relief to which the prevailing party may be entitled.

IN WITNESS WHEREOF this Agreement has been executed by each of the parties hereto on the date first above written.

SIGNED, SEALED AND DELIVERED   )
IN THE PRESENCE OF   )
)
(16)_____   ) _____(17)
Witness   ) Seller
)
_____   ) _____(18)
Witness   ) Purchaser
)
)

EXHIBIT "A"
AMOUNT AND PAYMENT OF PURCHASE PRICE

(a) Consideration.

As total consideration for the purchase and sale of the purchased shares, pursuant to this Agreement, the Purchaser shall pay to the Seller the sum of _____(19)_____ Dollars ($_____), such total consideration to be referred to in this Agreement as the "Purchase Price."

(b) Payment.

The Purchase Price shall be paid as follows:

iii. The sum of ____(20)_____ Dollars ($_____) to be delivered to Seller upon the execution of this Agreement.

iii. The sum of ____(21)_____ Dollars ($_____) to be delivered to Seller at Closing.

iii. In lieu of cash, transfer of the following purchaser-owned assets:

LIST	FAIR MARKET VALUE
_____(22)_____	_____(23)_____
_____	_____
_____	_____

Strategy #157:

SPLIT "COMPOUND INCOME"
WITHOUT CONCERN FOR THE
"ATTRIBUTION RULES."

The "attribution rules" that apply to income on an investment asset you have transferred to a family member — assuming you have not already used a strategy to avoid the attribution rules — do not apply to the income received on the "reinvested" money.

When you give or lend an income-producing investment to a family member, the income generated from the investment may, as discussed above, be attributed to you for tax purposes.

However, that family member still has use of the income received. If he or she reinvests that income and it, in turn, generates even more income, what you end up with is compound income. The compounded income is taxed at the tax rate of the new owner — the family member — not to you, the original owner or donor.

As an example, suppose you give your spouse $100,000, which earns $15,000 in interest. You would be attributed the $15,000 income and pay taxes on it according to your tax bracket. However, your spouse has the $15,000. Reinvested with the same return, your spouse will earn $2,250, taxable at the spouse's tax rate during the following year. Over the years, the amount of compound income will increase dramatically, as shown in the example chart following, since more and more of the additional money in the investment account will be from the compounding.

In the example, the investment amount transferred to your spouse is $100,000; the rate of return is 15%, tax deferred until the investment is sold:

YEAR	YEARLY AMOUNT TAXABLE TO YOU	YEARLY REINVESTMENT, REINVESTED BY YOUR SPOUSE	INCOME ON RETURN TAXABLE TO YOUR SPOUSE	TOTAL YEARLY RETURN ON THE REINVESTMENT
1	$15,000	$0	$0	$15,000
2	15,000	15,000	2,250	17,250
3	15,000	32,250	4,840	19,840
4	15,000	52,090	7,810	22,800
5	15,000	74,900	11,235	26,235
6	15,000	101,135	15,170	30,170
7	15,000	131,300	19,700	34,700
8	15,000	166,000	24,900	39,900
9	15,000	205,900	30,900	45,900
10	15,000	251,800	37,800	52,800

The above chart also illustrates how compound interest makes your money work hard for you, instead of you working hard for your money. At the end of 10 years, the $100,000 gift to your spouse has become $404,600 ($100,000 gift + $251,800 compound cash appreciation + $52,800 current year income).

Strategy #158:

SPLIT YOUR INVESTMENT INCOME WITH CHILDREN 18 OR OLDER TO REDUCE YOUR TAXES.

If you have children or grandchildren who are 18 or older in the year, you can split your investment income with them without having to worry about most of the attribution rules.

Income generated by the gift investment will generally be taxed at the child's tax rate, which is usually lower than yours. The end result is that more after-tax dollars will be available for the child's use — such as education, books, clothes, etc. All you have to do is transfer ownership of the investment to the child or grandchild. If you are acquiring a new investment, one that you don't already own, you could simply buy the investment — shares in a business, for example — directly in the child's name. Any income from the investment would generally be considered by Revenue Canada as the child's. If you already own the investment, you can transfer ownership to the child, but you are subject to the capital-gains exposure if the investment has appreciated in value. (See Strategy #151.)

If you transfer an investment asset to a child or grandchild younger than 18, any income earned by the investment before the year the child reaches 18 will be attributed to you. However, capital gains from the appreciation of the investment after the transfer can be taxable to the child at his or her rates.

For example, suppose you give your 15-year-old child 500 shares of stock with a current market value of $6,000. You bought the shares for $2,500 and the shares are paying a dividend of $1 each. When the child reaches 18, the shares are worth $15,000, but the annual dividend hasn't changed since you gave the investment to the child. What are the tax consequences?

First, the capital gain at the time of the gift is $3,500. If you have capital-gains exemption remaining, you may use it and perhaps pay no taxes. Otherwise you will be responsible for taxes on the capital gain according to your tax bracket. Until the year in which the child reaches 18, you will also have to pay taxes at your tax rate on the annual $500 dividend, even though the child receives the money. In the year the child turns 18, the dividends are no longer attributed to you. Further income is generally taxed at the child's rate, and any capital gains above the $6,000 market value at transfer would also be the child's tax responsibility.

If you use this strategy, you must be prepared to give up control of the investment since it will legally belong to the child after the transfer. If that is unacceptable to you, consider, with proper legal advice, setting up a trust.

Also note that where rental or other assets on which depreciation has been claimed are transferred, previous depreciation claims may become taxable.

Strategy #159:
PUT A SECOND HOME IN THE NAME OF AN ADULT CHILD
TO CLAIM A SECOND PRINCIPAL-RESIDENCE EXEMPTION.

Since 1981, the principal-residence exemption has basically been restricted to one residence per family. However, it may be possible to claim a principal-residence exemption if your second home is owned by a child 18 or older in the year, or a younger child if he or she is married.

Even if the child is too young to qualify for the principal-residence exemption, putting ownership of the home in the name of the child can still save taxes. It is possible for the child to claim his or her own lifetime capital-gains exemption on the home's appreciation if the home is sold while the child is still a minor. Once the child reaches the age of 18, a full principal residence exemption may be available. (Note that for an adult child to claim an exemption under his or her own name for a second residence, that child must actually use the residence as his or her place of habitation.)

Strategy #160:
CREATE AND CLAIM TAX DEDUCTIONS FOR
A SIDELINE FAMILY BUSINESS.

Revenue Canada recognizes as "business income" any income generated from activities such as:

- a profession
- a calling
- a trade
- a manufacture or undertaking of any kind whatsoever, and an adventure or concern in the nature of trade, but does not include income received from an office or straight employment.

Revenue Canada has further indicated that:

"Business activities include hunting, trapping, babysitting, self-employed commission sales agents, etc. where the activity is carried on for profit or with a reasonable expectation of profit."

With those parameters in mind, one of your best methods of income splitting and increasing tax deductions is the establishment of a family business.

With a family business, it may be possible to convert what might otherwise be personal expenses into business expenses, making them tax deductions. For example, your business may require the use of a video camera and recorder, a computer, a business car, office furniture, and other items of equipment you may already own or intend to buy. Their use in your business makes them tax-deductible expenses.

But bear in mind that a tax deduction may not be claimed for expenses related to the personal-use portion of the cost of a particular asset.

With a family business you can hire your spouse and children and pay them a salary commensurate with what you would pay a non-family member for the same service.

Additional deductions can include, for example, entertainment and promotional activities, office expenses, and certain portions of travel and entertainment.

It is possible for these deductible expenses to result in outright business losses. If so, these losses may be deductible against other sources of income.

A lower-income spouse may consider starting a business in which tax losses are anticipated. These tax losses may be of little or no use directly to the low-income spouse, but the higher-income spouse can take tax losses as tax deductions. That spouse can therefore profit by setting up the business under the higher-bracket spouse's name.

In this strategy, the lower-income spouse would be paid a tax-deductible salary. This in effect takes the income received by the high-earning spouse from his or her employment and redistributes it to the lower earner, who is taxed on the same income at a lower rate.

Children may also be employed by the sideline family business. Salaries paid must be "reasonable" — what you would expect to pay to a non-family member for performing the same service (cleaning, bookkeeping, filing, and so forth).

For further discussion on setting up a family business, see Chapter 18.

Chapter 13

STRATEGIES

FOR YOUR

RRSP

Don't look back — something may be gaining on you.

Satchel Paige, *How to Keep Young*, 1953

Objective: Use your RRSP to create a million-dollar nest egg.

In the next 20 years, as the baby-boom generation matures, the number of people expected to leave the work force for retirement is expected to double — a phenomenon unprecedented in this century.

The effects of this trend will be felt all though the work force and the economy. In particular, those individuals looking to enjoy their senior years in pleasant surroundings will be doing so at a time when the federal and provincial governments are expected to be more cash-hungry than ever. (All those vacancies in the work force are going to further deplete tax revenues — aren't they?)

Add to this the statistic that 47% of all seniors who retired in the '80s did so on fixed incomes — with little or no margin for the ravages of inflation — and you soon see the value in planning now for an enjoyable, financially trouble-free retirement later.

Although the government does offer retirement benefits of its own — CPP, OAS, and so on — it is the stated long-term policy of Canadian policymakers to pull back, over the coming years, from the burden of public responsibility for retirees.

The government would much rather that Canadians looked after their own retirement plans. To assist in this goal, the government has created what promises to be the most generous tax deduction of the '90s — the RRSP (Registered Retirement Savings Plan).

Strategy #161:
MAKE THE MAXIMUM POSSIBLE YEARLY CONTRIBUTION TO YOUR RRSP.

It's no wonder the Registered Retirement Savings Plan is, by far, Canada's most popular tax shelter. Contributions made to an RRSP are tax deductible. Second, investment earnings compound tax free. Only when money is withdrawn from your RRSP is it taxable — that usually occurs when you retire and have dropped to a lower tax bracket. The tax-free-compounding feature, moreover, allows you to build greater wealth in half the time.

The maximum RRSP contribution is the lesser of 18% of your earned income or the following amounts:

1991	$11,500
1992	12,500
1993	13,500
1994	14,500
1995	15,500
1996	15,500 (indexed)

Earned income is based upon your previous year's income — this means that your contribution for the 1992 taxation year, for example, is based on your declared earned income in 1991.

Practically, this means that during the "RRSP season" of January–February 1993, when most people begin to worry about RRSP contributions for the previous year's return, your contribution limits will relate back to what you earned in 1991, not 1992!

Since 1989, "earned income," the figure on which your contribution limits are based, no longer includes retirement income, pension income, death benefits, or taxable withdrawals from RRSPs or DPSPs (Deferred Profit Sharing Plans). Very generally, then, this term really applies to income from a job, business income, taxable alimony and maintenance payments, but (with the exception of rental income) not "investment" cash flow.

In addition, if you are among the 37% of the work force who look forward to a private pension, there is an additional reduction in your RRSP contributions known as a "PA" or Pension Adjustment. Starting in 1991, the PA has become so difficult to calculate without professional help that the government has taken an unusual step — you will be notified of your total possible RRSP contribution by the federal government.

Here is an example of an RRSP calculation (assuming the PA is not applicable):

If your earned income for 1990 was $65,000, 18% of which would be $11,700, you would be permitted to save for retirement through your RRSP $11,500, the limit allowed for your 1991 return. If your 1990 earned income was $30,000, you could put $5,400 into your RRSP for 1991. (Alternatively, you may contribute to an RRSP for your spouse — see Strategy #163.)

The combined benefits of a tax deduction at time of contribution plus tax deferral for the accumulated, compounded earnings are extraordinary. In order for you to appreciate how fast pre-tax invested dollars can grow with the earnings themselves being deferred or sheltered, see Table 13-1.

Consider this illustration:

If your combined federal and provincial tax bracket is 40%, then for every $1,000 you put into your RRSP, you would only be out of pocket $600. The additional $400 would be obtained from payment of that much less in taxes. What's more, $6,000 out of your pocket in an RRSP ($1,000 yearly contribution at 10%) would grow to $17,531 within another 10 years. That's equivalent to a taxable interest rate of return of 16.7%, i.e., the interest you would have had to earn if you were still paying taxes at your normal rate. An RRSP gives you the "effective" higher interest rate automatically!

Note also how RRSPs perform best with higher rates of return on the RRSP-selected investment. An investment of $3,000 per year at 10% for 30 years gives you $542,830 in your RRSP. Increasing the rate of return to 15%, however, gives you $1,499,870 — a difference of 275%, while the actual rate of return is only 50% higher!

In addition, a brand-new feature of RRSPs now permits you to contribute more to each "future" year's plan if your current cash position should not allow a contribution now. Restrictions apply after seven years.

For example, assume that in 1991 you made $22,000 in "earned income." This means you have a maximum contribution limit in 1992 of about $4,000, leaving aside the "Pension Adjustment." Also assume, however, that cash is tight that year and you only contribute $2,000, leaving a balance of $2,000 in your "seven-year carry-forward account."

Now assume that in 1992 you were making slightly more earned income (salary was $27,800) and your 18% limit for 1993 calculates out to about $5,000.

Should you choose to contribute only $4,000 that year — the 1993 taxation year — you still have a $3,000 carry-forward account to be used in the future.

But don't let these catch-up rules lull you into a false sense of security. It is one thing to know that you have extra contribution room in your RRSP for the coming year; it is quite another to actually have that money inside your RRSP working for you NOW.

Also, from a practical point of view, if you lack the cash to properly fund your RRSP now, what assurance do you have that you will be able to fund it fully next year and, at the same time, fund the excess passed along from this year? Because of the new rules, the problem compounds from year to year — the tighter your cash position now, the more room accumulates in future years, and the less likely you are to ever find the extra dollars to fully use up your excess contribution room!

Overall, the best strategy is to use your maximum limits in each year. This may even mean you have to borrow to do so.

Table 13-1
GROWTH OF YOUR RRSP INVESTMENTS

ANNUAL CONTRIBUTION $1,000 AT BEGINNING OF YEAR

RETURN ON INVESTMENT

NO. OF YEARS IN RRSP	5%	10%	15%
10	$13,207	$17,531	$ 23,349
20	34,719	63,002	117,810
30	69,761	180,943	499,957

ANNUAL CONTRIBUTION $3,000 AT BEGINNING OF YEAR

RETURN ON INVESTMENT

# OF YEARS	5%	10%	15%
10	$ 39,621	$ 52,593	$ 70,047
20	104,157	189,006	353,430
30	209,283	542,829	1,499,871

ANNUAL CONTRIBUTION $11,500 AT BEGINNING OF YEAR

RETURN ON INVESTMENT

# OF YEARS	5%	10%	15%
10	$151,881	201,606	268,513
20	399,268	724,523	1,354,815
30	802,251	2,080,844	5,749,505

Strategy #162:

**CONTRIBUTE IN THE PRESENT YEAR
FOR THE PRESENT YEAR, NOT IN THE
PRESENT YEAR FOR THE PAST YEAR.**

The bulk of Canadians contribute this year for savings to their last year's return (that is, they contribute in February of this year for a deduction from last year's income). The economics of compounded interest say that this is foolish — by contributing early in the present year to this year's tax plan, you end up with the same ultimate credit but, depending on the RRSP plan you have chosen, your plan will compound from 10% to 20% faster than the old way.

Strategy #163:

**CREATE A SPOUSAL RRSP TO DECREASE
TAXES ON RRSP WITHDRAWAL.**

A spousal RRSP is an RRSP that is owned by your spouse, but where you make the contributions. By using a spousal RRSP, you can claim a deduction against your own taxable income. When the money is withdrawn, it will generally be taxable to your spouse, not to you. This strategy is advantageous when your spouse will be in a lower tax bracket than you at the time the RRSP is collapsed (withdrawn). Normally, the combined contribution you make to your and your spouse's RRSPs cannot, together, exceed your basic maximum contribution limits for the year, however.

Also, if your spouse has earned income, his or her contributions to an RRSP do not change your basic contribution limits.

Example: Let's say that your spouse will be in the 27% tax bracket when he or she starts receiving RRSP funds and you are in the 45% bracket. The 18% difference represents $180 less taxes paid for each $1,000 withdrawn. In this case, it is in your interest to channel your funds, to the limits of your own contribution ceiling, to a spousal plan.

Where, as is often the case, it is possible that one spouse will have little or no income in retirement, it would be folly NOT to set up a spousal RRSP as early as possible. Otherwise, the spouse with low income (or no income) will not even be able to take advantage of the "basic" tax personal credits (usually about $6,000 a year) while the spouse with the RRSP income will be paying tax at his or her highest personal rate.

If you opt for this strategy, beware a special "attribution" rule that kicks in if your spouse collapses such a plan within three years of your funding. In this case — if the plan is collapsed in that time — part or all of the income in the collapsed plan is taxed in your hands, not your spouse's!

Strategy #164:
MAKE YOUR SPOUSE THE DESIGNATED BENEFICIARY ON EVERY RRSP YOU ESTABLISH.

With a few exceptions, assets in your RRSP automatically become taxable on your death unless your spouse is the beneficiary. So whenever you set up an RRSP, it is usually best to name your spouse as beneficiary in the plan.

Strategy #165:
PUT HIGH-TAX INVESTMENTS IN YOUR RRSP AND HOLD LOW- OR NO-TAX INVESTMENTS PERSONALLY.

Which investments you choose for your RRSP and which you choose to hold personally can have a big influence on the amount of taxes you ultimately pay. Higher-taxed investments include bonds and other interest-bearing investments. Investments that may qualify for capital-gains status (stocks, some bonds, mutual funds) may receive more favoured capital-gains treatment in that some of the gain may be totally tax free (if you still have any unused lifetime exemption) and the rest will be taxed at the preferred capital-gains rate (currently 75% of the gain).

Therefore, hold the high-taxed investments in your RRSP since your earnings will compound tax free, and hold the tax-favoured investments personally. You will win both ways.

The tax breaks on the tax-favoured items would be lost if you held them in your RRSP. Also — a feature particular to RRSPs — you must pay tax on all the money the plan yields on its collapse regardless of whether the gain is initial capital, capital gain, or interest.

Strategy #166:
**BEGIN CONTRIBUTING TO YOUR RRSP
NOW INSTEAD OF LATER.**

You can't be too young to begin an RRSP. Read the next statement carefully. It will amaze you.

IF YOU INVEST $2,000 IN AN RRSP EACH YEAR BETWEEN THE AGES OF 20 AND 26, AND NEVER INVEST ANOTHER CENT, YOU WILL HAVE MORE MONEY WHEN YOU REACH AGE 65 THAN IF YOU WAIT UNTIL YOU ARE 26 AND INVEST $2,000 EACH YEAR FOR THE NEXT 40 YEARS WITHOUT RRSP TAX PROTECTION. THE LONGER YOU LEAVE THE MONEY INVESTED, THE GREATER THE EFFECT OF THE TAX-FREE COMPOUNDING.

Look at these figures. Both assume 15% return on investment, 43% tax bracket.

AGE	RRSP CONTRIBUTION	TAXABLE INVESTMENT	RRSP VALUE	TAXABLE INVESTMENT VALUE
20	2,000	—	2,300	—
21	2,000	—	4,945	—
22	2,000	—	7,987	—
23	2,000	—	11,485	—
24	2,000	—	15,507	—
25	2,000	—	20,134	—

26	2,000	2,000	25,454	2,180
30	—	8,000	44,518	13,046
35	—	10,000	89,526	33,120
40	—	15,000	180,038	64,006
50	—	20,000	728,043	184,648
60	—	20,000	2,947,240	470,250
65	—	10,000	5,926,898	736,584
Totals	**$14,000**	**$80,000**		

Strategy #167:
CHOOSE AN RRSP WITH A LOW FEE, OR NO FEE.

Most RRSPs must have a trustee — someone who is certified by Revenue Canada to be responsible for your plan. Depending on the type of RRSP you buy, the fees for managing your RRSP can range from zero (bank plans based on simple deposits) to several hundred dollars for load fees on mutual fund investments.

The good news is that, as the public becomes more aware of the advantages of the RRSP, it is becoming a buyer's market. As the RRSP market heats up, financial institutions are becoming more interested in getting your business than in making money on your fee. When you choose an RRSP investment, inquire up-front what the charges are, and select the highest-quality investment with the lowest fees.

In the case of mutual-fund-based RRSPs — one of the most popular RRSP-type investments — be aware that there are both broker fees and load fees to consider. The load fees are fees charged by the fund manager, who ultimately gets your money. Typically these fees are charged on sign-up (front load); on withdrawal or transfer from the fund (back load); and, in some extraordinary cases, double fees are charged at each end of the transaction!

In addition, the brokerage firm or financial institution that handles the order also has its own fees. For example, buying a no-load fund via a broker instead of directly from the fund will often result in a broker's fee anyway. Broker's fees can vary widely, and some brokers have minimum charges, so this too bears watching. (Note that commissions are a two-way street. When the underlying investment is disposed of, or the plan collapsed, there will be a second commission to pay as well.)

Strategy #168:
IF YOU DO PAY AN RRSP FEE, PAY IT "OUTSIDE" YOUR RRSP.

Many plans with fees "conveniently" take their fees off your principal. This is very convenient — for the plan. For you, it wastes a possible deduction.

Arrange to pay all fees for your RRSP by cheque from funds not inside the plan, and based on current Revenue Canada administrative policy, they should be 100% deductible on your tax return.

Strategy #169:
OPEN A SELF-ADMINISTERED RRSP TO EARN
15% PER YEAR.

The advantage to a self-administered RRSP is that you control the money, choosing your investments for maximum potential profit.

When you want to change investments, you can do so without taxes.

Anyone who qualifies for an RRSP may open a self-administered account. A self-administered RRSP puts you in control, letting you choose from a wide variety of RRSP-eligible investments, including Government of Canada bonds, stocks listed on a Canadian stock exchange, qualifying Canadian corporate bonds, and mutual funds. Mortgages are also eligible to a certain extent.

Before you switch to a self-administered RRSP, carefully check out the terms of the investment plan you are considering to make sure it qualifies as an RRSP investment. If you make an error, the consequences could be disastrous. (The institution managing your self-administered RRSP may flag the problem for you, but don't rely on them. Ultimately, the risk of choosing the wrong investment and being hit with government penalties on discovery is yours and yours alone.)

Also make sure the plan you pick really makes you the boss. Although brokerage houses often offer low-fee, self-administered plans, you may be limited to investments that the brokerage sells for a commission.

Determine if there are charges per transaction or if a number of fee-free transactions are allowed. Some plans charge extra fees for specific types of investments, such as mortgages and options.

Using RRSP self-administered investments, such as mutual fund families, along with the Charles J. Givens Money Movement Strategy, can generate an average 15%-per-year return within your plan — with no current taxes from year to year.

SELF-ADMINISTERED RRSPS: 12 KEY QUESTIONS TO ASK

Here are 12 key questions you should ask before setting up a self-administered RRSP:

1. What is the minimum annual fee?
2. If the fees depend on the size of the plan, are they based on the cost of investments (book value) or market value? If the latter, the fees will increase if the investments perform well.
3. What are the transaction charges?
4. How many fee-free transactions are allowed?
5. Are there extra fees for certain types of investments (including mortgages, options, etc.)?
6. Are there "qualified" investments that cannot be traded in the account (such as mortgages or options)?
7. Can I use my stockbroker?
8. When and how is interest paid on cash balances?
9. How frequently do I receive reports on the account and what is the format?
10. Does the institution provide an up-to-date list of qualified investments?
11. Does the institution advise on which investments are qualified and resolve any other problems?
12. Can I choose whether to pay administration and other charges directly (in which case they are tax-deductible) or have them deducted from my accounts?

(Source: *RRSP Strategies*, by David Louis, Hume Publishing Company Limited)

Strategy #170:
BORROW THE MONEY TO FUND YOUR RRSP.

The tax and investment advantages of your RRSP are so powerful that if you borrow the money to make your investment, you could end up borrowing almost free. This particularly makes sense if you repay your loan within a year. The longer you take to repay the loan, the less value will be obtained by using this strategy. Don't forget that you will also have your tax rebate to pay down the loan.

Let's say this year you are short of cash but don't want to lose your RRSP opportunity. You borrow $3,000 at 11% interest and put the money in an RRSP account in a mutual fund family.

Although under current tax law you cannot take a deduction directly for the interest you pay on the money you borrow for the RRSP, you may take deductions for the money you contribute. If you are in the 40% tax bracket, the deduction for your contribution saves you $1,200 in taxes.

The interest on the loan if you pay it back in twelve equal payments of $265 is $182. This year, you have actually saved $1,018 more from the deduction for your contribution than the interest you paid ($1,200 − $182 = $1,018).

In addition, through your mutual fund investment, you have given yourself the opportunity the first year to earn another 12% to 20%, which will continue to compound tax free, giving you potentially amazing results.

Strategy #171:
USE YOUR RRSP TO DOUBLE YOUR LIFETIME INCOME.

If you earn less than $50,000 per year, your objective through your RRSP is to double the money you are going to earn during your lifetime from the day you begin contributions to the day you retire. In other words, you want your RRSP account to have as much waiting for your retirement as you earn in salary from now until retirement.

Let's look at how much you will have to contribute to realize that dream.

REQUIRED YEARLY RRSP CONTRIBUTION TO DOUBLE YOUR LIFETIME EARNINGS — 15% RETURN

YEARS TO RETIRE-MENT	YOUR EARNINGS PER YEAR								
	$10,000	15,000	20,000	25,000	30,000	35,000	40,000	45,000	50,000
20	1,750	2,625	3,500	4,375	5,250	6,125	7,000	7,875	8,750
30	600	900	1,200	1,500	1,800	2,100	2,400	2,700	3,000
40	200	300	400	500	600	700	800	900	1,000

Strategy #172:

TAKE ADVANTAGE OF THE SPOUSAL RRSP "PENSION ROLLOVER."

In certain instances, you are allowed to make additional tax-deductible contributions to your spouse's RRSP over and above the normal contribution limits of 18% of your earned income.

Between 1989 and 1994, this rule applies: If you receive periodic registered pension or deferred profit-sharing plan withdrawal payments, you will be able to enlarge your spousal RRSP contribution limits by up to $6,000 per year.

This rule can be useful for spouses of different ages. The general rule is that any RRSP must be collapsed by the end of the year in which the holder turns 71. ("Collapsed" doesn't necessarily mean you have to take the plan into income that year — there are a number of options available to allow you to keep your funds sheltered.)

In this case, if you have qualifying pension income but are no longer able to maintain your RRSP (you are over 71), you can transfer the income, to the $6,000 maximum, into your spouse's plan and get the offsetting deduction on your own return. Not only do you defer tax, the money is building tax free in your spouse's plan.

Strategy #173:

NEVER ANNUITIZE YOUR RRSP; INSTEAD, REINVEST IN AN RRIF.

Annuitizing means that you give your entire RRSP account to an insurance company, usually in return for their promise to make monthly payments to you for the rest of your life.

The problem with annuitizing your RRSP is that the interest paid by the insurance company based on your reinvested RRSP will be low relative to other possible investments. In addition, since no one knows how long you will live, you are averaged in with the life expectancy of everyone else. You are really getting no deal whatsoever.

Why would anyone accept this low return after working a lifetime to put their money aside? For some reason, the mind reacts positively to the notion of monthly income, no matter how little. It is treated like a gift or lottery winnings instead of something that is deserved and earned. You would never make an investment without knowing the true interest rate, so why would you want to consider turning your hard-earned money over to an insurance company that may give you an average return on your investment of much less than you could achieve using the Givens money strategies for the rest of your life?

As a result of recent tax changes, Canadians now have another option called a Registered Retirement Income Fund (RRIF), which has significant financial advantages over an annuity.

Unlike the annuity — where your RRSP money is kept and invested by an insurance company — Registered Retirement Income Funds give you a wide choice of investments for your own RRSP, many of which can significantly increase your investment return. There are even self-directed RRIFs available.

Another important advantage of an RRIF is that you can usually make emergency withdrawals. Most annuities either do not build in this privilege or impose heavy financial penalties if you do choose to make a withdrawal.

Strategy #174:
IF YOU DO BUY AN ANNUITY WITH YOUR RRSP, BUY WHEN INTEREST RATES ARE HIGHEST.

If you prefer to go the annuity route, the last possible time you can convert your RRSP into an annuity is the end of the year in which you turn 71. However, it usually does not make sense to wait until then.

The best time to buy an annuity is when interest rates have peaked. Since the return you receive on an annuity is highly sensitive to long-term interest rates, you will get a better return on your annuity if you time your conversion to match interest-rate peaks. High interest rates, 12%+, could occur years before your own RRSP maturity deadline.

If you are approaching the RRSP deadline and you think that interest rates have yet to peak, one strategy is to convert to an RRIF that holds short-term investments. When you think interest rates have peaked, you can then move your money into longer-term investments or use the money to buy an annuity.

Once your money is inside an RRIF, there is a legal requirement that a certain portion be taken into income each year. The formula for this is:

VALUE OF RRIF JAN. 1 ÷ (90 – YOUR AGE)

For example, you are 70, you have $150,000 in your RRIF: $150,000 ÷ (90 – 70) = $7,500 must be taken as income.

Once you have taken out this minimum, the balance is yours to do with as you like. This could mean leaving it in the RRIF, putting it in an RRSP if you are young enough to have one, or buying an annuity.

Another strategy to be considered when you think rates have peaked is to take a portion of the funds in your RRSP and purchase the annuity such that the payments go back into your RRSP, where they accumulate tax free. Depending on your age at the time you use this strategy, the flow of funds back into your RRSP will increase its value to the point where you might consider buying another annuity a year or two later if rates remain high or go higher.

Strategy #175:

USE YOUR RRSP FOR "FAST CASH" WITH LITTLE OR NO TAX CONSEQUENCES.

Another less-obvious benefit of having one or more RRSPs is that they can yield cash easily and, from a tax point of view, efficiently.

Consider the 45-year-old schoolteacher who started her RRSP program when she was in her late 20s. She maintains four separate RRSP plans, one of which has about $15,000 in it that has been compounding tax free for her year after year. Most people use their RRSP program to save for their retirement years, but it doesn't have to be that way. Our schoolteacher can arrange a six-month leave of absence, collapse this one plan, and take a dream vacation she'll remember for years to come. The $15,000 will have to be taken into income the same year. However, because she will have lost six months of employment income, her total taxable income for the year will be considerably lower — she will be in a lower tax bracket — and the tax due on her RRSP vacation will be much less.

Here is another way to get cash out of your RRSP. Say you have

$25,000 of blue chip stock that qualifies for an RRSP sitting around, stock that has been producing income for years and is worth about $5,000 more than what you originally paid for it. Also assume that one of your RRSPs is a savings-account type with $25,000 cash in it. If you transferred the money to a self-administered RRSP and "swapped" the stock for the cash, you would end up with the following consequences:

1. You still have the stock, only now it is sitting in your RRSP where the future gains are sheltered until you collapse the plan (or swap again).
2. You have a capital gain of $5,000 because the swap was deemed to take place at "fair market value."
3. You have $25,000 in cash you didn't have before, tax free and ready to spend.

Strategy #176:

DON'T LOSE THAT $1,000 PENSION-INCOME CREDIT.

If you are over 65, one of the few major benefits left to you is that you may receive $1,000 of so-called "pension" income (generally, annuities purchased with RRSP or RRIF funds) tax free if you are in the lowest tax bracket. Be sure to adjust your tax plan so that you have at least this amount of pension income to take into income — and then shelter it with the credit. If you don't have the income coming in, but you do have an RRSP, one option is to consider using one of your RRSPs to purchase an annuity providing at least $1,000 of income. (Purchasing the annuity with RRSP funds is itself a tax-free rollover.) To make sure that your spouse can use the same credit for his or her tax planning, use a spousal RRSP to "split" your income so that, later on, your spouse will have the means to create pension income that also qualifies for the credit. (See also Strategy #163.)

Strategy #177:

WITHDRAW FUNDS FROM YOUR RRSP IN SMALL, "BITE-SIZE" BITS AND BEAT THE WITHHOLDING TAXES.

With RRSPs, the size of the withdrawal, not the size of the plan, determines your withholding tax.

All RRSPs will have tax withheld when a plan is fully or partially collapsed. These fees are not penalties but, rather, prepaid taxes. You treat them just as you would at-source payroll withholding when you complete your April return.

You can have as many plans as you like, and you can collapse each plan totally or partially. If you have significant funds in a plan, you are better off withdrawing no more than $5,000 at a time — the with-holding on $5,000 is at the lowest federal rate, 10%, and does the least damage to your cash flow. (A lump-sum withdrawal of $20,000 from the same plan would see federal withholding at the 30% rate, for example; different rates apply to Quebec.)

Strategy #178:
**CONSIDER MAKING AN $8,000 "ERROR" IN
YOUR RRSP CONTRIBUTIONS.**

Because RRSP contribution limits have become so complex in recent years, the government is aware that taxpayers may inadvertently overcontribute to their plans throughout the year, and not be aware of the error. From 1991 on, the government has set a limit of $8,000 on these overcontributions. Therefore, at any one time you can have as much as $8,000 "extra" within your tax-sheltered RRSP without trig-gering any of the fairly severe penalties the government generally applies to taxpayers with overcontributed funds.

Potentially, such funds would be "double-taxed," that is, you may not get any tax deduction for the year of contribution, and you may be taxed at your full rate whenever the RRSP is collapsed. However, it is now possible to avoid this by "drawing down" the overcontribu-tion — that is, applying the overcontribution to future years' RRSP contribution limits as they materialize.

Chapter 14

_____

WORKING FOR
TAX DEDUCTIONS

The objective of the employee is to work just hard enough
so as not to be fired, and the objective of the company is to
pay just enough so the employee won't quit.

Anonymous

Objective: Use your job to create tax deductions and minimize paycheque withholding taxes.

When I was an employee back in the '60s, I was always told that employees get no tax breaks and most employees still believe that. While exorbitant sums are withheld from their paycheques, most act blessed if they get a refund, no matter how small. Employees may "get" no tax breaks, but there are many ways to use a job to "create" sizable tax deductions and significantly reduce withholding taxes.

Planning your financial affairs to reduce the taxes you will pay is a complex process. The Canadian tax rules are designed to be the most stingy when it comes to tax write-offs for salaried employees. This section will provide you with strategies that will assist you in understanding principal tax provisions applicable to your position as an employee — strategies you can use to minimize your tax burden.

You will discover tax-planning opportunities that you may not have known existed, or feared to use because of worries that Revenue Canada would come after you.

Fear not! These are not tax loopholes. The strategies are tax rules and incentives taken directly from the Income Tax Act, implemented by law to encourage certain activities. My definition of a tax loophole, by the way, is a tax incentive that has become so popular that legislatures want to change the rules.

When it comes to employment income in Canada, my experience

has been that there are two basic — and somewhat unpleasant — starting points:

1. If the employer provides a benefit, that benefit is usually taxable income to the employee.
2. If the employee pays expenses out of pocket, the expenses are usually not deductible.

So, while you have considerably less flexibility with employment income compared to other income sources, following are some strategies that will definitely make your employment life less taxing.

Strategy #179:
DEDUCT YOUR JOB-RELATED AUTOMOBILE EXPENSES.

If you are like most Canadians, your car is not an asset. It's an expense. Sure, in accounting terms the vehicle is called an asset, but what you owe the financing company is a liability. Chances are what you owe exceeds what you could sell the car for — unless you use my strategies for buying a car (see *Financial Self-Defense,* by Charles J. Givens, Simon & Schuster, 1990).

Your car expenses include interest on any loans you made to buy the car, insurance, maintenance and repairs, oil and lubricants, licences, parking and garage expenses, and last, but certainly not least in today's economy, gasoline.

You can generally claim your job-related automobile expenses (including capital cost allowance on your car) if you meet these three requirements:

1. Your employment agreement requires you to pay all or part of your travelling expenses.
2. You are not receiving a non-taxable automobile allowance from your employer when you use your car for company business.
3. You are regularly required to perform job tasks away from your employer's place of business or in a number of different places.

Your employer has to verify that you meet the above criteria on Revenue Canada's Form T2200, which you must file with your tax return. Your first step, then, is to get your employer to agree that you meet the criteria and to sign the form.

DECLARATION OF CONDITIONS OF EMPLOYMENT

Particulars of employee – To be completed by employee

Family or Last Name	Usual First Name	Social Insurance Number

Home Address	Business Address

If you use your motor vehicle in the performance of your assigned duties, indicate
1. the make and model of the vehicle used
2. the number of kilometres (KM) driven for employment use in the year
3. the total number of KM travelled by the vehicle in the year while it was owned or leased
4. the number of days in the year the vehicle was owned or leased
5. the number of days in the year the vehicle was used for employment

Conditions of employment – To be completed by the employer

1. Period of employment during 19 _____ From 19 _____ To 19 _____

2. Area of travel _____

3. Was this employee ordinarily (habitually) required to carry out the duties of employment away from your place of business or in different places? (Refer to Interpretation Bulletin IT-522)   ☐ Yes   ☐ No

4. Did the terms and conditions of this employee's employment contract require him/her to pay any portion of the expenses incurred in the performance of assigned duties? (Refer to Interpretation Bulletin IT-352R and IT522)   ☐ Yes   ☐ No

5. Was this employee required by his/her duties to be away for at least 12 consecutive hours from the municipality and, if there is one, metropolitan area of your business, where he/she ordinarily reported for work?   ☐ Yes   ☐ No

6. a) Was this employee wholly or partly paid by commissions or other similar amounts fixed by reference to the volume of sales made or contracts negotiated?   ☐ Yes   ☐ No
   b) If yes, indicate
     (i) the amount received: $ _____
     (ii) the type of property sold or contracts negotiated: _____

7. a) Did this employee receive an allowance or a reimbursement for expenses incurred in the performance of assigned duties?   ☐ Yes   ☐ No
   b) If yes, indicate
     (i) the amount received in the form of a fixed allowance (i.e. a flat monthly allowance) for
       A) motor vehicle expenses $ _____
       B) travel expenses $ _____
       C) other (specify) _____ $ _____
     (ii) the amount received upon presentation of proof of payment of
       A) motor vehicle expenses $ _____
       B) travelled $ _____
       C) other (specify) _____ $ _____
     (iii) the amount received computed according to a rate per KM:
       A) rate
       B) KM travelled   _____ /KM
       C) total amount $ _____ KM
     (iv) the amount charged to the employer (i.e. credit card) for
       A) motor vehicle expenses $ _____
       B) travel expenses $ _____
       C) other (specify) _____ $ _____

8. Please indicate the specific expenses and the amount entered in item 7 b) which are included in the box titled "Employment income before deductions" on the T4 slip. _____

9. a) Was this employee required to incur other expenses in the performance of his/her duties for which he/she did not receive any allowance or reimbursement?   ☐ Yes   ☐ No
   b) If yes, specify the type(s) of expenses: _____

10. a) Was this employee required under his/her contract of employment to
     (i) maintain an office away from your place of business?   ☐ Yes   ☐ No
     (ii) provide an assistant or substitute?   ☐ Yes   ☐ No
     (iii) provide supplies that were consumed directly in the performance of the duties of his/her employment?   ☐ Yes   ☐ No
   b) (i) Was this employee reimbursed or is he/she entitled to a reimbursement, for any of the expenses indicated in #10 a)?   ☐ Yes   ☐ No
     (ii) If so, please indicate to which of the expenses the reimbursement relates, and whether the reimbursement is reflected in #7 b) above, and to what extent _____

Employer declaration

I hereby certify that the above-named employee was employed by us under the above conditions of employment for the period indicated.
Name of employer _____
Person from whom additional information can be obtained:
Name _____ Tel. _____ Address _____
Date _____ 19 _____

Signature of employer or authorized officer

Form prescribed by order of the Minister of National Revenue   (Français au verso)

The second step is to keep a log of all of your employer-related car use and all of the above-listed expenses. Many stationery stores sell "automobile expenses" books that are small and can be stored in your glove compartment. A small spiral notebook will work just as well. Record your beginning mileage now and at the end of the year — or when you sell or trade the car. Thereafter, write down the mileage at the beginning and end of each year. That's the total number of miles you drove the car.

You must then log each trip you make that relates to your employment. The mileage you record for your employer divided by the total number of miles driven during the year represents the amount you can deduct using this strategy.

Here's an example. Let's say that your odometer reading on January 1 last year was 17,872. On New Year's Eve, it was 54,921. Your total mileage for the year was (54,921 − 17,872), or 37,049 kilometres.

The job-related driving you did during the year, based upon your log, was 29,639 kilometres. That means that 29,639 ÷ 37,047, or 80%, of your mileage was job-related and therefore deductible. The expenses you had during the year and the capital cost allowance which you may claim in respect of the employment-related use of your automobile were:

loan interest	$2,184
insurance	872
repairs	553
oil changes/lubricants	257
gasoline	2,505
garage rent	1,200
licence	78
Total expenses for the year	$7,649
×	80%
Deductible job-related auto expenses	$6,119
capital cost allowance	6,000
capital cost allowance	× 80%
	$4,800

Even in the lowest combined federal and provincial tax bracket, this strategy would have saved you almost $3,000 in taxes. Remember, travel to and from work is not allowed as a deduction.

Use form T777(E) to report your automobile expenses.

Similar rules apply where the car is leased instead of owned, and they can become complicated. Generally, however, if the leased car was valued at less than $28,235, the lease payments are less than $650 a month, and no unusual deposits or lease prepayments were made, the application of this deduction will be similar to the calculations above.

Starting in 1991 (for income earned in 1991) employees who can deduct a portion of their car costs, as above, may also claim back the GST (Goods and Services Tax) portion of those costs. The current GST rate is 7%. Generally, this refund will equal 7/107 of the depreciation or leasing costs so claimed. Note also that employees mirror the GST eligibility of their employer in this respect — if the employer would not ordinarily be able to claim a GST refund because of the nature of the business occupation, then the employee may not either (see below).

The mechanism for the refund is to file a special claim with the Excise Office of Revenue Canada — the branch of the government that looks after GST. Don't overlook the fact that any GST refund when received is included as income in the filing for the subsequent taxation year.

Because of the nature of the GST legislation — certain classes of business are excluded completely — employees of the following may not claim back GST for work-related expenses even if the expenses themselves are deductible:

1. Companies unregistered for the GST doing less than $30,000 volume a year
2. Banks, trust companies, lenders, insurers, financial institutions
3. Health-care providers
4. Charities
5. Government

Strategy #180:
DON'T LEASE A CAR EVEN IF ALL (OR A PORTION) OF THE COSTS ARE DEDUCTIBLE.

Every major study done on the costs of leasing vs. buying shows that leasing costs you on average 20% to 30% more, even when any tax breaks are taken into account.

If you think about it, it makes sense. When you buy a car, even if

you finance the payments, you are doing the labour part, the processing of your own purchase so, in essence, you are getting the financing
"wholesale."

Leasing is another story entirely. Here someone does the work for
you but you still pay the piper. In a perfect world — perfect for the
lessor, that is — the lessor makes money not only on the car but also
on the financing package. And, if he is doing his job right, he will
pocket a few extra dollars on your trade (if you have one); on the
buy-out (if you ask for one); and on the maintenance contract (if you
accept one).

The best — and only — argument for leasing generally has to do
with cash flow. In other words, leasing frees up your cash to be invested in appreciating assets, not depreciating ones. But, on close
examination, this doesn't hold up. The first thing you notice when
you shop for a lease is the more money you are willing to put as a
downpayment (sometimes called a prepayment) the more reasonable
your monthly payments become. But if you wanted to put a lot of
money down, you would purchase a car in the first place, wouldn't
you?

Strategy #181:
DEDUCT THE EXPENSES OF AN OFFICE IN YOUR HOME
WHEN YOU USE IT FOR YOUR EMPLOYER.

The employees' home-office deduction is one of the most overlooked
write-offs in the Income Tax Act. While it's true that Revenue Canada
has placed hurdles between you and your deduction, with a bit of
planning, this deduction can save you big tax dollars.

Here are the rules — if you meet all of the following conditions,
you may deduct office expenses:

1. Your contract of employment requires you to maintain an office and pay
   the expenses.
2. Your employer has not and will not reimburse you for these expenses.

As is the case with automobile expenses, your employment
agreement must require that you have an office away from your
principal place of business. In order to substantiate the requirement, you must file form T2200, signed by your employer, with
your tax return. In practice, Revenue Canada usually accepts the

form as certification of your right to deduct office expenses — however, the form itself does not constitute your Conditions of Employment agreement. For your own protection, for example, in case of a Revenue Canada reassessment after a job termination, a written employment agreement would be helpful to your case in the event of a dispute with Revenue Canada.

If you rent your home, claim a portion of the rental expenses, prorating everything based upon square footage or number of rooms. For example, if you rent a five-room house, one room of which is used as an office for your employment income, then 20% of the rental expenses would be deductible.

If you own your home, you should determine all of your expenses for heating fuel, electricity, cleaning, etc., and calculate the "office-use portion," which is deductible. Among expenses specifically excluded by Revenue Canada are mortgage interest and capital cost allowance on the building.

Under current tax proposals, the employee home-office deduction will be subject to similar restrictions to those applying to self-employed individuals. As a result, starting in 1991, one of these two requirements must be met in order to claim the deductions:

1. The home work space must be your principal place of business.
2. You only use the work space to earn income from your business and you use it on a continuous and regular basis for meeting customers or others in the course of performing your employment duties.

Strategy #182:
DEDUCT PROFESSIONAL FEES AND UNION DUES.

In Canada, entrance fees — those expenses required to get you initially into a profession — such as real estate courses required to become licensed, are usually non-deductible expenses. Among the often overlooked expenses that are job-related are annual professional association dues.

If your employer doesn't pay the membership dues for you, the dues become a tax deduction for you. Generally, you may deduct annual professional and membership dues, if they are reasonably regarded as applicable to your employment income and provided also that they are annual dues, and the professional status is recognized by statute. Such payments need not be essential to hold your job, but there must be a reasonable degree of relationship between the payments and your job. For example, a chemical engineer, employed by a company to sell chemical products, is considered by Revenue Canada to satisfy this requirement, for membership in a chemicals-related professional association.

Take the deduction on form T1, Step 3.

Strategy #183:

PAY YOUR SPOUSE OR KIDS A DEDUCTIBLE SALARY TO HELP WITH YOUR JOB.

The Income Tax Act allows you to deduct reasonable salary expenses you pay for an assistant, if you are required by your contract of employment to pay for additional help. The rule would allow you to hire family members and pay them a deductible salary.

Such salary expenses may be deductible to you and are taxable to your spouse or kids who are working for you. You are required to withhold income tax, Canada or Quebec Pension Plan contributions, and Unemployment Insurance premiums from your "assistant's" salary. You may deduct the employer's portion of the Pension Plan and Unemployment Insurance remittances for your assistant as an expense. Taxes can be saved if the family member is in a lower tax bracket than you are.

If you work for a smaller company, you may be able to convince your employer to hire the family member directly, trading off some of your salary to the family member (provided that the pay is reasonable in relation to the family member's services). The resulting tax benefit would be quite similar, but the inconvenience and record keeping would be considerably less.

How much tax can be saved? If you are in the highest combined federal and provincial tax bracket and the family member hired as your assistant is in the lowest (earning less than about $27,800 annually), in round numbers you can save about $200 in taxes on every $1,000 paid in salary to the family member. That's roughly equivalent to a pre-tax salary bonus for you of more than $350 for each $1,000 of salary.

What are some of the jobs your family members might perform? The list is extensive:

- answer the telephone
- write letters, answer correspondence

- file papers
- clean office
- make appointments
- record business activities
- follow up with clients
- maintain appointment log
- keep expense records
- assist (whatever you do)

Moreover, using this powerful strategy, your designated family member "assistant" now has money to invest in an RRSP of his or her own, providing further tax shelter to what was originally a highly taxed salary!

To claim these job-related expenses, file form T2200 with your tax return.

(See Chapter 13, Strategies for Your RRSP.)

Strategy #184:

DEDUCT THE COST OF JOB-RELATED SUPPLIES.

You may take deductions for the cost of supplies consumed directly in the performance of your job, provided that your Conditions of Employment agreement requires you to supply and pay for these expenses.

For supplies to be deductible, they must be used directly while performing your employment duties, and your employer must not now or ever reimburse you for your supply purchases. Among the expendable supply items whose cost should be deductible would be stamps, pens and pencils, stationery, paper clips, etc.

Basic guidance by Revenue Canada limits the supplies you may deduct to materials that are used directly in the performance of your employment and are then unfit for further use in the performance of any similar employment.

Revenue Canada specifically excludes the following: monthly basic telephone rate for your home telephone, calculator, briefcase, computer, special clothing used in your employment, and any types of tools.

As with other deducted expenses from job-related employment income, when you declare deductions for supplies, you must file form

T2200 with your return, whereby your employer certifies your conditions of employment.

The GST portion of these expenses may also be claimed back following the general guidelines in Strategy #179.

Strategy #185:
ESTABLISH A "KEY PERSON" PENSION PLAN.

If you are a senior employee (in terms of the salary you receive and the number of years you've been with the company), it may be possible to set up a special "key person" pension plan, which can be specially designed for you.

One important advantage of a key person pension plan is that you can trade off a fair amount of your annual salary as contributions to the plan. These contributions are tax-sheltered as they are paid into the plan.

Although these contributions may decrease your RRSP limits, the tradeoff may be worth it, since you may be able to increase the total amount of deductible contributions that can be made toward your total retirement plan. A number of executive compensation consultants specialize in these types of plans.

Strategy #186:
COMBINE A PERSONAL MOVE WITH A JOB RELOCATION.

Many Canadian taxpayers have literally been taken to the cleaners for failing to take, or overlooking, the moving-expense deduction. "Well," you think, "in our case, my wonderful employer took care of us. Our company paid the mover, flew me and the family down to look for a new home, paid our motel bill — even gave us some money to buy our meals. Too much extra paperwork anyway!"

What about the $200 you spent on a hotel the night before you moved in? What about the $50 you gave your friend for driving one of your cars to the new location — with the house plants loading up the back seat, floor, and front passenger seat? How about the real estate commission?

If you recorded and deducted these expenses, it would have meant a tax savings of well over $4,000 assuming your salary is in the $40,000-or-above range.

One of the most overlooked tax write-offs is the moving-expense deduction. If you are a salary or wage earner, a self-employed person, or a student attending a post-secondary institution, you may qualify to deduct moving expenses from income earned at your new location if:

- you move to begin business or employment at a new location;
- you move to attend classes full-time at a college, university, or other post-secondary education institution;
- your move brings you at least 40 kilometres closer to your new school or place of work.

It isn't necessary for you to actually change companies, just job locations — in effect, a job transfer.

You can deduct:

- travel expenses, including meals and lodging, for you and your family;
- transportation of household goods;
- storage of household goods;
- temporary board at both old and new locations for a period of up to 15 days;
- costs of selling your old home;
- costs associated with breaking a lease in order to move;
- some costs relating to a home purchase at your new location, including cost of legal services, land transfer, and title registration taxes (if you're selling or have sold your old home).

A number of moving expenses aren't deductible. For example, Revenue Canada will not allow deductions for losses on the sale of your old home, expenses for work done to make your former home more saleable, or house-hunting trips.

You may claim as deductions all Revenue Canada-approved moving expenses up to the amount of income received at the new location (carrying forward the balance, if any, to next year). Where the employer specifically offers a reimbursement of expenses, this amount must be included in your income at the new location, if you wish to claim moving expenses as a deduction.

For example, if your move cost you $1,500,

(a) and your income during the year at the new location (you moved in late November perhaps) was $1,200, the amount of moving expenses you may deduct is only $1,200. The remaining $300 may be carried forward to be deducted from your income earned in the following year at the new location.

(b) and your employer reimbursed you $800, you may deduct the $1,500 from the combined new salary plus reimbursement, in this case ($1,200 + $800) or $2,000. This means that you would show $500 in net income after this particular deduction.

If you have moved or are contemplating a move, you'll want to obtain a copy of Revenue Canada's Interpretation bulletin IT-178R2, as well as form T1-M.

Strategy #187:
INVESTIGATE STOCK PURCHASE
AND OPTION PLANS.

The Income Tax Act offers a number of tax advantages to employee share purchase and option plans.

For example, if you work for a Canadian-controlled private corporation (e.g., a corporation whose shares are not listed on a Canadian stock exchange and which is not controlled by non-residents or public corporations), special tax rules allow you to receive shares of your company (or a related company) without an immediate tax benefit.

This is an exceptional bonus because, generally, when shares are purchased through a company plan to purchase shares below market value, you are otherwise considered to have received an immediate taxable benefit equal to the difference in value between the fair market value at the time of purchase and the acquisition price.

Dividends received on the shares will be eligible for the usual dividend tax rules — taxed at relatively low rates (approximately 30% for top-bracket taxpayers).

The difference between the acquisition cost and fair market value constitutes the taxable benefit. However, if the shares qualify for the special Canadian-controlled private-corporation rules, the taxable benefit doesn't occur until you sell, exchange, or give your shares away. Keep them for at least two years and there is an additional 25% deduction of the tax benefit. (Only 75% of the benefit will be taxed.)

Any appreciation over fair market value from the time the stocks are acquired will generally be eligible for capital-gains status, including capital-gains exemption.

Strategy #188:
USE THE HOME-RELOCATION-LOAN TAX BREAK.

If your employer gives you a low-interest or no-interest loan, you can incur additional tax as a result. However, income tax rules provide an exemption for home-relocation loans made by an employer to an employee.

The conditions for this tax break are similar to those for the moving-expense deduction. Also, it only applies to the first $25,000 of an interest-free or an equivalent low-interest loan received from the employer. The exemption is available for up to five years. You must use the proceeds to buy your new home.

Strategy #189:
TAKE REIMBURSEMENTS INSTEAD OF SALARY
OR BONUSES.

Reimbursements are one way of getting a break on certain expenses that might not otherwise be deductible. The following items, assuming they are not claimed as separate deductions by the employee, could be reimbursable by an employer without triggering a taxable benefit to the employee (if such a benefit were triggered, the benefit would be included in income as though received in cash, and the tax advantage is lost):

1. Moving expenses, including those which may not be acceptable for ordinary deductions, such as reimbursement for the loss on a sale of your old home.
2. Dues (professional, social, athletic)
3. Convention and seminar expenses
4. Tuition fees for job training
5. Job-related books and equipment
6. Trips for business purposes
7. Up to $25,000 worth of group life insurance (term)

Look through this list and prepare a list of your own for your employer of all things for which you would like to be reimbursed — items that have some benefit to your employer. For example, say there is a job-related seminar being given in Montreal. If the seminar is business related, the full expenses may be deductible by your employer and there may be no taxable benefit to you. (It may even be possible for your spouse to accompany you, if an effective arrangement can be made for his/her assistance in a business capacity.)

On the other hand, your employer may take the position that, while sending you to the seminar is helpful, it is not really a decision he is predisposed to make on his own. If you really want to go, therefore, suggest to your employer that you would "trade" either future salary or a seasonal bonus for the trip. In this situation, the cost of the trip to you is considerably less than if you went on your own.

Another "perk" to ask for is an interest-free loan. Although such loans do, by themselves, result in a taxable benefit, your strategy is to use the money for further investment only. If the loan is put towards a potentially profitable investment, the deemed benefit could be 100% offset by the interest deduction, so that the net cost of the loan to you would be nothing.

Think about this for a moment — even the most conservative investments are "winners" if the cost to you is free!

Strategy #190:
ENCOURAGE YOUR EMPLOYER
TO START A GROUP RRSP.

As I have already demonstrated, the advantages of the RRSP program are powerful (Chapter 13). I explained how RRSPs offer such potent tax advantages that you come out ahead even if you have to borrow to fund yours.

An even better way to invest in an RRSP is to have your employer set up a plan that meets the needs of most of the employees in the company. The contributions to the plan would be made by at-source deductions handled by the company comptroller.

The advantage of this approach is more than mere convenience — your employer can fill out the necessary forms to persuade Revenue Canada that you may now reduce your at-source tax prepayments to compensate for the deductions you will claim on your RRSP.

This is the best of both worlds — not only do you get the advantages of your RRSP but you get to fund the plan with your own money, before Revenue Canada gets a chance to stake its claim!

Chapter 15

TRAVEL THE WORLD ON DEDUCTIBLE DOLLARS

Money is a guarantee that we may have what we want in the future. Though we need nothing at the moment, it ensures the possibility of satisfying a new desire when it arises.

Aristotle, *Nichomachean Ethics*

Objective: Make your vacations and trips tax-deductible.

One great way to take tax-deductible trips in Canada and around the world is through your business or profession. If you don't have a small business, start one. You'll find all the necessary instructions in Chapter 18.

Imagine visiting Honolulu, New York, or even Hong Kong, and having the government pick up a good portion of your travel expenses! Following these strategies, you may be able to enjoy the privilege by making your vacations and trips tax deductible.

Strategy #191:
BECOME A SEEKER OF KNOWLEDGE.

Expenses incurred while in pursuit of knowledge, education, contacts, clients, or suppliers while travelling within Canada may be deductible, as well as many of those relating to conventions, seminars, or education abroad. This chapter contains strategies you may be able to use to create deductions for business travel.

Note, however, that while most of your expenses may be fully deductible, the cost of your meals while travelling is only 80% deduct-

209

ible. Therefore, add up your total food expenses and multiply by .80 to determine your food deduction. If you are travelling by train, plane, or boat and the meals are included in the ticket price, the 80% rule doesn't apply.

This 80% rule is faithfully carried over to the GST as well. Therefore, assuming you are in business and GST-registered (see Chapter 30), 80% of your GST for food is reclaimable directly from the government when you file your next GST return.

Strategy #192:

TAKE ADVANTAGE OF BUSINESS CONVENTION WRITE-OFFS.

If you own a small business or are a professional, subsection 20(10) of the Income Tax Act allows you to deduct up to two business-related conventions per year, provided they are held by a business or professional organization. In fact, it is not even necessary that you be a member of the organization, simply that the organizers meet the test themselves.

Choose places you have always wanted to go in other provinces, or even Las Vegas, Atlantic City or Florida. With all the conventions these days put on by everyone from trade associations to independent educators, you will be able to make two tax-deductible trips per year to places you have always dreamed of going — and get some great deductible education to boot.

The conventions must be at locations that are consistent with the "territorial scope" of the organization offering the convention. This means that if you attend a convention outside of Canada offered by an international organization, your expenses will normally be deductible. But if a Canadian organization has an out-of-Canada convention, the deductions may be disallowed.

To get the deduction, simply follow the rules in Interpretation Bulletins IT357R2, IT131R2, and IT-518 under Meals, Entertainment, and Convention Expenses.

Use some caution when it comes to very exotic locations. For example, Revenue Canada is more likely to allow expenses for a convention in Vancouver than a junket to Tahiti. Your basic tax strategy always applies. If you feel you should be allowed the deduction, take it.

Strategy #193:
ORGANIZE YOUR OWN CONFERENCE TO EARN A DEDUCTIBLE TRIP FOR YOU AND YOUR COLLEAGUES.

You can organize a private seminar with a number of colleagues to discuss current events in your profession or to share business methods and strategies. Set your goal as getting away from ringing phones and other distractions. Holding the seminar at an out-of-the-way retreat solves the problem and simultaneously creates a deduction for related travel.

After you've finished your business, you can enjoy the nightlife or theatre, or involve yourself in other activities without losing the deduction as long as the primary purpose of the trip is business-related.

Keep good records and have minutes typed as to what was discussed and at what times and for how long the meetings were held.

Strategy #194:
START A SMALL IMPORTING COMPANY FOR PROFIT AND DEDUCTIBLE INTERNATIONAL TRAVEL.

A great way to make your international travel deductible is by starting a small importing company. Your total investment? Two empty suitcases. Take them with you to the United States, Mexico, South America, the Far East, or Europe. While you are at your destination, your tax strategy is to go shopping for items you can take back to Canada and sell for a profit. While visiting the marketplaces and bazaars, you buy the beautiful handicrafts and handmade items that are so inexpensive overseas and so incredibly expensive when you see them in the gift shops and department stores back home. These are your imports and that's what goes in the suitcases. Pick the things you know your friends would love to have in their homes.

When you get home, have a party and invite all your friends right down to your distant acquaintances. They are your customers. After you serve the "tax deductible refreshments," bring out all your beautiful imports — with a price tag on them. You will find, like so many who use this strategy, that you'll sell out the first night, and make more than enough profit to pay for your next trip. At tax time, claim a deduction for the business-related portion of your travel expenses.

My first experience at importing came during my first trip to Mexico. I was 26, and two friends and I scraped together enough gas and hotel money to get us from Nashville to Monterrey, Mexico. With the couple of hundred extra expense dollars, I bought leather coats for $8 each and beautiful coloured ceramic plates that sell in gift shops for $30. They cost me just $2. Everything I brought back was gone instantly as my friends grabbed for their favourites as if they were at a bargain-basement sale. This strategy is subject to the requirement that you have a reasonable expectation of profit (Strategy #210). Be sure to check for customs restrictions, import duties and other expenses.

Strategy #195:
BECOME AN "OUTSIDE AGENT" FOR A TRAVEL AGENCY.

You can have the benefits of a travel agent or agency without changing careers or starting your own agency. By acting as an "outside agent" for any travel agency, you qualify to receive part of the travel agency's commission — up to 50%. The travel agency normally receives 8% to 10% of the cost of the airline tickets, and 10% or more commission on the ground arrangements, such as hotels and tours. Choose a destination you would like to visit, and one that your friends and associates might also enjoy. Print simple brochures or fliers that explain your adventure and distribute them to fellow employees, club members, or even neighbours. The travel agency can furnish you with "shells" — partially printed brochures with colour pictures and blank areas for insertion of time, date, and specific information about your trip.

As an outside agent you will have the chance to travel free. When the travel agency acts as your representative with the airline, you'll get one complimentary trip for every 15–20 people who pay the regular price. The commission income from your trip will show your intent to make a profit and allow you to claim a tax deduction for any extra expenses you incur. Call the travel agencies in your area and find one that is anxious to get you started.

I enjoy travel so much I finally bought a travel agency. While in Amsterdam recently, I pulled out my travel agent's business card at the beautiful Amstel Hotel and was promptly given a 50% discount on my entire stay — from $200 per night to $100 per night. The previous month, I flew on American Airlines round-trip, first-class from Orlando, Florida, to Sacramento, California, for only $300, far less than the regular first-class fare of $1,200. On a recent safari to Africa, the regular cost of the land arrangements was cut by half, from $3,400 per person to $1,700, and the first-class airfare was 75% off, all tax deductible, of course, since I own the travel agency.

During the '70s, I personally took hundreds of people to Hawaii, Mexico, England, Ireland, France, and South America. As an outside agent putting the trips together, I knew I would enjoy myself. My share of the commissions amounted to about $5,000 per week plus free airfare and hotels. Not a bad way to travel!

Following the strategy above, you can get the same bargains by becoming a successful "outside agent."

Chapter 16

OFTEN OVERLOOKED

DEDUCTIONS

AND CREDITS

The new legislation is more complex than anything ever seen before in this country, a complexity that aids tax collection and harms taxpayers.

Arthur Drache, *Financial Post*

Objective: Maximize your tax deductions and credits.

Strategy #196:
CLAIM THE EQUIVALENT-TO-MARRIED TAX CREDIT.

Every year thousands of Canadian taxpayers overlook one of the most lucrative tax credit opportunities. The Canadian tax system offers a substantial credit to individuals whose spouse's income is significantly lower, resulting in a situation where one spouse is effectively supporting the other.

You don't have to be married to claim this tax advantage, since the Canadian tax system may also recognize "equivalent-to-married" status.

Unfortunately (or fortunately, depending upon your viewpoint), in order to claim the credit you must be single, legally divorced, or — if you are still married — you must not support, live with, or be supported by your spouse (ignoring deductible alimony).

In order to be eligible for the tax credit, which is worth about $1,300 in tax savings (taking provincial tax into account and based upon 1991 information), you must also maintain and live in your own residence (you can be a tenant renting) and you must have a dependent living with you. The dependent has to be someone you support and must be a resident of Canada (not applicable in the case of your child). The following qualify: a relative younger than 18 (your children, grandchildren, sisters, brothers, nieces, nephews), a parent or grandparent, or a relative who is physically or mentally ill and is dependent upon you by virtue of that illness.

When you meet these requirements, you may be eligible to claim the equivalent-to-married tax credit. (Additional provincial tax credits may also be available.) Complete Schedule 6 to determine the amount of your equivalent-to-married tax credit and attach it to your T1 Tax Return.

Strategy #197:
TAKE ADVANTAGE OF TRANSFERABLE TAX CREDITS.

Canadian Tax Reform of 1988 provides that certain tax credits can be transferred to the other spouse if one spouse doesn't need them to reduce his or her tax exposure. These include the pension and age tax credits and the disability credit, as well as the tuition and education tax credits. (The disability, tuition and education tax credits can also be transferred to supporting individuals other than the spouse.)

To calculate the amounts you may transfer from one spouse to the other, complete Schedule 2 and attach it to the T1 Tax Return to which the transfer is being made. The amount transferred must be entered on your T1 return during Step 4, Calculation of Total Non-Refundable Tax Credits.

Strategy #198:
TAKE ADVANTAGE OF SPECIAL RULES FOR
MEDICAL EXPENSES.

Many taxpayers do not take full advantage of the tax opportunities relating to uninsured medical expenses. Because of the general rule that medical expenses can only be claimed if they are in excess of 3% of net income, many high-income earners simply pitch out their medical receipts. What they don't realize is that there are special rules that may enable them to claim such tax credits anyway.

Here are some solutions:

1. A new rule allows the medical expense credit to be claimed for expenses in excess of $1,571 per year (in 1991 — this amount is indexed every year). This will be of obvious benefit to high-income earners who would otherwise be subject to the 3%-of-net-income restriction.
2. Where both spouses have tax exposure, the lower-income spouse should generally claim the medical expenses of the higher-income spouse. That way, more medical expenses may be allowable to the lower-income spouse since the 3%-of-net-income limit will be lower.
3. You can claim medical expenses for any 12-month period that ends in the year. This will be important if you want to get as far above the 3%-of-net-income limit as possible. Of course, you cannot claim the same expense twice. For example, assume you had major medical expenses last December that extended into the new year for three or four months. Realizing the expenses for December were insufficient to gain you the medical reduction, you simply did not claim them. You could now claim the expenses of December to April on your current tax return.

Example: John Jackson shows $40,000 as taxable net income for the year. He had a lot of dental problems during the year and, including some trips to the doctor, his medical bills came to $1,800. The general rule is that John can claim the excess over 3% × his net income; that is, the amount that is left after subtracting (3% × $40,000) or $1,200:

$1,800 − $1,200 = $600 claim (the remaining $1,200 is "lost")

If John's wife Sally shows net income of $12,000 for the year from her part-time job, it would be to everyone's advantage to have Sally claim both her own expenses (say, $500) and John's ($1,800).

Total medical expenses for both spouses claimed on Sally's return: $2,300.

Sally's limit: 3% × $12,000 = $360

$2,300 − $360 = $1,940

"lost expenses" = $360

Using this strategy, only $360 of expenses is denied to the family. If John and Sally had claimed each set of expenses separately:

John's allowable expense, if separate: $600 ($1,200 lost)

Sally's allowable expense, if separate: $500 − $360 = $140 ($360 lost)

Total medical expenses disallowed by separate filing: $1,200 + $360 = $1,560

Therefore, by combining their deductions on the tax return of the lower earner, the Jackson family "loses" only $360 of deductible expenses. By filing separately, they "lose" $1,560 in medical expenses. This strategy earned an additional $1,200 in medical expenses worth $204 (17% of $1,200) as tax credits.

Examples of allowable medical expenses may include:

- Non-government health plan premiums
- Seeing-eye and hearing-ear dog expenses
- Certain medical devices, as listed under the Income Tax Act, e.g., artificial limbs
- Eyeglasses, hearing aids, dentures, pacemakers, artificial limbs, prescription drugs, crutches
- Doctors', dentists', registered nurses' fees

Obtain Interpretation Bulletin IT-225R, Medical Expenses, for more information. Remember to keep all receipts!

Strategy #199:
MAKE THE MOST OF CHARITABLE DONATIONS.

Charitable donations that exceed $250 per year are eligible for a special 29% federal tax credit, whereas the first $250 of charitable donations will be eligible only for a 17% credit. The maximum you may be eligible to claim in any one year is 20% of your net income.

As a result of this rule, consider the following:

1. Lump your charitable donations into one calendar year to get above $250.
2. One spouse should claim the other spouse's charitable expenses, if this will allow the claiming spouse to pass the $250 threshold.
3. If you are under the $250 threshold one year, consider saving your claims until next year if next year's claims would then exceed $250.
4. Claim your oldest unclaimed donations first. You do not have to claim the full amount of any year's donations as any unused donations may be carried forward up to five years.
5. If you live in Canada but work across the border, you may be eligible to claim donations to American charitable organizations to the extent they do not exceed 20% of your U.S. income.

6. You may also claim donations other than cash. Refer to these Revenue Canada publications:

IT-288R, "Gifts of Tangible Capital Properties to Charity and Others"

IT-297R, "Gifts in Kind to Charity and Others"

IT-244R2, "Gifts of Life Insurance Policies as Charitable Donations"

Cancelled cheques and photocopies are not acceptable proof of payment. Official receipts are required for all donations except those shown on your T4 information slips. See Revenue Canada Interpretation Bulletin IT-110R2, Deductible Gifts and Official Donation Receipts.

The method the government has chosen to handle charitable donations is quite unique. The two rates given — 17% for the first $250, 29% for the balance — mirror the highest and lowest marginal rates in the Canadian tax system. This has some peculiar effects. For example, if the donor is someone in the lowest marginal rate category, they will get a credit on their first $250 of donations equal approximately to their true tax cost. However, additional donations actually end up with a net tax "bonus."

Example: Ted makes $25,000 a year and is in the 17% federal tax bracket. This means that if Ted donates $250 to charity he is giving up money that would have had a 17% tax cost to him and getting a credit of 17% (provincial taxes aside). However, if Ted donates another $100, he receives a credit of 29% ($29) for money that would have had a tax cost of only 17% ($17), so, since the credit he gets can be used against other income, in effect, he comes out $12 ahead on his tax bill.

Here is an example of charitable donation "carry-forward":

Frank has a net income of $20,000, which means that his "cap" for purposes of charitable donations is 20% × $20,000, or $4,000 a year. In 1990 Frank donated $5,000 to charity. In 1991 Frank donated $2,000 to charity.

The maximum Frank was allowed to take as a tax credit on his 1990 return was $4,000. The extra $1,000 ($5,000 − $4,000) is carried over to 1991. In 1991, assuming the same net income, Frank can still credit only a maximum of $4,000 a year. That year, 1991, he still has his $1,000 carry-forward plus $2,000 in current year tax credits, for a total charitable donation of $3,000. Frank can take a credit for the entire $3,000 that year since he is still under the $4,000 "cap."

Strategy #200:
DON'T MISS THE SPECIAL TAX RULES FOR CAPITAL GAINS.

If you are reporting a capital gain, you should be aware that there are a number of special rules that may reduce the taxable amount of the capital gain:

1. V-Day rules. If you owned the particular property before 1972, when capital gains were first taxed in Canada, you are usually entitled to treat the asset value at the end of 1971 (the "V-Day Value") as the cost of the property for tax purposes.
2. Reserves. Any time you can defer a tax liability, do it! If you have sold an investment for a capital gain, but you are not entitled to receive cash proceeds until after the end of the year, special rules relating to "reserves" allow you to defer a portion of your capital gain until a later return. Using these rules, recognition of the full amount of the capital gain may be deferred up to five years. But it is necessary that at least ⅕ of the capital gain be recognized in the year of sale and in each of the subsequent four years.

    For example, assume you have a capital property that cost $5,000 and sold for $14,000 (with sale expenses of $1,000), paid for by the buyer with $2,000 down and $2,000/year for six years.

    Although your capital gain is actually $8,000 (that is, $14,000 − $6,000), you need only take into income $1,600 in the year of sale, and $1,600 in each of the four succeeding years.
3. If you have sold for a profit "personal use" property (e.g., a car, a boat, and so on), special tax-reducing rules may apply. Notably, you can usually claim $1,000 as your tax cost, even if the property actually cost you less.
4. The first $200 of capital gains or losses due to fluctuations in foreign currency are tax-exempt for individuals.

Strategy #201:
CLAIM APPLICABLE FOREIGN TAX CREDITS.

If you have investment income from the United States or another foreign country, don't forget to claim a foreign tax credit on your return, if foreign taxes have been withheld on your out-of-country income.

Also, don't forget that a provincial foreign tax credit can be claimed by filing Form T2036.

Strategy #202:
CLAIM YOUR SPOUSE'S DIVIDEND TAX CREDIT.

If your spouse has a very low taxable income, he or she may be able to eliminate tax exposure without having to claim the dividend tax credit. If this is the case, the credit will simply go to waste.

However, there is a strategy that can allow you to claim your spouse's dividend tax credit. You can transfer your spouse's dividends to yourself, provided that the transfer will increase the amount of your married tax credit. (The calculation of the married tax credit is based on the notion that the lower your spouse's income, the higher the possible credit. Therefore, by taking the dividends into your own income you are reducing that of your spouse's, thereby increasing the ceiling on the married tax credit that you yourself may now claim.)

Of course, by reporting your spouse's dividend, your income will increase. However, the increase in the married tax credit — and corresponding tax saving — may compensate for this. You may now be better off since you can claim the dividend tax credit for your own return, and use it to effectively reduce the tax due on Canadian corporate dividends.

Chapter 17

MAKING YOUR RECREATIONAL ASSETS DEDUCTIBLE

True, you can't take it with you, but then, that's not the place where it comes in handy.

Anonymous

Objective: Find big tax deductions for your recreational assets.

The great outdoors! Who can resist it? Exploring rivers, lakes, and cruising ocean waters for the big catch, while waiting for the National Film Board camera crew to arrive; donning the wings of eagles and flying three-dimensionally free in a personal and private plane; getting close to nature at the seashore, or high in the mountains in your own plush home on wheels. These are the dreams that inspire us to work harder. Vacations and leisure-time activities cost money. But from my own experience, I can assure you that you can significantly reduce the cost of owning and operating recreational assets by making your boat, plane, or motor home legally tax deductible.

Strategy #203:
USE YOUR BOAT, PLANE, OR MOTOR HOME IN YOUR SMALL BUSINESS TO CREATE TAX DEDUCTIONS.

What is now a hobby — flying, fishing, or sailing — may be turned into a tax-deductible small-business enterprise if there is a reasonable expectation of profit related to these activities. (For further discussion, see Strategy #210.) As you will see in later Strategies, assets used in a business that contribute directly to the production of income can result in tax deductions, even if you own them personally, to the extent that there is business use of the assets.

Here is a good example. My friend Tom lives and breathes fishing. He would rather fish than eat, except for eating fish. Year after year, weekend after weekend, he trailers his 23-foot Sea Craft behind his Ford van from his home in Richmond, Virginia, to fertile fishing grounds in the Chesapeake Bay over 100 kilometers away. Continually pouring money into gas, maintenance, fishing tackle, and motel expenses left Tom feeling as if he was working for his boat, instead of the other way around.

One day, while bobbing about in two-foot swells, Tom and I began to discuss what he could legally do to be able to take tax deductions for some of his expenses. Tom was already selling his catch to local restaurants, often at a handsome profit, which meant that he was in a tax-deductible business. He had never thought of taking the deductions.

Tom also wrote to manufacturers of fishing rods, reels, and lures to see if he could become a distributor, and received several enthusiastic replies, especially from the smaller companies. He was excited and well on his way. He bought several samples at wholesale (50% off) and began to show them to fellow fishermen. He used his boat to house, display, and demonstrate his new line of fishing equipment. Not only has Tom picked up some unexpected income from his venture, his expensive hobby has now become a personally and financially rewarding, tax-deductible small business.

Look how Tom benefitted the first year alone from his small fishing-related business:

Item	Cost	Cash Spent	Annual Tax Deduction	% Business Use
Boat	$26,000	$ 4,000	$ 1,950	50%
Boat fuel	1,800	1,800	900	50%
Van fuel	900	900	450	50%
Sample costs	750	750	750	100%
Cost of van	12,000	2,000	1,800	50%
Motels, food	2,800	2,800	1,400	50%
TOTALS		$11,250	$7,250	

Fishing for income is a way of life for many Canadians. You are therefore subject to more restrictions than in the United States. For example, you need a commercial fishing licence to sell game fish. There are also limits on your catch. However, Canada publishes a tax guide specifically for those who generate income from fishing. If you have a passion for fishing, why not turn it into a small business?

Here's another creative example of how to make your recreational assets deductible. Bart, a member of my organization, always loved flying, but didn't feel he could afford to own a plane. He estimated that he could buy a used, four-seater Cessna for about $22,000. Even though the cost of fuel and maintenance was slightly out of his budget at the time, Bart reasoned that if he could make a good part of his expenses tax deductible, he could afford the plane immediately.

Bart combined his interest in flying with another interest, photography, and started a small business he calls "Aerial Photos by Bart." He printed brochures and business cards and contacted realtors, the Chamber of Commerce, and the city planning commission about his new venture. He also ran ads in the classified section of the newspaper offering to give guided air tours for new families moving into the area. (For this he was required to get an additional licence.) His weekend, part-time business is thriving, and he was able to convert two hobbies into a fun and profitable business. Most of all, he was able to afford his dream of owning his own plane.

There are countless other ways to use recreational assets in a small business and take advantage of the potential tax deductions and profit potential. Here are a few ideas:

- Using your plane for flying lessons.
- Sailing lessons on your sailboat.
- Chartered fishing trips on your fishing boat.
- Water skiing lessons using your boat and tax-deductible skis.
- Using your motor home as the principal office for your small business or to display products or services offered.
- Using your motor home as a travelling billboard with your ad painted on the side.

Note that you may also deduct the business-use percentage of the interest you pay on the loan to purchase recreational assets, since business interest is generally deductible. However, limitations on interest deductibility and depreciation claims may apply to most vehicles.

Strategy #204:
USE THIRD-PARTY LEASING TO MAKE RECREATIONAL ASSETS DEDUCTIBLE.

Third-party leasing means offering your boat, motor home, or airplane for rent at fair market rental value, using someone other than yourself as the leasing agent.

When you are renting through a third party — another company normally in the business of leasing — my advice is that you treat your recreational asset as being used for business purposes the entire time the asset is available for rent, whether rented or not. So, if you use the asset for two weeks per year and it is available for rent the balance of 50 weeks, you should base your claim on 11½ months or 23/24 of the total available tax deductions. (Certain capital-cost-allowance restrictions may apply.) Leasing agents can be found for boats at most marinas, for planes at flight services or the flight booking office at any airport, and for motor homes in the Yellow Pages under Recreational Vehicles — Sales and Service.

If you are active in the leasing business, approving all leases, formulating a business plan, contracting for maintenance, doing regular inspections and keeping the business records yourself, you would then qualify to take all expense deductions as allowed under the Income Tax Act against current income from all sources (subject to restrictions for capital cost allowance).

(Note: If you are leasing your recreational asset as a business, use Revenue Canada Form T2124(E) to report your income and expenses.) See also Strategy #210.

Chapter 18

START YOUR OWN
SMALL BUSINESS

*By working hard eight hours a day, you may eventually get
to be boss and work hard twelve hours a day.*

Robert Frost

**Objective: Start a small business for fun, profit, and huge tax
deductions.**

While I was in the Soviet Union in 1985, I had a lengthy conversation with one of the Soviet tourist guides. "What do you do," I asked,
"if you want to start your own business in the Soviet Union?"

"Defect to the West," she answered matter-of-factly.

How fortunate, I thought, that we live in a country where small-business opportunities are so easy to come by. You, too, are blessed
to be living in Canada where you are free to become whatever you
are willing to work toward achieving.

My father started his first business when he was 10, sitting in the
limbs of oak trees in La Grange, Illinois, waiting for rattlesnakes to
come along so he could trap them with a forked stick around the base
of the head. He would then stuff them into a burlap bag and cart the
snakes off to a local laboratory where they were sold for 17 cents
apiece. He was always positive, aggressive, and incredibly calm
under pressure — three winning characteristics for all successful entrepreneurs.

My own entrepreneurial experience has taught me that success in
business is 80% marketing and only 20% dependent on your product
or service.

My first crack at the wonderful world of self-employment was a
carry-out food service founded by me and my neighbour, J. Allen
Furguson. I was 11. Al had a gas hot plate and refrigerator in his
basement. So during the summer months we fixed lunch for all the

neighbourhood housewives who hated to cook three meals a day. Day after day we cooked a batch of hot dogs and hamburgers and delivered them semi-hot throughout the neighbourhood for a quarter apiece. After gutsy negotiations with the grocer on the corner, we could buy three pounds of hamburger for a dollar, instead of the normal 38 cents a pound, and a loaf of bread for 14 cents. Soon I was hooked. I liked the independence and freedom of choice that business brings. Unfortunately, I didn't stick with it. Why should I have worked for pennies when I could live in luxury off my 50-cents-a-week allowance? Besides, there was baseball.

You get many great returns for starting your own business. Check those that are important to you:

- Sense of accomplishment.
- Desire for wealth or greater income.
- A sense of freedom and independence.
- An opportunity to be creative.
- A chance to meet people.
- A chance to turn work into fun.
- A chance to be your own boss and stop working for others.
- An opportunity to transform personal expenses into legitimate tax deductions.

Strategy #205:

TAKE THIS BUSINESS-POTENTIAL QUIZ TO DETERMINE YOUR BUILT-IN ENTREPRENEURIAL SKILLS.

WHAT IS YOUR BUSINESS POTENTIAL?

	YES	NO
1. I thrive on constant change	___	___
2. Working to accumulate wealth is the most important thing to me, even if I have to work for someone else to do it.	___	___
3. I enjoy work, particularly if it allows me to improve on my ideas.	___	___
4. I wouldn't want to spend many years developing an idea.	___	___
5. If the situation calls for it, I can make a decision and it is usually a good one.	___	___
6. I love buying lottery tickets.	___	___

7. If I undertake a venture that is well planned but somehow unsuccessful, I view it as a setback or that I just ran out of time.   ____   ____

8. I can convince people to go along when I am trying to accomplish something.   ____   ____

9. I sometimes run out of energy.   ____   ____

10. Investing in the stock market is exciting to me.   ____   ____

11. Being organized is important, but not the most important factor in an entrepreneur's success.   ____   ____

12. I have often been at odds with my employer(s) on many issues. I may even have to leave or I may get fired.   ____   ____

13. I have many ideas and enjoy exchanging them with other people.   ____   ____

14. I consider myself a nonconformist, but I abide by the laws and rules.   ____   ____

15. I tend to set realistic and achievable goals.   ____   ____

16. Only if someone gets me going can I get things done.   ____   ____

17. There can be no value in suffering.   ____   ____

18. Because of what people may think, I'm not willing to try outrageous and stupid things.   ____   ____

19. Because I never say things unless I mean them, people can rely on me.   ____   ____

20. Looking back at my childhood, I was an enterprising kid.   ____   ____

Answering yes to questions 1, 3, 5, 7, 8, 10, 12, 13, 14, 15, 19, 20 and no to questions 2, 4, 6, 9, 11, 16, 17, 18 would give you a perfect score. If you answered 18 or more questions correctly, you definitely have what it takes to start your own business.

Strategy #206:
TURN ANY SMALL BUSINESS INTO A TREMENDOUS TAX SHELTER.

A business can be part-time or full-time, require a large capital investment or no investment, can have no employees or many employees, and can be run out of a home, apartment, retail store, or office.

This small-business strategy should be considered by everyone who works for someone else or who is retired. The possibilities are endless and so are the financial opportunities and benefits — if you understand the rules. A small business, even run part-time from home, can create thousands of dollars of tax shelter every year. I am familiar with many situations where tax write-offs are in the $6,000 to $10,000 range.

In a small business, the personal things you own and do become fully or partially tax deductible. To emphasize the importance of a small business as part of your tax strategy, here is a list of things that are not normally tax deductible but may become deductible through your small business:

- Your automobile or van
- Your automobile expenses — gas, insurance, parking and tolls
- Your interest on loans for assets used in your business
- Your home expenses
- Salaries paid to your children or spouse
- Your boat, motor home, or airplane
- Your home computer
- Your domestic and foreign travel
- Your entertainment
- Your videotape recorder
- Your books and subscriptions
- Your educational audio and videotape courses
- Your calculator, typewriter, cassette recorder
- Your repairs to your automobile or other equipment
- Your utilities and telephone
- Your gifts to customers, potential customers, and associates

These deductions are just a sampling of the tax power of operating a small business; there are many more potential deductions. If you are not getting tax deductions for these expenses, plan to start a small business immediately, even part-time. If you already have a small business or if you are a professional, there are strategies and tax techniques we will cover that your tax advisors never told you about.

Any business idea creates the opportunity to succeed financially. Small businesses started with little capital, and winning ideas have resulted in the creation of thousands of new millionaires and multimillion-dollar corporations; McDonald's, Apple Computer, and Texas Instruments are well-known examples. As the old Coca-Cola bottles stated so clearly, "No deposit, no return." If you don't experiment with new ideas you have no chance of success at all.

For those who are beginners, we will first concentrate on starting a part-time business. You'll discover how to make many things in your life legally tax deductible through the small-business tax umbrella. If you own your own business already, use the strategies in this chapter as your business-tax-strategy checklist.

When you have a small business, many business-related activities may become legally tax deductible, even if you derive pleasure or fun in the process. If the business initially generates little income, it may still generate hundreds or thousands of dollars of tax deductions that can be used to shelter income from your job, investments, or retirement plan.

To take advantage of these tax opportunities, your venture must have a "reasonable expectation of profit." (For more information, see Strategy #210.)

Strategy #207:
MAXIMIZE BUSINESS-RELATED DEDUCTIONS.

As a general rule, you are allowed to deduct all business-related expenses. The deduction is called "capital cost allowance" (CCA). For example, if you use a capital asset in your business activities, all or part of the cost is deductible by depreciation. Capital assets used in your business can include:

Asset	Depreciation Rate (%)
aircraft	25
auto equipment	30
automobiles	30
boats	15
buildings	4
calculator	20
cash register	20
cassette recorder	20
computer hardware	30
computer software	100
fax machine	20
fences	10
home computer	30
moulds	100
office furniture	20
photocopier	20
refrigerator	20
telephone system	20

tools	20
tools (under $200)	100
typewriter	20
uniforms	100
video camera	20
videotape recorder	20

Note: The above are general CCA rates for the type of asset listed. Specific rates for these assets may differ from the rates listed, depending on a number of circumstances.

THE HALF-YEAR RULE

Instead of giving you a full year's depreciation during the first year you own and use a capital asset in your business, tax rules usually treat the asset as if you owned it one-half of a year no matter when it was available for use in the business. You usually get half of the normally allowable depreciation, i.e., 10% on a 20%-rated asset and 15% on a 30%-rated asset.

THE DECLINING-BALANCE METHOD

There are several possible methods of computing depreciation. Canadian tax laws require the use of the declining-balance method. Instead of taking a fixed, equal percentage each year, you multiply the applicable percentage times the undepreciated balance of the cost of an asset.

For instance, if the depreciation rate is 20%, each year you multiply 20% by the undepreciated balance.

Example: You buy a $700 VCR, which is used exclusively for deductible business purposes.

1st Year Depreciation

$700	cost
× 20%	depreciation rate
$140	full-year depreciation
× .5	(only 1/2 can be used the first year)
$70	1st year depreciation

2nd Year Depreciation

$700	cost
−70	1st year depreciation
$630	undepreciated balance
× 20%	depreciation rate
$126	2nd year depreciation

3rd Year Depreciation

$700	cost
−196	total of 1st + 2nd year depreciation ($70+$126)
$504	un-depreciated balance
× 20%	depreciation rate
$101	3rd year depreciation

In the case of 30% assets like computers, you use 30% of the un-depreciated balance each year instead of the 20%, with a first-year depreciation of 15% or half the normal 30% amount.

The following depreciation tables show you how much you can deduct each year based on the type of asset.

20% assets		30% assets	
Year	% Deductible	Year	% Deductible
1	10.0%	1	15.0%
2	18.0%	2	25.5%
3	14.4%	3	17.9%
4	11.5%	4	12.5%
5	9.2%	5	8.7%
6	7.4%	6	6.1%

THE PERCENTAGE-USE FORMULA

If you use an asset 100% of the time in your business plan, 100% of the cost of the asset is deductible through depreciation. Often, however, you will use the asset part-time in your business and part-time personally. In that case, Revenue Canada requires that you determine with some accuracy the percentage of time you use the asset for each purpose — deductible and personal. Once you determine the deductible percentage for the year, multiply the deductible percentage times the maximum allowable depreciation for the year.

In our previous example of the $700 video recorder, notice that the second year's maximum allowable depreciation is $126. If you used the asset 40% of the time in your business, your allowable depreciation would be 40% of $126, or $50.

Look at the depreciation tax form T2132 that follows and you will see how you take your depreciation deductions each year.

Revenue Canada **Revenu Canada**
Taxation Impôt

T2132
Rev. 90

CAPITAL COST ALLOWANCE SCHEDULE (DEPRECIATION)

- A separate Capital Cost Allowance Schedule is required for each business.

- Attach one completed copy of this schedule to your income tax return and keep a copy for your records.

- The *1990 Business and Professional Income Tax Guide* has information to help you complete this schedule.

Social insurance number

Name

Address

Postal code

(1) Class number	(2) Undepreciated capital cost at beginning of 1990*	(3) Cost of additions during 1990 (Area A Column (5))	(4) Proceeds from disposals during 1990 (Area B Column (6))	(5) Undepreciated capital cost after additions and disposals (Column (2) plus Column (3) less Column (4))**	(6) Enter 1/2 of the amount, if any, by which Column (3), exceeds Column (4). If Column (4) exceeds Column (3), enter NIL	(7) Column (5) minus Column (6)***	(8) Rate %	(9) Capital cost allowance for 1990 (Column (8) X Column (7) or a lesser amount)	(10) Undepreciated capital cost at end of 1990 (Column (5) minus Column (9))
8	–	5,800		5,800	2,900	2,900	20%	580	
10.1	–	13,000		13,000	6,500	6,500	30%	1,950	
12	–	900		900	450	450	100%	450	450
							TOTAL	2,980	

* You must reduce the beginning undepreciated capital cost of the related property by the amount of any 1989 investment tax credit carried back to other years as well as any 1989 investment tax credit deducted and/or refunded in 1989.

** A negative amount in this column must be added to income as "Recapture." A positive amount must be deducted from income as a "Terminal Loss" if there is no property left in the class. "Recapture" and "Terminal Loss" do not apply to passenger vehicles included in Class 10.1.

*** If you disposed of a Class 10.1 passenger vehicle and meet the conditions explained in Chapter 5 of the *1990 Business and Professional Income Tax Guide*, enter in this column 1/2 of the amount from Column (2).

DETAILS OF ADDITIONS AND DISPOSALS DURING 1990

AREA A – ADDITIONS

(1) Class number	(2) Kind of property	(3) Total cost*	(4) Personal portion	(5) Business portion (Column (3) less Column (4))
5		$ 3,000	$ 1,200	$ 1,800
10.1		13,000		13,000
8		4,000		4,000
12		900		900

* Refer to Chapter 5 of the *1990 Business and Professional Income Tax Guide* to determine the capital cost of property.

AREA B – DISPOSALS

(1) Class number	(2) Kind of property	BUILDINGS (3) Proceeds of disposal	OTHER PROPERTY (4) Proceeds of disposal (Amount not to exceed capital cost)	(5) Personal portion (if applicable)	(6) Business portion (Column (3) or Column (4) less Column (5))

ADDITIONS AND DISPOSALS OF LAND DURING 1990

Additions: Total cost $

Disposals: Total proceeds $

(Note: You cannot claim capital cost allowance on land.)

(FRANÇAIS AU VERSO)

Strategy #208
BEGIN A SMALL BUSINESS AS A SOLE PROPRIETORSHIP INSTEAD OF A CORPORATION.

The easiest form of business to create is a sole proprietorship; that is, you or your spouse doing business in your own home. Most at-home, part-time businesses should start as sole proprietorships. The cost of incorporating and the paperwork involved are usually not worth the expense at this point. In fact, if you anticipate initial business losses, a corporation could actually be to your disadvantage as tax losses of your corporation cannot be written off against your personal income.

As your business grows and becomes highly profitable, you can later consider incorporation. In the meantime, an inexpensive small-business liability policy could protect you from personal liability.

Starting a business as a sole proprietorship usually involves only a simple registration form and fee. Contact your provincial government switchboard to determine which office in your area processes these forms.

When filling out the form, you will be asked to specify what name you wish to run your business under. Note that simply filling out the name does not give you any special rights to use that name that you would not otherwise have. For example, running a business out of your home as Esso Oil or Burger King might cause you problems later on with the legal owners of those names!

Strategy #209:
USE BUSINESS "PAPER" LOSSES TO TAX SHELTER JOB AND INVESTMENT INCOME.

With a sole proprietorship, you are your business; all legitimate tax deductions in excess of business income reduce your personal taxes from all sources. Look on page 1 of your T1 individual tax return and you'll notice that business profit or loss is included with your other income from your job or investments. A business becomes a personal tax shelter when your business shows a "paper" loss. Your personal taxable income is reduced by the amount of the loss, and your personal income taxes are reduced accordingly.

For example, if your first-year business income is $2,000 but your deductible expenses are $10,000, the $8,000 difference reduces your taxable income from your job, investments, or pension income.

Strategy #210:
OPERATE YOUR ACTIVITY AS A BUSINESS, NOT A HOBBY.

Note that the fundamental definition of a business in Canada is an enterprise run with a "reasonable expectation of profit." In the event of an audit by Revenue Canada you would be required to show that, even though your business showed a loss for the taxation year, it was your honest and reasonable intention that one day the business would show a profit in its own right in the not-too-distant future.

In order to be a business you must have a product or service that you offer regularly to the public. In fact, for tax purposes, you are a business if you sell a product or service for profit, whether you actually call yourself a business or not.

This expectation of a profit is what differentiates a business from a mere hobby. A hobby is an activity that may produce income, but is operated primarily for pleasure without the intent of making a profit.

As a true business, you may deduct your operating expenses as allowed under the Income Tax Act, no matter how great or small your income. If you have more income during the year than expenses, the difference is your taxable profit. If you have more expenses than income, the difference is your tax loss. With a hobby there can be no loss for tax purposes.

You show your intent to operate as a business by following these steps:

1. Talking regularly to potential or actual customers and keeping a list.
2. Establishing that you regularly offer your product or service to the public.
3. Opening a separate bank account.
4. Keeping good records of income and expenses.
5. Printing business cards and flyers or brochures, and otherwise operating in a professional manner.
6. Being able to produce business plans or budgets which show a genuine expectation of profit.
7. Being able to demonstrate you have the expertise to run the business properly.
8. Being able to show that you have sufficient capital to generate profits.

Strategy #211:

COMPLETE THE "BUSINESS START-UP CHECKLIST" AS A GUIDE TO GETTING STARTED.

_____ Obtain Revenue Canada publication "Business and Professional Income Tax Guide" and read it thoroughly.

_____ Choose a business idea based on your interests, abilities and the amount of time you want to spend.

MY SMALL BUSINESS IDEAS:

_____
_____
_____
_____
_____

_____ Choose a business form — sole proprietorship, partnership or corporation. Sole proprietorship is the simplest.

_____ Set up your business record-keeping system. Simple record-keeping books are available at any office-supply store. Obtain copies of all Revenue Canada Interpretation Bulletins, Forms, guides and other publications appropriate to your business.

_____ Choose a business name.

BUSINESS NAME IDEAS

_____
_____
_____

_____ Set up an interest-bearing business chequing account using one of the asset management account sources listed in the investment section of this book.

_____ Print business cards and flyers.

_____ Offer your product or services for sale to friends and others.

_____ Learn everything you can about business from books, magazines, tape courses, seminars, and trade publications.

_____ Get business-educational materials from the Charles J. Givens Organization.

Have fun. It's only work if you don't like what you're doing.

Strategy #212:
LEARN THE TRUTH ABOUT BUSINESS DEDUCTIONS.

There are so many myths and misunderstandings about how to start and run a business that confusion prevents many people from ever getting started. Here are the facts:

1. You don't need to operate your business full-time or incorporate to take tax deductions.
2. There are no tax requirements regarding how much money you must invest or that you must invest any money at all.
3. If you are a sole proprietorship without employees, you do not need to obtain a Source Deduction Remittance account number.
4. You are allowed to take tax deductions on assets you buy and use in your small business, even if you buy the assets on credit.
5. If you use assets only part-time in your business, you may still deduct a portion of the cost. (See, for example, Strategy 223.)
6. Investments in real estate should usually be treated as a capital investment, not a small business.
7. Managing your own personal investments or collectibles is usually not considered a business.
8. Having a small business does not automatically flag your return for audit.
9. You may claim more tax deductions than income. Your business is entitled to show a loss for different phases of its growth.
10. Your automobile or other assets do not have to be in a business name in order to take the tax deductions.
11. Record keeping and tax forms for a small business are easy.
12. You don't need any special licences or permits before you can take tax deductions.
13. Being in business also entitles you to claim back from the government GST expended for goods or services used by the business, although you will have to register separately with the GST office in order to do this — see also Chapter 30.

Strategy #213:
CHOOSE A SMALL-BUSINESS IDEA THAT IS EXCITING, FUN
AND IN ALIGNMENT WITH YOUR INTERESTS AND ABILITIES.

There are no limits to the number of ideas for creating a small business, even those that require little or no capital. If you need ideas for your small-business venture, use the small-business ideas below to get your mind moving.

The important thing is to pick something you love to do or make and turn it into a small business.

SMALL-BUSINESS IDEAS

Services:

- Automobile tune-up
- Automobile washing, waxing
- Carpet cleaning
- Care for ill or elderly
- Catering
- Clown for children's parties
- Consulting (in anything)
- Dance instruction
- Day care for children
- Doing anything for anyone
- Flower arranging
- Foreign language teaching
- Interior decorating
- Lawn maintenance
- Maintenance for real estate investors
- Manager for musical groups
- Office janitorial service
- Painting/wall papering
- Party organizer for adults or children
- Pet boarding
- Photography—portraits, weddings
- Real estate sales
- Real estate property management
- Roommate locating
- Tool, saw, and scissor sharpening
- Teaching — golf, tennis, music
- Tutoring
- Typing
- Videotaping—parties, weddings

Products:

- Cake baking and decorating
- Candle making
- Catering
- Christmas tree ornament making
- Dressmaking
- Jewellery making
- Making and delivering office lunches
- Quilt making
- Used books or records—buying and selling
- Woodworking from your woodworking shop

Multilevel marketing:

- Amway
- Herbalife
- NSA
- NuSkin
- Prepaid legal services
- Shacklee

MAXIMIZING BUSINESS DEDUCTIONS

The following strategies will help you create the maximum deductions for your small business.

Strategy #214:

BEGIN MARKETING IMMEDIATELY TO MAKE BUSINESS START-UP COSTS DEDUCTIBLE THIS YEAR.

Expenses you incur after your business begins are generally deductible in the year you spend the money. As far as capital purchases go, you are generally limited to half of the allowable Capital Cost Expense in the first year. The unclaimed half is effectively picked up in later years, however. Begin marketing your product or service immediately to establish the starting date of your business.

Canadian tax law generally requires you to claim expenses you prepay in the year(s) in which you receive the related benefit, however. So if your fiscal year-end is December 31, and in the middle of December you prepay January's rent on your business premises, you must claim the expense in the following year.

Strategy #215:

HIRE YOUR SPOUSE AND CREATE A DEDUCTIBLE RRSP.

Provided that your spouse (or any other family member, for that matter) provides bona-fide, business-related services for your business, a reasonable tax-deductible salary may be paid.

When you employ your spouse, certain everyday expenses may become tax deductible as well:

- life insurance premiums, in certain circumstances,
- tuition for job-related education, and
- business-related travel and entertainment, subject to some restrictions.

While your spouse will usually have to pay taxes on his or her own salary, he or she may be in a lower tax bracket than you are. And though you may lose a tax exemption for your spouse, the strategy can still pay off, especially if a larger salary can be justified, and you're in a high tax bracket. In addition, your spouse may now be eligible to contribute to an RRSP in order to further shelter his or her income.

Strategy #216:

HIRE YOUR CHILDREN AND GRANDCHILDREN, AND MAKE ALLOWANCES AND GIFTS DEDUCTIBLE.

As a teenager, I arose at 4 a.m. every morning to deliver the newspaper to subscribers in my hometown. When everyone paid, my net profit was $7.40 a week for a daily four-mile bike ride. Eventually, my father offered me an evening job with his home-improvement business. I was moving up the corporate ladder. Instead of riding four miles in the morning, I began riding four miles every afternoon to the C.J. Givens Company, where my after-office-hours responsibilities included sweeping floors and taking phone messages. Boy, did that make me feel important! I felt more like a business executive than a part-time janitor. My father also felt great, taking a tax deduction for each of the five dollars he paid me once a week.

If you have or start a small business, even part-time, hire your children or grandchildren — you may be able to turn what would otherwise be non-deductible allowances, gifts, and expensive handouts into tax-deductible salaries.

Depending on ages, the kids can perform many tasks including:

* Cleaning the business office
* Answering the phone when you are away
* Stuffing and addressing envelopes
* Keeping track of inventory
* Delivering products
* Running business errands
* Entering data on the computer

You can pay deductible salaries to children to perform jobs either for your small business or to help you in your regular employment (see Strategy #183) as long as the salaries are reasonable for the legitimate business-related services that they perform. Pay two children or grandchildren salaries of $20 per week each for three or four hours of work instead of giving them non-deductible allowances, gifts, and handouts, and you have created a $2,000-per-year, legal tax deduction. The money the kids earn can be used for school lunches, clothes, entertainment, or investments.

As an example, hire your two children to work in your small business and pay them each $20 per week: $10 is used for entertainment and allowances, $10 each goes into an investment account in their names. Your tax deduction is the amount you pay the children. (Two children × $20 per week each × 52 weeks = $2,080; 40% combined federal and provincial tax bracket × $2,080 deduction = $832 cash tax saving.)

Any salary paid to your children must be shown in their own individual tax returns, however. Using this strategy, the kids are involved, having fun, and learning responsibility, and you are pocketing over $800 a year from the tax savings!

Bob, another member of my organization, started a small business and hired his 11-year-old son, Jeff, who had a knack for computer programming, at $10 per hour to write simple business programs. Jeff works three hours a week. Can Bob legally take a tax deduction for the $30 per week he pays his son? Yes, as long as Jeff actually does the work. Bob would have to pay a programmer from outside the family as much as $25 to $50 an hour for programming services, so he is within the rules. It doesn't matter that Jeff is only 11.

By using this strategy, Bob created a $1,500-per-year tax deduction (50 weeks × $30 per week). His home computer is now tax deductible because he is using it in his small business, and he is enjoying the benefit of working on an important project together with his son. Since the $1,500 is Jeff's only income, Jeff pays no income tax.

RULES FOR HIRING FAMILY MEMBERS

1. The family members must do the work for which they are paid. It would not be proper to pay a family member for work not performed simply to claim a tax deduction, nor would it be proper to pay a salary for non-business work. Cleaning your home office is a business function. Cleaning the bedroom isn't.
2. You may pay a family member a deductible salary of up to the amount you would have to pay a non-family member to do the same job. The pay cannot be unreasonable for the work performed. Squelch any tendency to overpay a family member in order to claim a greater tax deduction. Someone from outside the family must be paid a minimum wage, so no matter how menial the job, minimum wage is not unreasonable.
3. Salaries paid to children under 18 are not subject to Canada Pension Plan contributions.
4. Typically no at-source tax withholding is required if the family member is paid under $6,500 per year. However, the minimum amount changes from province to province and from year to year.
5. Salaries are treated as tax-deductible wages by you as the employer, and as taxable income by your family-member employees. You lose the tax advantages if you pay wages to a family member in a higher tax bracket.

6. The pay should be periodic. I suggest that you pay family members by cheque at least once a month, as you would any employee. If you were to pay a year's worth of wages in the last month of the year, it may look suspicious to Revenue Canada. Do not pay by cash.

Strategy #217:

PAY YOUR CHILD A SALARY OF UP TO $2,617 AND STILL CLAIM A DEPENDENCY TAX CREDIT.

Based upon 1991 information, each claim for the first two dependents younger than 18 on your tax return is worth a $69 tax credit, provided they earn less than $2,617 each, saving you up to $138 in taxes. Each additional child will give you a tax credit of $138.

A child who earns more than $2,617 (up to $3,005) can still earn you partial tax credit (see your T1 return).

Strategy #218:

USE YOUR AUTOMOBILE IN YOUR SMALL BUSINESS TO MAKE IT DEDUCTIBLE.

Because your automobile represents one of your largest personal expenses, it is also one of your biggest potential tax deductions. One method of making your automobile deductible is to use it in your small business.

If you use your automobile 90% of the time for business, 90% of the cost of running it is deductible. The 90% rule might apply to a two-car family that allocates one car for personal use and the second, usually more expensive car, almost exclusively for business.

If you use one automobile for both personal and business purposes, you must allocate by percentage the amount of deductible business use and non-deductible personal use — for example, 55% business use, 45% personal use.

Cash expenses you may deduct (based on percentage business use) include: gas, oil, lubricants, insurance, lease payments or interest on loan used to purchase the car, and repairs. You may also be able to claim Capital Cost Allowance based on percentage business use.

Parking and body-shop fees are also deductible if the car was in business use at the time the expense was incurred.

Note that Capital Cost Allowance is based on: percentage business use × the acquisition price of the car × the rating for the asset class (in this case 30%). So if you purchase a $20,000 car that you use 50% for business, you could potentially deduct up to $20,000 × 30% × 50%, or $3,000 in one year. However, in the year of acquisition, your maximum CCA would only be $1,500 — this is the so-called "half-year rule."

Other rules:

1. Generally, for cars costing in excess of $24,000, CCA may not be taken on the excess.
2. Monthly interest deductions may not exceed $300.
3. For leases, the maximum monthly lease payment for tax purposes may not exceed $650 (assuming 100% business use).

Strategy #219:
BORROW TO BUY YOUR CAR.

If your car is used for business, consider borrowing to purchase the car. The percentage of the interest relating to business use is fully deductible, subject to the restriction referred to in Strategy #214.

Strategy #220:
BUY AN AUTOMOBILE INSTEAD OF LEASING.

You are usually better off in the long run buying rather than leasing a business automobile if you make it tax deductible. Leasing allows you to write off only the business percentage of the lease payment.

Owning allows you to use the Capital Cost Allowance deduction, based on business use, which will usually be greater than the lease deductions.

For current purchases, automobiles are class 10.1 assets, depreciated at a maximum rate of allowance of 30% with a limit of $24,000. As a shortcut to determining the maximum amount of your automobile deduction, use the following table and tax form T2132.

AUTOMOBILE BUSINESS-USE MAXIMUM-EXPENSE DEDUCTIONS
SIMPLIFIED CALCULATION TABLE

YEAR	BUY (CCA)	Loan Interest	Total Deduction	LEASE Maximum
1	30% (24,000) = $7,200 × 1/2	$3,600*	$7,200	$7,800
2	30% (20,400) = $6,120	$3,600	$9,720	$7,800
3	30% (14,280) = $4,284	$3,600	$7,884	$7,800
4	30% (9,996) = $2,999	$3,600	$6,599	$7,800
5	30% (6,995) = $2,098	$3,600	$5,698	$7,800
6	30% (4,897) = $1,469	$3,600	$5,069	$7,800

* Maximum deductible interest payment is $300 per month. Maximum monthly lease payment deduction is $650.

The above table assumes that the car you buy to use in your business costs at least $24,000 — which is the maximum capital cost allowance — and the same quality of car can be leased for no more than $650 per month (the maximum allowable lease payment deductions for business use). Note that during the first two years, the allowable business write-off for buying is $16,920 compared to $15,600 for leasing.

Strategy #221:
USE YOUR ASSETS IN YOUR BUSINESS TO MAKE THEM DEDUCTIBLE.

Using your own equipment, such as home computers, videotape recorders, cassette recorders, calculators, tools, or furniture in your business may make these assets deductible.

If you already own the assets when you begin using them in your business, generally your tax deductions will be computed by depreciating the market value at the time they are converted to business use using the CCA declining balance method, based on the percentage of time you use your assets for business and the Capital Cost Allowance class to which they belong.

For example, you start a business which requires the almost full-time use of the personal computer that you have had for two years.

You paid $5,000 for the computer and it has a market value today of $3,000. Therefore, since computers are in the 30% class, the maximum possible amount you could deduct as CAA is: 90% (business use) × 30% × $3,000, or $810. (Due to the "half-year rule," however, you could only take half of this amount in the first year.)

If you buy an asset and begin using it immediately in your business, even part-time, you may depreciate the business portion of its use.

It is important to understand the difference between personal and business use. Here are some examples:

Your computer is used for business when used for record-keeping, business projections, or computing your business tax deductions. Your videotape recorder is used for business when you buy or rent videotapes that relate to any phase of your business. Your video camera can be deductible if you use it for business at conventions, lectures, for practising sales presentations, or in any other way that relates to your business.

Computer and video supplies are generally deductible when used for business purposes. The furniture in your business office, whether at home or at a separate location, can be depreciated. Your typewriter, filing cabinet, computer software, or cassette recorder are also depreciable if used in your small business.

Any tools or equipment are deductible when used even part-time for a business purpose, such as:

- musical instruments used in a band
- a lathe and drill press in a home woodworking shop
- a sewing machine used in making quilts or other items to sell
- steam cleaning machine used in a part-time carpet-cleaning business
- cameras and dark-room equipment used in a photography business.

Note: When a personal asset is converted for business use, tax rules specify that there is a "deemed sale" at its then-current market value. This will form the basis of future Capital Cost Allowance claims. If the cost for tax purposes is less than the current value, there could be capital-gains exposure; also, the depreciation base for the particular asset may be restricted under certain technical rules. In most instances, though, these rules will not come into play, as the value of assets converted to business use will be less than the original cost — i.e., due to depreciation of the asset's value.

For more information on what constitutes a legitimate business, see Strategy #210. Also, see paragraph 1 of Strategy #222.

Strategy #222:
UNDERSTAND THE CCA CALCULATION.

Capital Cost Allowance, or depreciation, means deducting the cost of the business portion of an asset at the rates allowed by the Income Tax Act. These rates represent a rough estimate of the declining value of your depreciable assets. Most capital assets can be depreciated, although there are a few exceptions, such as raw land. To calculate your CCA deduction for an asset used in a business you must know:

1. Your depreciation base — This is technically known as your "Undepreciated Capital Cost" or UCC. Your original UCC is usually the amount you paid for the property. When you inherit or receive property as a gift (other than from your spouse), your UCC is usually the market value at the time you obtained the asset. As you depreciate an asset, your UCC reduces based on the cumulative depreciation claimed. Improvements increase the UCC. If you convert personal property to business use, your UCC is usually the fair market value of the property on the date you make the change (special rules apply if the property has appreciated over its original cost when converted, but this is usually not the case).
2. Date placed in service — The date the property is available for use in your business generally determines the first year you can start claiming Capital Cost Allowance. You are, however, allowed in most cases only one-half of the normal CCA deduction in the first year. This formula is often called the "half-year rule."
3. Capital Cost Allowance — The original cost of equipment and buildings used to earn income cannot be claimed as a lump-sum operating expense. However, to recognize that over a number of years such properties will wear out or become obsolete, you may claim a portion of the UCC each year as a deduction. The deduction allowed each year is called Capital Cost Allowance (CCA). Income tax regulations group different assets into a number of "CCA classes," most of which have an annual percentage CCA rate. For example, the normal rate for most office equipment is 20% per year of the UCC at the beginning of the year (see point one). In a small business, you are typically concerned with the CCA for cars, computers, office equipment, furniture and fixtures. The following table gives you the classes of various types of equipment and buildings you may use in your business.

Example: You purchase a car for $10,000. Class is 30%.

Year One depreciation: $3,000 reduced by half-year rule to $1,500.

Year Two undepreciated capital cost is ($10,000 − $1,500) or $8,500. You may depreciate up to 30% this year or $2,550.

Year Three undepreciated capital cost is ($10,000 − $1,500 − $2,550) or $5,950. You may depreciate up to 30% of this or $1,785.

CAPITAL COST ALLOWANCE CLASSES*

Allowances may only be claimed on property used to earn income.

Where property is used partly for business and partly for personal purposes, you may claim Capital Cost Allowance on the business portion only.

CLASS 1 (4%) Most buildings acquired after 1987, including component parts such as electrical wiring and fixtures, plumbing, heating, and central air conditioning.

CLASS 3 (5%) Most buildings acquired after 1978 and before 1988, including component parts such as electrical wiring and fixtures, plumbing, heating, and central air conditioning.

The cost of an addition or alteration to a building described above may also be included in this class. If the building was included in this class because it was acquired after 1978 and before 1988, the cost of additions or alterations may also be added to this class. However, the total cost of any additions or alterations made after 1987 are limited to the lesser of
- $500,000, or
- 25% of the building's capital cost on December 31, 1987.

Any amount over this limit belongs in Class 1.

CLASS 6 (10%) Fences, greenhouses, and wooden wharves. Most buildings acquired after 1978 belong in Class 1 or Class 3, but buildings made of frame, log, stucco on frame or galvanized or corrugated iron (including component parts) may

be included in Class 6, if built without footings or other base support below ground level.

The cost of an addition or alteration to a building described above may also be included in this class. If the building was included in this class because it was acquired before 1979, the first $100,000 of additions or alterations may also be added to this class. Any amount over $100,000 belongs in Class 3.

CLASS 7 (15%) Canoes, rowboats, scows and most other vessels, and their motors, furniture and fittings. Additional information is available in Interpretation Bulletin IT-267R and Special Release, *Capital Cost Allowance — Vessels.*

CLASS 8 (20%) Assets not included in any other class, including fixtures, machinery and equipment and even certain buildings or other structures.

Most outdoor advertising panels or bulletin boards acquired after 1987.

CLASS 9 (25%) Electrical generating equipment with a maximum load capacity of not more than 15 kilowatts, portable electrical generating equipment, radio transmission and receiving equipment and aircraft, including furniture, fittings, equipment attached to the aircraft acquired after May 25, 1976, and spare parts.

CLASS 10 (30%) Automotive equipment (except automobiles used in a daily car rental business or taxis, both of which are Class 16 [40%]). Included are vans, trucks and tractors, portable tools costing more than $200 acquired by a business offering them on short-term rentals, harness or stable equipment, sleighs, wagons, and trailers, most general-purpose electronic data-processing equipment and systems software, contractor's movable equipment, and mechanical equipment for logging operations.

CLASS 10.1 (30%) A motor vehicle owned by an individual (other than a trust) or a passenger vehicle owned by any other taxpayer.

CLASS 12 (100%) Chinaware, cutlery or other tableware, kitchen utensils costing less than $200, linen, uniforms, dies, jigs, patterns, moulds or lasts, tools costing less than $200, the cutting or shaping part of a machine (for example, saw blades), medical or dental instruments costing less than $200, computer software (but not including systems software which must be included in Class 10), and a video cassette acquired after February 15, 1984, for the purpose of renting, and that is not expected to be rented to any one person for more than seven days in any 30-day period.

CLASS 16 (40%) Taxicabs, vehicles used in a daily car rental business and coin-operated video games or pinball machines acquired after February 15, 1984.

CLASS 17 (8%) Roads, parking lots, sidewalks, airplane runways, storage areas or similar surface construction.

CLASS 22 (50%) Most power-operated, movable equipment for excavating, moving, placing or compacting earth, rock, concrete or asphalt acquired before 1988.

CLASS 38 (30%) Most property acquired after 1987 that is power operated, movable equipment for excavating, moving, placing or compacting earth, rock, concrete or asphalt. (In 1988 the rate was 40%, in 1989 it was 35%. As of 1990, the rate is 30%.)

Leasehold interest (Class 13) Capital Cost Allowance may be claimed on a leasehold interest in a property, but the maximum rate depends on the nature of the leasehold interest and the terms of the lease.

Patent, franchise, concession or licence for a limited period (Class 14) The amount of capital cost allowance that may be claimed is the lesser of:
- the capital cost of each property apportioned over the life of the property, and
- the undepreciated capital cost of the property of the class at the end of the taxation year.

Wind-energy conversion equipment (Class 34) Equipment that generates electrical energy from wind and that was purchased after February 25, 1986, to be used in a business may be eligible for full write-off in the first three years at the rates of 25%, 50%, and 25% respectively.

To be eligible for this special write-off, wind-energy equipment must be certified by the Minister of Energy, Mines and Resources. Eligible items can include fixed-location wind-driven turbines, related generating, control, conditioning, and transmission equipment, support structures, and a powerhouse.

SOURCE: 1988 Business and Professional Income Tax Guide, Revenue Canada Taxation.

Strategy #223:

USE CAPITAL COST ALLOWANCE FORM T2132 TO COMPUTE AND CLAIM ALL DEPRECIATION DEDUCTIONS.

Your key to Capital Cost Allowance deductions is Tax form T2132. The total amount of your form T2132 deduction is entered on T2124 for income and expenses from a business.

Example: Jim and Sue start a small business in which they use their home computer 60% of the time. The cost of the computer was $3,000 and it was purchased this year along with some business software for $900. They also buy a second car that they allocate 100% of the time for business. Cost: $13,000. They realize that the maximum deduction the first year is 15% for the automobile. Other equipment already owned, such as furniture and small machinery, used in the business has a value of $4,000 when placed in service and qualifies as Class 8 property. How much is their total form T2132 deduction?

The final tally looks like this:

Computer	$3,000	class 10	30%	60% use=$540
Software	900	class 12	100%	100% use=$900
Car	13,000	class 10	30%	100% use=$3,900
Furniture	4,000	class 8	20%	100% use=$800

The total depreciation available under CCA is $6,140. Following the half-year rule, however, the allowable CCA deduction in their first year of business will be 50% of this, or $3,070, saving them over $1,200 in combined federal and provincial taxes (assuming a marginal tax rate of approximately 39%).

Strategy #224:

USE A SIMPLIFIED RECORD METHOD TO ALLOCATE BUSINESS AND PERSONAL USE OF ASSETS.

Record-keeping requirements are not complicated. For home computers and video recorders/cameras, the simplest, most effective system is to keep a pocket-sized spiral notebook by the equipment. You need only three columns:

1. Date
2. Amount of time used
3. B for business/P for personal

Strategy #225:
TAKE DEDUCTIONS FOR REPAIRS TO BUSINESS ASSETS.

Repairs to assets are potentially deductible when the assets are used even part-time in your business. When you use your assets only for personal reasons, your repairs and maintenance are not deductible. Major repairs may sometimes be considered to be of a capital nature and therefore will be added to the UCC of the particular asset and depreciated rather than being currently deductible.

(In the case of body repairs to cars, Revenue Canada's policy is that the accident must take place while the vehicle is in business use, however).

Strategy #226:
CREATE A DEDUCTIBLE OFFICE IN YOUR HOME.

If you start a small business at home, use part of your home for a deductible office and storage area. You may deduct a reasonable portion of your home expenses, including light, heat, water, insurance, and property taxes. Whether you own or rent, you may apportion these expenses between business and non-business use.

For example, measure the square footage of floor space used, and deduct the business portion. If you own the house, you may also claim some Capital Cost Allowance, based on square footage occupied for the business, and mortgage interest. One of these two requirements must be met in order to claim the deductions:

1. the home work space is your principal place of business, or
2. you only use the work space to earn income from your business and you use it on a continuous and regular basis for meeting your clients, customers, or patients. Rule 1 says "your principal place of business," not "your principal business." So if your home is the "headquarters" for your sideline business, you have probably met the requirement.

Note, however, there is a rule stating that all expenses relating to a home office are not deductible to the extent they exceed income from the business. So if you earned $50,000 in salary and ran a part-time home business that showed only $2,000 in income, the maximum deduction you could make for running your business office out of your home would be $2,000. However, excess deductions can be carried forward to the next year.

Also, be warned that taking a home business deduction for CCA might interfere with the tax-free capital gain to which all Canadians are entitled when the principal residence is sold for a profit. For most people, a good guideline would be to take all home office re-lated expenses *except* CCA.

Strategy #227:
MAKE YOUR SOCIAL-CLUB, COUNTRY-CLUB, AND HEALTH-CLUB MEMBERSHIPS DEDUCTIBLE THROUGH BUSINESS USE.

If you use your club for business purposes, you may deduct the busi-ness portion of your expenses. Initiation fees and dues are not deductible, but meal and entertainment expenses at the club are (sub-ject to the 80% deductibility rule, i.e., only 80% of the expense is deductible for tax purposes). Entertaining current or prospective cli-ents is considered business use.

The required record keeping is simple. Keep a club section in your appointment book that lists the dates you use your club and if the use was personal, business, or a combination. Also keep track of entertain-ment expenses, such as drinks, green fees, tennis-court fees, and meals. If you are prospecting for clients or customers, list the names of the people you talk to, whether they become customers or not.

Entertainment deductions are taken under meals and entertainment expenses.

Strategy #228:
TAKE DEDUCTIONS FOR YOUR BUSINESS-RELATED BOOKS, MAGAZINES, NEWSLETTERS, AND TAPE COURSES.

Purchasing books, magazines, newsletters, or audio- and videotape courses that allow you to maintain, update, or upgrade your business skills could make these items tax deductible if you start a small business.

Much of what you already wish to read may be tax deductible if you start a small business. Here are some examples of worthwhile business-related publications that you may be able to deduct:

Magazines:

Venture	*Nation's Business*
Money	*Newsweek*
Entrepreneur	*Fortune*
Maclean's	*Canadian Business*

Books:

There are dozens of books currently available at your bookstore in the business and social-sciences sections that relate to starting a business, business management, business ideas, marketing, advertising, accounting, record-keeping, and success attitudes.

Audio- and Videotape Courses, Seminars, and Workshops:

High-impact, adult education in the future will not be done in traditional classrooms spanning several years, weeks, or evenings, but will use new types of media and meeting facilities. Keeping up and getting ahead is already being done at home with audio- and videocassettes or in multimillion-dollar hotel meeting and conference rooms, through seminars and workshops. When videotape courses, seminars and workshops relate to your business or career, the cost can be deductible.

Strategy #229:
TAKE DEDUCTIONS FOR YOUR BUSINESS
TRAVEL EXPENSES.

Planning your trips or vacations around a legitimate business purpose could make at least part of your travel expenses tax deductible. What better way to travel than with tax savings covering part of the cost? When it comes to business travel deductions, a few simple guidelines could keep you from being audited or losing the deductions. Although you may have lots of fun and enjoyment on your trips, the primary purpose of the deductible trip must be business related.

The expenses of your spouse or other family members on the trip could be deductible if they are co-owners or employees of the business and have a business purpose for being there. The travel expenses of your spouse or other family members are not deductible if they are simply travelling with you. Your spouse's expenses could be deductible if your spouse is involved in business-related activities such as entertaining, or secretarial work, or if those you are doing business with also include spouses and it would be inappropriate for you to be without your spouse.

My advice is to claim a deduction, as business travel expenses, for hotels, rental cars, airline fares, automobile expenses, meals, entertainment, and any other business-related expenses. The main categories or purposes of potentially deductible business travel are:

- Attending a convention or conference
- Attending a trade show or association meeting
- Attending a business-related educational program
- Setting up distributors for your product or services
- Buying trips for products to resell
- A shareholders or partners meeting, even in a small, closely held business
- Meetings with current or potential business investors
- Visits and discussions with owners of similar business to keep your business skills sharp

---

Strategy #230:
MAKE INTEREST DEDUCTIBLE AS A BUSINESS EXPENSE.

Tax deductions for interest are possible when you treat interest paid as a business and not as a personal expense. Business interest is generally deductible, consumer or personal interest is not.

When you borrow money to purchase an automobile, video recorder, computer, or other asset for use even part-time in your business, the business interest portion (i.e., the % of interest matching the % of time the asset is used for business) can be deducted. (Certain interest deductibility restrictions may apply in the case of money borrowed to purchase an automobile.) Your small business once again creates deductions out of previously non-deductible expenses.

TAX-DEDUCTION STRATEGIES CHECKLIST
FOR SMALL-BUSINESS OWNERS

Starting a small business is fun, profitable, and certainly tax smart. Here is a summary of the strategies for maximizing possible tax deductions:

1. Hire your kids to work in the business.

2. Hire your spouse to work in the business.

3. Use your automobile in your business to create deductions through Capital Cost Allowance, gas, repairs, insurance, parking, and interest.

4. Use your home computer, videotape recorder, cassette recorder, furniture, typewriter, or other assets, even part-time, in your business.

5. Set up your business office in your home.

6. Use your social or athletic club for business purposes such as meetings, entertaining, and finding new customers.

7. Books, subscriptions, newsletters or tape courses that relate to business in general or to your particular business could be deductible.

8. Repairs to any asset you use in your business could be deductible.

9. Plan a trip around a business purpose, such as staff meetings, visiting customers or suppliers, and setting up a sales organization.

10. Use your boat, plane, or motor home directly in your business.

11. Interest deducted as a business expense rather than a personal expense could give you interest deductions you might otherwise lose.

Part III

POWERFUL

INVESTMENT

STRATEGIES

Chapter 19

THE TEN BIGGEST
INVESTMENT MISTAKES

The trouble with the profit system is that it has always been highly unprofitable to most people.

E. B. White, *One Man's Meat*, 1944

Objective: Learn to recognize investment schemes, scams, and bad advice.

By understanding the 10 worst investments and how they earn that distinction, you will find it easier to develop your winning approach to investment wealth. Left out of the "10 worst investments" list are those that border on fraud or are actually fraudulent. The investments chosen for our list are considered legitimate, but have downside risks or costs that far outweigh any apparent benefits.

Strategy #231:
KEEP YOUR MONEY OUT OF VACANT LAND.

Undeveloped land, sometimes called vacant or raw land, will continue to be a less than optimal investment for the next few years. The lowered value is caused by the shift in agricultural production from small farms to major farming operations. In addition, land, unless leased, produces no income but does create negative cash flow through property taxes and loan interest. A lot in an appreciating area, or one on which you eventually intend to build for yourself, is an exception and can be a good investment.

257

Strategy #232:
DON'T THROW MONEY AWAY IN TIME-SHARING.

Time-sharing is a real estate investment, usually one condominium unit, co-owned by as many as 25 investors. Each investor may personally use his unit during designated weeks, which are chosen as part of the transaction. Two "unit weeks" are usually sold for between $8,000 and $25,000. Owners, instead of being confined to the use of their own unit, usually have the right to trade for the use of other units in other complexes.

Time-sharing has a bad reputation because of developer defaults and bankruptcies. To combat the well-deserved negative press, developers have coined a new term, "interval ownership," to replace "time-sharing," but a rose by any other name is — well, you know. The latest marketing twist is the "membership" concept. The purchaser owns nothing except the right to use a unit for a week or two each year. Because the purchaser owns nothing, the price is often half of the cost of time-sharing. Is this concept saleable? Yes. Is it a good value? No!

There are four major drawbacks to time-sharing:

The Cost

A developer who sells two weeks to 25 investors for $10,000 each has generated $250,000 for one unit. The cost plus reasonable profit for building the unit may have been only $80,000, so the purchasers have overpaid by 300%. The payments at 12% interest would be $1,200 per year, plus maintenance fees. Renting luxury accommodations at most resorts costs far less, with no maintenance fees or headaches of ownership.

The Maintenance Fees

The developer charges yearly maintenance fees per owner of $300 to $500, built in, of course, to the monthly payments. One of the developer's goals is always to sell out the project and retire comfortably on the income from maintenance fees never used for maintenance.

The Promises

There are already on record hundreds of defaults because the developer wasn't able to sell enough "unit weeks." The developer goes bankrupt, the project remains uncompleted, leaving the unit purchasers holding the bag. Purchasers usually lose their down payment, plus any monthly payments already made. If the purchaser paid cash, the entire amount may be lost.

The Investment Pitch

The salesperson usually implies that the purchaser is making a good investment and that the "unit weeks" eventually can be sold at a big profit. Today there are thousands of "unit weeks" on the market that can't be sold at any price.

Strategy #233:
NEVER USE LIFE INSURANCE AS AN INVESTMENT.

Buy life insurance as if you were going to die tomorrow, and invest as if you were going to live forever. Life insurance and investing, both necessary parts of a good financial plan, have little in common. Life insurance companies got into the investment business for one major reason: There are bigger profits in selling investments than in selling insurance.

Unlike your bank, which can tie your money up for only a few days to a few years, insurance companies have discovered methods to tie up your money for almost your entire lifetime at a low rate of return. Put $2,000 into a "universal life" policy, withdraw your money after one year, and the surrender charge can be as much as $1,000!

The best strategy is to buy term insurance and build your investment wealth by choosing the correct investments and strategies yourself.

Strategy #234:
STAY AWAY FROM INDIVIDUAL STOCKS AND BONDS.

Buying 100 to 1,000 shares of a stock, or pumping $1,000 to $25,000 into one or two bond issues, is far more risky than investing in stocks and bonds through mutual funds. Buying individual stocks and bonds also means paying commissions. You pay no commissions by using one of over 175 no-load mutual funds you will learn about later.

Strategy #235:
NEVER INVEST IN BONDS WHEN INTEREST
RATES ARE RISING.

Bonds are good investments only when they are appreciating due to declining interest rates. When the prime rate is rising, any long-term bond will lose 10% of its principal value for every 1% increase in the prime rate. From March 1987 to October 1987, while the prime rate rose from 7½% to over 10%, bond investments dropped 10% to 20% in value. Stay away from financial advisors who tell you bonds are always a good, safe investment for those who want income.

Bond investments include:
Individual Bonds — corporate, zero coupon.
Bond Mutual Funds — high yield, fixed income, government securities.

Strategy #236:
DON'T INVEST IN INFLATION HEDGES
SUCH AS PRECIOUS METALS.

Precious metals (gold and silver) are investments only for the most aggressive investors. Traditionally, gold and silver have been called a hedge against inflation. Inflation hedges are always investment losers. For instance, when adjusted for inflation, the real value of gold hasn't changed in a hundred years. For example, the price of a good tailor-made suit has almost always been one ounce of gold. Your loss in an inflation hedge comes when you sell your investment and pay capital-gains tax on your profits.

Scared investors often invest in precious metals as a hedge against economic collapse or hyper-inflation, basing their reasoning on the Great Depression. The Great Depression was not even close to an economic collapse; 75% of all workers remained employed and real estate appreciated an average of 3% per year even in 1933 and 1934. Of course, no depression is a pleasant time, but it was not the end-all doom period it was painted to be. There is no impending economic collapse, no matter how many books and newsletters predict one. Therefore, all defensive investing will cause investment losses.

Strategy #237:
DON'T FALL FOR INVESTMENT PHONE PITCHES.

Now you can buy your investments over the phone, but don't! Dozens of phone "boiler rooms" have been created to sell off-the-wall investments. High-pressure sales pitches are conducted by highly commissioned phone-room managers using minimum-wage telephone solicitors. The bait is the belief you are being let in on some new investment secret or opportunity not generally known to the public. Included in the wide range of these investment pitches are:

- precious metals
- cellular phone lotteries
- commodities
- industrial-grade diamonds
- bids on government land leases
- tracts of land in desolate areas

These schemes make big promises and deliver little, other than the opportunity to lose your money. Incredibly enough, tens of thousands of investors fall for these investment gimmicks every year.

Strategy #238:
NEVER USE A COMMISSIONED FINANCIAL
SALESPERSON AS A FINANCIAL ADVISOR.

Paying big commissions will turn almost any winning investment plan into a marginal one at best, often into a loser. Today's smart investor learns to work directly with financial institutions like no-load mutual fund families, eliminating the need for the middleman.

A commissioned investment salesperson should never be used as a financial advisor for two reasons:

1. Bias — The salesperson will always recommend as your investment solution the investments he or she sells, whether or not these are the investments you should be using.
2. Lack of Investment Knowledge — Brokers and other licensed salespeople are required to know only two things: the securities laws and how to sell investments successfully. Although the various provincial securities commissions do require brokers and salespeople to abide by the "know the client" rule and to ensure that investments are "suitable" for the client, too many strategies recommended by investment salespeople are either too risky or 20 years out of date.

The *Wall Street Journal* recently published an article, based on a copy of a brokerage-firm memo, that stated the only requirement to keep your job as a broker with the firm is to produce $100,000 in commissions for the company. A better approach would be for each firm to require its salespeople to produce a 20% after-commission return for investors and to collect commissions only on investments that actually return what the salespeople promised! Most brokers and financial planners have appalling records when it comes to making investors any real investment wealth.

And what about Chartered or Certified Financial Planners? Be careful. Some "certified" financial planners have taken only a home-study course, and most have very little money of their own to manage. If you want to learn how to make money, you will learn the most from someone who has plenty of it.

Strategy #239:
DON'T OVER-LEVERAGE IN VOLATILE INVESTMENTS
SUCH AS COMMODITIES.

Commodities are the riskiest of all legal investments. Greed is the commodities' drawing card. Investors can put up as little as 5% of the purchase price of the investment in order to control the entire investment. An investor can buy a $10,000 commodities contract for only $500. The leverage seems interesting until you look at the validity of the investment. The average price fluctuation in the commodities market is 1% per day. If the investor puts up only 5% and is leveraged by a factor of 20 to 1, the value of his investment will fluctuate an average of 20% per day — great news if the price goes up, disaster if the price of the commodity drops. Even if the price drop is small, the investor's capital may be wiped out. In the casinos of the world, this condition is known as "gambler's ruin." Ninety-five percent of commodity players eventually lose money.

There is no safe strategy for profiting in commodities. When the value of the investment drops below the 5% margin requirement, the investor is required to put up more money or lose the investment and receive a bill for the difference. These margin calls have wiped out the entire assets of many investors.

In one famous Canadian court case involving commodities, a husband and wife acquired a "short" position in sugar futures on the advice of their broker. (They were gambling that sugar prices would decline. If they did, the couple would make money.)

Unfortunately, the market went against them — the price of sugar futures rose and their "paper" position worsened daily.

In such a situation, the investor will typically close out his position and take his medicine. In this case, the broker advised the couple to hang on to their position, since he expected the market to drop over the longer term. He also advised trying to make back some of their immediate paper losses by going "long" in sugar futures (the exact opposite of the original strategy) via quick buy-and-sell trades done between the start of the trading day and the end (known in the industry as "day trading").

The broker's thinking was that the fast profits made on these new "long" day-contracts would protect the couple while they waited for the market to ultimately reverse itself and make their short position profitable.

Unknown to the husband and wife, this approach placed them in additional jeopardy. If any of their newly acquired "long" contracts remained in their brokerage account at the official close of the business day — through oversight — these would automatically be applied by the broker's computer to offset their older "short" sugar contracts (which were losing money) and so finalize or trigger the very losses they wanted to avoid.

That was exactly what happened. Several of their "long" day-trades were accidentally left unsold in their account at the close of a particular business day. The brokerage computer immediately offset these against the outstanding "short" sugar contracts and so triggered an immediate loss for the unhappy investors of over $35,000.

This case went to the Ontario Court of Appeal. The court ruled that, even though the husband and wife had signed a contract that broadly exempted their broker from liability for bad advice, the quality of the advice given, and service rendered, was so bad the contractual protection could not help the brokerage firm. Not only did the couple not have to pay the $35,000 that they had "lost" in that final and unfortunate computerized transaction, the judge awarded them an additional $33,000 in damages representing the lost profits they would have made if their day-trading had been correctly handled on that fateful day.

Based on this story, it is clear that commodity trading is hardly a safe or predictable financial investment. If you want excitement, go to Disney World. If you want security, avoid the commodity game completely.

Strategy #240:
DON'T BUY OVERLY SPECULATIVE INVESTMENTS SUCH AS PENNY STOCKS.

Penny stocks are highly speculative securities sold by fast-talking brokers and securities representatives. They are usually sold over the telephone for less than $10 a share. These are stocks of companies that have no earning history and could even be fictitious.

Imagine, 20,000 shares of stock at only pennies per share. What a deal, right? Wrong! Authorities estimate that the epidemic of penny stocks is costing the public hundreds of millions of dollars per year.

Penny stocks normally sell for less than $1 per share, although sometimes the price can be bid up to where it exceeds a dollar.

Very often, the company that issues the stock publicly will hype the stock with talk about new inventions, discoveries, or technological breakthroughs made by the company. Penny-stock brokers often suggest to their prospects that they can double or triple their money in a short period of time. It's an opportunity that can't wait, and the investor doesn't have time to think about it or confer with an advisor — he must act now!

With many penny stocks, there is as much as a 100% difference between the ask, which is the price at which the broker will sell the stock to the investor, and the bid, which is the price at which the broker will buy the stock from the investor. In this scenario, the stock would have to double to allow the investor just to break even!

Penny-stock brokerage firms control as much as 95% of the market activity of a single stock, allowing them to manipulate the price. Because most penny stocks cannot be found in the newspaper listings, it's very difficult for the investor to determine what a penny stock is really worth.

A TYPICAL STOCK-MANIPULATION SCHEME

Brokers are instructed to come up with twice as many buy orders as sell orders, thus moving the price of the stock up. Meanwhile, investors are strongly discouraged from selling the stock. Before the story behind the stock fades, the insiders who bought the stock at a much lower price sell their stock at the now-inflated price. The price of the stock then collapses and investors are left with stocks of little or no value.

Penny stocks are extremely risky and, therefore, should only be sold to qualified investors who can afford to lose all of the money invested. Most of the time the stocks are sold to investors without sufficient qualification through high-pressure phone pitches.

In Canada especially, because of this country's long fascination with mining and mining investments, penny stocks are a gold mine. For the brokers, at least! Be particularly wary of stocks traded on the smaller exchanges such as the Vancouver exchange. Although such exchanges are now more regulated than they were a few years back, they are still dangerous places for the unwary and inexperienced. One office worker from Toronto, who should have known better, purchased 12,000 shares of a stock trading at $0.50 on the Vancouver exchange for a total investment of $6,000. Because he was leaving town for several days, he elected to use a device known as a "stop loss" in order to protect his investment. He told his broker to program the brokerage computer so that his position would be sold if the value of the stock dropped by 50%, or to $0.25 a share.

In most situations, a "stop loss" provides good protection in the event of a major problem with the security. When this fellow returned from his trip, three days later, his broker told him that the stock had dropped as low as $0.18 and his position had been sold at $0.20, for a total loss of 12,000 × ($.50 − .20) or $3,600. However, when he looked at the trading results for the day, he saw his stock trading back at $0.48. The stock had declined by over half its value and then rebounded, all within 48 hours! Needless to say, reputable stocks traded on reputable exchanges do not behave that way!

The only people who consistently make money in penny stocks are the brokerage firms, brokers, and insiders. The next time a smooth-talking penny-stock broker calls to let you buy from his "bargain basement," politely decline. Remember, if it sounds too good to be true, it probably is.

Strategy #241:
AVOID OPTIONS AS A LEVERAGED OR HEDGED INVESTMENT.

An *option* is a right to buy or sell a specified number of shares of stock at a specified price on or before a specific day. A *put* is the right to sell. A *call* is the right to buy.

The investor pays a price for the option, which is forfeited if he or she does not exercise the option. The price an investor pays for the option is usually 2% to 10% of the price of the stock. Seventy-two percent of options are never exercised. The only realistic use of an option for a conservative investor would be to protect the profit on a stock already owned that could not or should not be sold at the present time.

Examples:

A. An employee is going to leave a company in six months and wants to cash in his stock, but cannot sell until he leaves. He is concerned that the price will drop during that period. He buys a put on his company stock, which gives him the right to sell at a guaranteed price. The cost of the option is like buying insurance.

B. An investor has a huge profit on a stock, is concerned the market is about to drop, but wants to sell the following year to defer the capital-gains tax for 12 months. He buys a put to protect his profits from a market drop. If the market drops he exercises his right to sell at the higher price; otherwise his risk is limited to losing the money he paid for the option.

There are now many mutual funds that use options as their primary investment or as a hedge against fluctuating prices. The mutual funds that use options as a hedge have poor overall performance records.

Strategy #242:
LEARN TO RECOGNIZE BAD INVESTMENT ADVICE.

How do you really know when your broker or financial planner is just a commissioned wolf in sheep's clothing? You can tell by the statements he or she makes and the strategies you are told to employ. You should recognize the following statements as bad investment advice:

THE BIGGEST LIES IN THE INVESTMENT BUSINESS

"Stocks and bonds are a good long-term investment."
There is no such thing as a good long-term securities investment. The best investments change as the economy and interest rates change.

"We'll diversify into different investments — some stocks, some bonds for safety."
Stocks and bonds are good investments at different times, but not at the same time.

"Government securities are always a good, safe investment for those who want income."
Government securities are bonds. Bonds drop about 10% in principal value for every 1% increase in the prime rate. Never invest in government securities when the prime rate is going up.

"It always requires bigger risks to make bigger profits."
Only amateur financial advisors believe this. Bigger profits in the range of 15% to 20% can easily be attained using knowledge and not risk. The investment strategies in this section will all earn you over 15% safely.

"This investment is a hedge against inflation."
If you just keep pace with inflation, your before-tax profit is zero. If you have to pay taxes on the phantom capital gains, you end up with a guaranteed loss of 19% or more.

"By using dollar cost averaging, we can avoid the fluctuations in the market and end up with potentially bigger profits."
Dollar cost averaging is the practice of making equal investments at equal intervals in the same stock, bond, or mutual fund. This strategy violates two rules of successful investing:

1. There is no such thing as a good long-term investment.
2. Every economy has one best type of investment.

"I've got a hot tip on a good stock."
Hot tips ruin most unaware investors. Stockbrokers are always the

least informed in a brokerage-firm hierarchy, and their hot tips usually lose investors' money.

"Zero coupon or remainder bonds are a great investment for your children."

Zero coupon or remainder bonds are sold as investments for tax shelters, and for children, because salespeople know you'll buy them. If not in a tax shelter, however, you or the kids will owe taxes each year on interest you do not actually receive. The best way to invest for children under 14 is mutual funds, averaging over 15%. Even with a 10% one-time withdrawal penalty the child's account will average over 15% per year.

"You should pay commissions because you get better financial advice."

A good financial advisor or money manager will earn you 25% per year after commissions, but those of this calibre only manage portfolios of $1,000,000 or more and spend most of their time on the ski slopes. If you have less than a million, you won't qualify to work with the best portfolio managers. One reason this book was written is to give you the same calibre of help, even if you don't have the big dollars.

"We should make some conservative investments and then take a few risks."

No risks are necessary for a knowledgeable investor. Using the winning investment strategies in this book, even a novice investor can expect to earn 15% or more per year while avoiding pitfalls and risks.

"A trust company or bank trust department should become the trustee for your estate."

Trust companies or bank trust departments have the worst track records of any estate managers, often losing 60% of an estate in five to ten years. Use as your trustee a lawyer, friend, or relative who will follow exactly the strategies you are learning now for building and preserving your estate.

"It is not possible to average 15% per year safely."

Nonsense! Tens of thousands of investors who have followed my strategies for two years or more have averaged 15% or more safely.

These strategies work, work for everyone, and work all the time.

Half the battle of successful investing is ridding yourself of common false or outdated investment beliefs, most of which we have reviewed in this chapter. From now on we will concentrate on the winning investment strategies.

Chapter 20

THE SECRETS OF
POWERFUL INVESTING

Money is the guarantee that we may have what we want in the future. Though we need nothing at the moment, it ensures the possibility of satisfying a new desire when it arises.

Aristotle

Objective: Accomplish the three major investment objectives:

1. **Maintaining up to a 20% safe investment return**
2. **No commissions**
3. **No taxes**

What is investing? Investing is putting your money instead of your muscle to work; yet, if there is any area of managing and making money that most people foul up, not just once, but over an entire lifetime, it is investing.

One of my personal fortunes was lost by listening to the dubious advice of a financial salesman. At 26, after losing a million dollars in my recording-studio fire, I decided to build my next fortune through investing. Genesco, the apparel conglomerate for which I designed computer software systems, offered a magnificent stock incentive plan to its management employees. My first 200 shares were bought for me by the company with another 200 shares on the payment-a-month plan. After buying in at $21 per share, the stock began to grow rapidly in value and split periodically. Being close to management computer systems, I began to see loopholes that would legally allow me to get my hands on hundreds of shares of Genesco stock financed totally by the company. With two thousand shares of stock, for which I had made only a few monthly payments, I was accumulating tens of thousands of dollars in stock equity during the company's most expansive era, and the stock skyrocketed to $70 per share.

I was hooked on the stock market. I thought I couldn't lose. What a learning experience I was in for! Borrowing money on everything I owned, including my home and cars, I bought shares in all the new stock issues of the mid-'60s. Margin accounts and undercollateralized loans enabled me to run $60,000 of borrowed capital into a stock fortune of $800,000 in just three years. I even considered a leisurely, full-time career as an investor.

Then the roof fell in. Every morning, the newspaper would show my newly found fortune dwindling at an ever-increasing rate. Every afternoon, I was in contact with the holders of my notes and margin accounts who wanted instant replacement for their disappearing collateral. My margin calls seemed to have margin calls! Companies in which I had invested heavily, like Performance Systems (Minnie Pearl Fried Chicken) and Continental Strategics, went bankrupt, leaving me only memories and worthless stock certificates. I was forced to trade my new custom-designed Cadillac for a three-year-old Volkswagen Beetle, rather than have the car repossessed for lack of payments. My home was finally sold with barely enough equity to pay back most of the borrowed money. The entire fortune was gone. I had tasted both the bitter and the sweet of investing and vowed that I would never again risk my money until I knew how to win without the risk of losing.

The investment principles I discovered over the next few years were enough to build a lifetime investment fortune without investment mistakes, and these principles can do the same for you. Powerful investing is one of the easiest of all strategies to master, but the misinformation, lack of information, potential for loss, and outright fraud that exist in the arena of investing are enough to destroy any good financial plan. Traditional investing has become a mixture of storing money and legalized gambling. Players are usually the losers, financial institutions the winners.

THE IMPORTANCE OF INVESTING

If you don't expect to win a lottery, and you don't have the option of inheriting vast sums of money, you have only five ways to increase your wealth:

1. Putting yourself to work — employment.
2. Putting other people to work — business.
3. Putting your ideas to work — inventing, marketing, or consulting.
4. Putting your money to work — investing.
5. Putting other people's money to work — leverage.

Working for someone else is the first money-making experience for most of us, beyond birthday gifts and the tooth fairy. There are two limiting considerations when you put your financial future in the hands of the "company":

- Your success is directly tied to the success and attitude of your employer, over which you have no control.
- Your income and lifestyle are limited by your experience, age, education, the opportunity for advancement, and your ability to sell yourself on the job.

If there are any two words that no longer belong together, they are "job" and "security." Putting together a powerful investment program will put an end to the lifelong dependency on others (employers or the government), even if you don't want the responsibility of starting your own company. In the '90s, a powerful investment plan is as essential to your lifestyle as a home or automobile. It can be your ticket to freedom, both during your working years and after retirement.

There are two approaches to investing — putting your money to work, and putting other people's money to work.

You put your money to work when you invest in:

- Stocks
- Bonds
- Mutual funds
- Guaranteed Investment Certificates (GICs)
- RRSPs
- Canada Savings Bonds
- Company pension programs
- Any other direct investment using your own money

You put other people's money to work when you:

- Buy a home with a mortgage
- Use a brokerage firm or mutual-fund margin account
- Take an option on a piece of real estate
- Borrow money for your business
- Invest in leveraged limited partnerships
- Borrow on the equity in your home to reinvest
- Expect any financial rewards from the use of borrowed capital

Putting your own money to work is direct and easy to understand, but limits your benefits to the profits that can be generated by your

own capital. Putting other people's money to work can be more profitable, but can also be more risky and difficult to understand. The
main benefit of OPM (other people's money) is that you can create
profits and/or tax deductions far beyond what your own capital
can generate. Using OPM is a step you will certainly want to consider once you have mastered the basics of investing your own
money.

Strategy #243:
USE THE EIGHT BEST INVESTMENTS TO AVERAGE UP TO 20% PER YEAR.

Powerful investing is not like saving money. In Canada, savers die
broke hoping for a pitiful 6% to 10% return that is instantly eaten up
by taxes and inflation. Smart investors, on the other hand, have
learned to earn 15% to 25% per year safely with no taxes and no or
low commissions. How? By using the eight best and safest investments in Canada, those you normally won't find at banks or from
investment salespeople.

The eight best investments and the average yearly returns you can
expect are listed below. In this section, you will learn all the strategies for successfully using each of these great investments.

Your objective as an investor is to put your money to work safely
and effectively, making yourself rich instead of making financial institutions rich. Through your choice of these investments you can
enjoy income, tax shelter, and maximum growth or any combination
you choose.

THE EIGHT BEST INVESTMENTS

INVESTMENT	STRATEGY	ACTIVE/ PASSIVE	AVERAGE YEARLY RETURN
1. No-load mutual funds	Money Movement	Passive	12%–25%
2. Mutual fund margin account	Leverage	Passive	25%
3. RRSP accounts	Self-directed accounts	Passive	15–20%

4. Your own home	Leverage & personal use	Passive	20%
5. Asset management chequing account (where available)	Legal float and debit card	Active	8%–14%
6. Employer's pension plan	Money Movement and payroll deducted	Passive	20%
7. Discounted mortgages	Guaranteed interest tax deferral	Active	30%
8. Residential real estate	Leverage and equity growth	Active	30%

Strategy #244:

**EARN 20% PER YEAR SAFELY BY USING ONLY
THE EIGHT BEST INVESTMENTS.**

Normal investment profits can be more than doubled with knowledge and without additional time or risk by using a combination of the eight best and safest investments. Chapter by chapter in this section we will cover them all. The last chapter will show you how to choose those that are right for your investment plan and objectives.

Strategy #245:

**PAY NO OR LOW COMMISSIONS BY WORKING
DIRECTLY WITH GOVERNMENT AND
FINANCIAL INSTITUTIONS.**

You cannot split your money with everyone else and expect to end up with much for yourself. Smart investors eliminate commissions by dealing directly with financial institutions and eliminating middlemen such as brokers and financial planners. Paying unnecessary commissions is like throwing $20 bills into your fireplace to heat your home. The job will get done but at far too great a cost.

Strategy #246:

USE TAX SHELTERS AND TAX STRATEGIES TO PROTECT YOUR INVESTMENT INCOME.

Most investors think the only strategies for investing without paying taxes are retirement programs. Any investment income can be tax sheltered. You have the choices of using automatically tax-sheltered investments, such as real estate, or creating tax deductions to match your investment income using any of the tax strategies in this book. Both methods can make your investments tax deferred or even tax free.

Whether you are a novice or a seasoned investor, you'll find all the secrets to building a powerful investment plan right here. There are no prerequisites. Your job is to organize or reorganize your investment dollars around a combination of these powerful, safe investments. Your decisions on which investments to choose will depend on your investment experience or lack of it, your financial goals, and the amount of capital you have. All eight investments are intended to remove risk and are appropriate no matter what your age.

Personal knowledge will eliminate risk and fear in your investment plan. Risk occurs most frequently when you act solely on the advice of others, without sufficient knowledge, making decisions without taking control.

THE GREATEST RISKS ARE TAKEN, NOT THROUGH THE INVESTMENTS CHOSEN, BUT THROUGH THE LACK OF PERSONAL KNOWLEDGE OF HOW TO USE INVESTMENT STRATEGIES CORRECTLY.

Chapter 21

THE 10% SOLUTION

A man who both spends and saves money is the happiest man, because he has both enjoyments.

Samuel Johnson

Objective: Start your million-dollar investment plan on a shoestring.

Without the discipline to take control of your financial future, there is no level of income you cannot outspend. Budgeting is certainly not the answer. The two most difficult personal promises to keep are certainly budgeting and dieting. Neither produces the instant reward or positive feedback so necessary for continued motivation. Budgeting is a plan requiring self-sacrifice now for some vague reward sometime in the not-so-foreseeable future. Budgeting never worked for me and it probably doesn't work any better for you. But there is a strategy I've discovered that allows you, without sacrifice, to build an investment fortune for your future. I call it "the 10% Solution."

Strategy #247:
**USE THE 10% SOLUTION TO GO FROM
PAYCHEQUE TO PROSPERITY.**

Ninety percent of the families in Canada are still living paycheque-to-paycheque, always finding too much month left over at the end of the money. Paycheque-to-paycheque is a symptom, not of a lack of income, but of a lack of skills needed to build wealth. You begin to feel as if there is no level of income you cannot outspend.

Beginning with your next paycheque, take 10% right off the top and send it to a mutual fund family. Do the same with every paycheque for the rest of your life. Write yourself the first cheque each month before

275

you pay the rent, mortgage, car payment, or buy the groceries. We were all taught to handle obligations backwards; to pay everyone else first and then enjoy and invest what was left over. The problem? There is never anything left over.

Always pay yourself first. The less money you think you have, the more important the strategy. Make the 10% Solution a personal challenge. Do it now. Don't wait for it to happen.

Two mutual fund families that will allow you to invest with low minimums are Altamira Investment Services and Central Guaranty Trust Co. Funds Services (see Chapter 24, No-Load Chart for addresses). With a pre-authorized monthly chequing plan, Altamira offers minimums as low as $50 per month and even has a Baby Bonus account allowing you to invest as little as $33 per month.

Under the Futurlink Plan at Central Guaranty Trust, paying $50 for 10 months or $500 over a one-year period entitles you to put in as little as $25 for each new fund you invest in (check your branch for details). By sending as little as 10% out of each paycheque and using the Money Movement Strategy (Chapter 23) to choose the right kind of mutual fund, you will double your money every three to four years. Do like everyone else does and put the same 10% of your cheque in a bank or credit union account and you will double your money only once every 10 years! Central Guaranty Trust will now debit your bank account automatically every month for the amount you want to invest — automatic wealth building.

"What do you mean, take 10% out of my paycheque?" you may be thinking. "I'm already spending 120%!" If you are, you won't even miss the other 10%. No one ever makes excuses for success. Excuses are only necessary when we forget or fail to do something. Excuses won't build wealth, action will. All successful people have discovered the same success principle: "Do It Now."

(Note: Money market funds will generally charge higher minimums than regular mutual funds and should not be considered.)

Strategy #248:
STORE 20% OF ONE YEAR'S INCOME AS ATTITUDE MONEY.

Have you ever noticed how directly your attitude is related to your bank account balance? You have if you are still on the paycheque-to-paycheque treadmill. A positive attitude and financial self-confidence are two of the most important wealth-building tools. The easiest method of maintaining the winning attitude that comes from cash in the bank is never to be without it.

Using the 10% Solution, make deposits in your mutual fund account until the balance is equal to 20% of one year's take-home pay. In writing, promise yourself you will never touch the money — not for overdue bills, emergencies, or any other logical reason. Why? As soon as the money goes, so does your attitude. You will find it far easier, attitude-wise, to have overdue bills with money available to pay them if you wanted to, than to have your bills totally paid and be back in the paycheque-to-paycheque rut.

You will always encounter tough months where the money goes out faster than it comes in. Your 20% is your attitude money, your dependable shelter during financial storms — never, never touch it no matter how tough it gets. Your more stable attitude will propel you past your short-term financial dilemmas.

Once you have reached the 20% quota, you won't have to deposit another dime in the account. If your goal is to double your income every four years or so, your 20% account invested correctly also will double in the same amount of time. Open a separate account for your future 10% deposits.

Strategy #249:
USE THE "RULE OF 76" TO DETERMINE
THE DOUBLING POWER OF YOUR MONEY.

How long does it take to double your money in an investment? — a long time in a 7% bank account, not so long if you're earning over 15% per year in a mutual fund family. But how long? The "Rule of 76" is the easiest way to determine the answer. Divide the number 76 by the expected return on your investment and the result is the number of years required to double your money if all of the earnings are reinvested and compounded. The short-term doubling power of money invested at 15% to 25% should give you the motivation to get your 10% Solution strategy started immediately.

**THE RULE OF 76
INVESTMENT TIME REQUIRED
TO DOUBLE YOUR MONEY**

$ Invested @	Number of Years
25%	3.0
20%	3.8
15%	5.0
10%	7.6
9%	8.4
8%	9.5
7%	10.8
6%	12.67

Using investment strategies like mutual funds and Money Movement, covered in this section, you will soon be doubling your money every three to four years, even starting with only 10% out of every paycheque.

USING THE 10% SOLUTION

Let's look at it another way. For every $1,000 you invest this year at 15% to 25%, the following chart will show you how much you will have accumulated during periods ranging from five to 20 years. What you see in the chart can be accomplished with just $83.33 per month ($1,000 per year), the amount that someone with a net income of $833.00 per month would deposit using the 10% Solution. Who said you have to have big money to make big money?

In my twenties, I wondered what it was I didn't seem to understand about getting wealthy. Why did some people seem to have the Midas touch, while I was still running to the bank with each paycheque to cover the cheques I had written the previous week? I had been taught that hard work would build wealth; but I couldn't work any harder. I had been holding down at least two jobs since I was 18 and there were no more hours in the day.

Then, one day, I found an answer in "Ripley's Believe It or Not" which said:

> If you sell a five-pound bar of iron right out of the blast furnace, it will be worth $6.00. If you turn the iron into

fishing weights, they will be worth $25.00. Transform your iron into fishing hooks, and they will sell for $250. Hammer the iron into hunting knife blades and you'll get $2,500. If, however, you transform your iron bar into watch springs, they will be worth $250,000 — one quarter of a million dollars.

I suddenly realized that working smarter instead of harder is what creates wealth. It doesn't matter what you are worth now; what matters is what you do with what you've got. Time and knowledge will do the work for you. Strategies like the 10% Solution help you turn your five-pound bar of iron into watch springs.

Begin your 10% Solution with your next paycheque!

FOR EACH $1,000 YOU INVEST

INVESTMENT RETURN	5 YRS	10 YRS	15 YRS	20 YRS
15%	$2,010	$4,050	$8,150	$16,380
20%	2,480	6,190	15,400	38,340
25%	3,051	9,313	28,422	86,736

Chapter 22

DEVELOP POWERFUL BANKING STRATEGIES

Most bankers dwell in marble halls, which they get to dwell in because they encourage deposits and discourage withdrawals.

Ogden Nash

Objective: Redesign your banking to take advantage of the best and newest products and services available.

A new banking product called the Asset Management Account is gradually being introduced in Canada.

Asset Management Accounts (AMAs) are cash and investment management accounts established by major brokerage firms, mutual funds, or other large financial institutions that give you the opportunity to gain better control of these assets. Depending upon the account, you may be able to trade securities, earn market interest rates on your cash reserves (often as much as twice what your bank pays), and write cheques to pay bills or for other financial matters without being charged, thereby accessing your money whenever you wish.

Some AMAs require no minimum deposit, while others want $10,000 to $25,000 just to open the account. Additional deposits can be made at any time. Asset Management Accounts have no minimum cheque requirements or limit to the number of cheques you can write.

Canadians can access existing AMAs in the United States via toll-free numbers. If you wish to invest dollars, in U.S. currency, on the other side of the border, an AMA is definitely worth thinking about.

Strategy #250:
USE AN ASSET MANAGEMENT ACCOUNT TO DOUBLE THE INTEREST YOU RECEIVE FROM A BANK CHEQUING ACCOUNT.

There are two profits in an AMA. The first is the variable interest paid on your account balance. Interest rates in Asset Management Accounts have averaged between 6.5% and 18% since 1980 in the United States; they are based on money market rates at which your money is invested. The second profit is an additional ½% to 1% created by the daily compounding.

Strategy #251:
IF AVAILABLE, CHOOSE AN ASSET MANAGEMENT ACCOUNT THAT OFFERS A NO-CHARGE CREDIT CARD.

A no-charge credit card tied into your AMA means that your charge account gets paid off "automatically." (Don't get too excited — if you don't have the cash in the account, the financial institution will likely create an instant loan to pay your charge bill, albeit at a preferred loan rate.)

Strategy #252:
CHOOSE AN AMA WITH A LOW YEARLY FEE.

Find the lowest fee around for features you want. Also, because your Asset Management Account is really an investment account, you should claim the yearly fees are tax deductible as a miscellaneous investment expense.

Strategy #253:
AVOID COMMERCIAL BANKS FOR YOUR BUSINESS CHEQUING ACCOUNT.

Many Canadian banks are unwilling — so far — to offer interest on the balances in business or corporate accounts. Since these same banks do, of course, charge chequing fees, this creates a nightmarish situation for business owners: substantial sums of money lying idle, collecting no interest, while the account itself is continually hit with chequing and statement fees.

Accepting this situation blindly could cost you large sums of money in lost interest. Consider these solutions:

1. Choose an Asset Management Account (as explained in this chapter).
2. Deal instead with a trust company or credit union.

Though these institutions do not publicize the service, they are willing and able to take a daily-interest chequing account, with statement privileges, and convert it to a business name. While you still get charged a regular statement fee plus (depending on the institution) separate fees for such things as money orders and overdrafts, chances are the interest you will earn on your balance will more than compensate for these charges. As well, many trust companies are experimenting with no-fee or low-fee accounts that further minimize these extra charges. Shop the trust companies and credit unions in your area and see what is available.

Strategy #254:
IF YOU ARE IN BUSINESS, TALK TO YOUR BANK OR TRUST COMPANY BRANCH MANAGER IN ADVANCE ABOUT OVERDRAFTS, CREDIT LINES, ETC.

Consider the different cases of Dave and Sally.

Both are small-business owners. Both are in the same business. Dave opened his business account at the most convenient bank, as always. He just filled out the forms, smiled at the clerk, and left. One day, while Dave was away in Florida on business, he received an urgent call from his secretary, who told Dave that some of his best suppliers had been phoning to say that their latest cheques from Dave had bounced. They were angry and wondering what was going on. Was Dave in financial trouble?

Dave called the bank long distance from Florida, and after much screaming and yelling, determined that the bank had made an error on Dave's last deposit. Dave had actually deposited $5,000, but the teller had missed a zero and the deposit came out to only $500. As a result, Dave's cheques were bouncing all over Toronto.

The bank ultimately admitted its error and grudgingly said they would reverse the NSF charges that were accumulating in Dave's account — charges over several hundred dollars by the time Dave called. They even said they would write letters to Dave's suppliers saying it was their fault. As far as the long-distance charges, aggravation, and bad feelings, there was nothing else they could really do.

Now let's look at Sally's case. When Sally opened her business account, she insisted on a personal meeting with the branch manager to establish "special instructions" up front. Sally brought to the meeting her personal financial statements as well as her business statements. She had two special requests to make of the manager:

1. Never bounce a cheque without telling her first and giving her a chance to fix things. No exceptions.
2. Put automatic overdraft protection of $1,000 on the account, secured by Sally's name only, without collateral. (Most managers have the authority to do this, but you have to ask.)

It took Sally three or four tries to find a bank manager who would agree to these conditions. Eventually Sally found a manager willing to make the proper entries on Sally's account so that, even if he himself were away from the branch, her instructions would be followed to the letter.

When the same situation that happened to Dave happened to Sally — a $5,000 deposit was entered incorrectly as $500 — here is what happened:

The first few cheques that were processed under Sally's account went through under her automatic overdraft. When that was used up, a clerk spotted the special instructions in Sally's file and put in a call to Sally's office. Sally, like Dave, was in Florida at the time, and it took her a few long-distance calls to pin down the problem. Once the bank realized what had happened, they adjusted that bank deposit, voided the overdraft and interest, and cleared the remaining cheques that were being held. Sally was still out the long-distance calls, but no damage was done to her business or her reputation — and that's what matters!

Strategy #255:
USE AN ASSET MANAGEMENT ACCOUNT FOR YOUR SMALL-BUSINESS CHEQUING ACCOUNT.

An AMA for business gives the business owner the best of all worlds — a high-interest, compounded return plus regular statements, and no charge for cheques.

Asset Management Accounts are new to Canada and are not available everywhere. One product that is available in most major centres across the country is the Wood Gundy Asset Advantage Account. This account has an annual fee of $200. It includes:

1. Daily compounded interest (prime less 2%)
2. Margin loans for any purpose (prime plus ¾%)
3. U.S. and Canadian no-charge chequing available
4. No-cost VISA card included
5. Comprehensive monthly summary

Strategy #256:
FOR PERSONAL USE AND CONVENIENCE, CONSIDER A U.S.–BASED AMA.

The best of the U.S.-based AMAs will happily accept Canadian customers. Though such a situation is impractical for business — cheques are issued and cleared in U.S. dollars through U.S. banks — it is of interest to anyone who maintains a U.S. investment portfolio, does some business in the United States, or simply enjoys the luxury of a U.S. chequing account when travelling through the United States.

The following U.S.-based AMAs are available to Canadians:

U.S. - BASED AMA'S AVAILABLE TO CANADIANS

Sponsor's Name	Account Name	Minimum Information Number	Minimum Initial Deposit	Balance Required	Cheques Returned	Yearly Fee	Debit/ Credit Card	Margin Accounts Available	Bus. Accounts Available
Declaration Cash Account	DCA	800-423-2345	Any[1]	None[2]	No	None[2]	None	No	Yes
Fidelity	Ultra Service/ USA	800-343-8721	25,000	10,000	Yes	60	MC Gold VISA Gold	Yes	Yes

1) Initial deposit less than $1,000: $15 opening fee
Balance under $2,500: $1.25 per-month fee plus $5.00 fee if over 5 cheques are written per month.
Balance of $2,500-$5,000: No monthly fee, $5.00 fee if over 5 cheques are written per month.
Balance over $5,000: No fees, unlimited chequing.

2) Balance under $2,500: $24 annual fee deducted quarterly.

Chapter 23

THE
MONEY MOVEMENT
STRATEGY

You don't buy a stock because it has real value. You buy it because you feel there is always a greater fool down the street who will pay more than you paid.

Donald J. Stockings
Securities and Exchange Commission, 1925

Objective: Time your investments in stocks, bonds, and money market instruments to safely earn 20%+ per year.

The Money Movement Strategy allows you to reach three important investment objectives:

1. To earn 20% per year safely.
2. To pay no commissions.
3. To pay minimum taxes on your earnings.

Every investor dreams of being in the right place at the right time — to get in on the beginning of a bull market and out before a bear market, or to own bonds when they are appreciating and to sell them before they drop. The Money Movement Strategy times your investment moves to accomplish these goals.

There are a few simple strategies for successful stock, bond, and money market investing that will turn you into a wealthy investor in a short time. Violate any of these rules and you will eventually lose money.

Strategy #257:
NEVER STORE MONEY.

A futile effort made by most conservative investors is the search for a good long-term investment. There are good investments and there are long-term investments, but when it comes to stocks and bonds there are no good long-term investments. The best investment this year will become the worst investment in two or three years as inflation and interest rates change. To become a successful investor, you must be willing to move your money, but only once every year or two.

Strategy #258:
INVEST IN STOCKS, BONDS, AND MONEY MARKET INSTRUMENTS ONLY THROUGH MUTUAL FUNDS.

A mutual fund is a group of a hundred or more stocks, bonds, or money market investments, all managed by the same company. When you invest in mutual funds, you own a small share of the fund's entire investment portfolio. Mutual funds give you the benefits of a diversified portfolio of stocks, bonds, or money market instruments without the risks, costs, or required expertise. The benefits of mutual fund investing make such a strong case that there is virtually no reason to invest in individual stocks, bonds, or money market instruments.

REASONS FOR USING MUTUAL FUNDS

1. Professional Management — Mutual fund managers are among the most knowledgeable financial people in the country. A full-time professional, not you, is responsible for choosing the stocks, bonds, or other investments.
2. Safety — A mutual fund is a group or portfolio of over a hundred stock, bond, or money market instruments all managed by the same company. You, as an investor, own shares in the entire portfolio. Because of the incredible diversification, a mutual fund investment is mathematically eight times safer than investing in any one stock or bond.
3. Easy-to-Evaluate — The track record of every mutual fund is a matter of public record. You simply check your newspaper for the previous day's

closing price (net asset value per share) just as you would for a stock. There is currently no effective way to evaluate stockbrokers, financial planners, or investment counsellors.

4. Control — Only those who are willing to exercise a measure of control over their investments can safely and consistently earn big profits. Those who turn control over to a broker, financial planner, or other investment salesperson generally do poorly. Mutual funds are an excellent vehicle for exercising control.

5. Income — You can choose to receive periodic income from any type of mutual fund: stock, bond, or money market.

6. Liquidity — You can withdraw part or all of your money any time you wish and receive it within a few days (24 hours for certain money market funds).

7. Investment Options — Your investment options are almost limitless through mutual funds. You can invest in stocks, bonds, money market instruments, overseas companies, and even precious metals.

Strategy #259:
USE ONLY THE NO-LOAD MUTUAL FUNDS.

A load is a sales commission and not a management fee. The load is paid to a broker, brokerage firm, financial planner, insurance agent, or anyone else who sells you the investment. By working directly with a no-load mutual fund and eliminating the middleman, you save 5% to 9% in commissions. Remember, you can't be splitting your money with everyone else and end up with much for yourself.

A true no-load mutual fund charges no commissions when you invest, and no commissions when you withdraw your money. Out of more than 600 Canadian mutual funds, more than 250 are no-load.

Where does the mutual fund make its money? All mutual funds, whether they charge commissions or not, charge an average of 1.5% to 2% per year for management fees and expenses. For this low fee the mutual fund:

- chooses the investments
- watches the markets for you eight hours a day
- keeps all necessary records of your account
- sends you periodic statements, usually monthly, about your account

No-load funds give you a great deal of investment help for very little money. The net asset value per share (NAV), quoted in the newspaper or on your statement, already reflects the deduction of the management fee.

The important question is: Does paying a commission in any way earn you extra profits? The answer is no. My research studies of mutual funds have shown that no-load and load funds perform equally well when the sales charge is disregarded. Often there are more no-load than load funds in the list of the top 20 best-performing funds. When you do include sales commissions in calculating mutual fund performance, load funds earn less.

Strategy #260:
PURCHASE NO-LOAD FUNDS DIRECTLY FROM THE FUND OFFICE OR AN AUTHORIZED AGENT.

Buying a no-load fund usually involves making contact directly with the business office of the fund or an authorized agent. Recently many brokerage firms have been offering their customers the "convenience" of buying no-load funds as a normal brokerage transaction under their existing account. Not surprisingly, there is a fee for this "service," which often works out to the amount you would have paid if the fund had been a load fund.

Such "convenience" ends up being costly, especially if the fund you have selected is a family fund — a number of different types of funds under one roof — with free telephone-switching privileges. Buying one of the funds from the family through a regular broker means paying a fee when buying and paying a double fee (selling/buying) whenever you switch. The difference could be hundreds or even thousands of dollars from your pocket, especially if you follow the Money Movement Strategy, which requires you to switch for maximum return whenever the economy changes direction.

Note: Some no-load funds do have an arrangement with brokerage firms where they actually repay the broker in some way for your business. Such arrangements end up being true "no-loads" in that they cost you nothing. Your best way to find out is to phone the fund office directly. Virtually all the major funds have a toll-free number for just this reason.

THE THREE CLASSIFICATIONS OF LOAD MUTUAL FUNDS

High-Load Mutual Funds are those that charge 4% to 9% commissions on the money you invest or withdraw. A front-end load means you pay commissions when you invest, reducing your principal. A back-end load means you pay commissions when you withdraw your money, reducing your earnings. Many back-end load funds become no-load funds after your money has been invested for five years or more.

Is there ever a time when your best choice of mutual funds might be a load fund? Yes, but only a back-end load fund. Let's say you want ongoing advice from a certain successful financial adviser but want to avoid paying commissions for the advice. When you invest in a back-end load fund, the adviser gets paid a commission by the mutual fund instead of you. As long as you stay with most back-end load funds for at least five years, you pay no commissions even when you withdraw your money. If you withdraw your money during the first five years, you are charged a yearly decreasing commission which enables the fund to recoup some of the money it paid to the advisor.

Low-Load Mutual Funds are those that charge 3% or less when you invest and no more than 1% when you withdraw or move your money. There are low-load funds that do make good choices for aggressive investors. Conservative investors should avoid low-load funds altogether. Most low-load funds do not pay commissions to salespeople but keep the money for advertising and extra profits.

No-Load Mutual Funds are ones that charge only 1% or less per year to offset marketing costs. Those who sell mutual funds will lead you to believe that it is better to pay 6% to 9% up-front rather than the small marketing fee each year. Mathematically, that is not true. When you pay an 8% commission up-front, only 92% of your money is actually invested. If you had a no-load fund, 100% of your money is invested and the 1% fee is taken from your earnings.

See the Mutual Fund Family Fact Sheets at the end of Chapter 24 for descriptions of nine mutual fund families containing 53 different funds.

Strategy #261:
CHOOSE THE RIGHT TYPE OF MUTUAL FUND
FOR EACH ECONOMY.

If the secret to safely investing in stocks and bonds is mutual funds, then the secret to making money in mutual funds is knowing that there are three entirely different types of funds — stock, bond, and money market. (See Strategy #268.) The Money Movement Strategy matches the right investment to the right economic climate, thereby creating an average investment return of 15-20% per year.

Strategy #262:

INVEST IN ONLY ONE TYPE OF MUTUAL FUND AT A TIME.

One and only one type of mutual fund is right for each economy. One major mistake made by most investors, often on the advice of an investment salesperson, is overdiversification: dividing investment capital among stocks, bonds, government securities, and money market funds. Overdiversification can cost as much in lost profits as underdiversification. An overly diversified investment plan operates like a seesaw; when one side goes up, the other goes down.

Strategy #263:

USE THE PRIME BUSINESS LOAN INTEREST RATE TO IDENTIFY THE SAFEST AND BEST MUTUAL FUND INVESTMENT FOR EACH ECONOMY.

What factor identifies the current economy and therefore the correct investments? Interest rates. More specifically, the prime interest rate. Eighty percent of the long-term increase or decrease in the value of stocks, bonds, and money market instruments is caused by changes in interest rates and is predictable. Short-term, nonpredictable increases or decreases are caused by speculation. The prime rate is the easiest of the interest rates to follow. Any change makes front-page headlines.

The prime rate moves slowly and does not change direction as often as stock prices do. Looking at the "Prime Rate Direction Changes Chart" and the "Prime Rate Changes" graph on page 297, you will notice that, if we consider direction changes of at least 1/2%, the prime rate has changed direction only 13 times in 10 years. Twice during the last 12 years the prime rate has continued in the same direction for more than two consecutive years, and changed direction an average of once every 11 months.

You must watch two components of the prime rate to choose the right investment:

1. Prime Rate Level — High or Low.
2. Prime Rate Direction — Up or Down.

Refer to the "Money Movement Strategy Chart" below and you'll see a curve that represents typical changes of prime interest rates over a three- to five-year period. This is one prime rate cycle. On the chart we've smoothed out the curve to demonstrate how the Money Movement Strategy works. The actual changes are shown on the graph of prime rate changes. The three shaded areas on the chart each represents one of the three investment climates. Notice that there are three places during the cycle where the shading changes. At each of these points you must move your money from one investment to another to maintain maximum safety and continued profits.

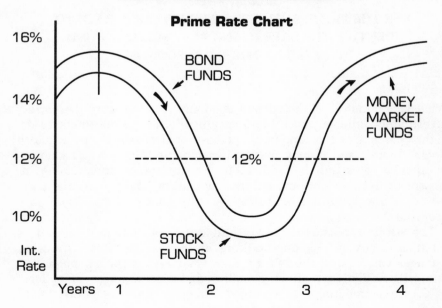

MONEY MOVEMENT STRATEGY

Strategy #264:

INVEST IN STOCK MUTUAL FUNDS ANY TIME THE PRIME RATE IS BELOW THE INVESTOR'S DECISION LINE.

There is always one of the three types of mutual funds — stock, bond, or money market — that will give you an average investment return of 20% per year or more. The prime rate indicates which one.

The points on the Money Movement Strategy Chart where the shading changes are the points at which you must move your money. Two of the three points are on the horizontal dotted line across the middle of the chart called the Investor's Decision Line (currently shown at 12%). The Investor's Decision Line does change, but only once every few years. The area below the Investor's Decision Line defines a bull market, a time when most stocks and stock mutual funds are on the rise. It is the point at which the big institutional investors get into the stock market, when the prime rate is dropping, and out of the stock market when the prime rate is rising. Currently over 80% of stocks are owned by just three groups of institutional investors: mutual funds, pension funds, and big corporations. When the big guys buy, stocks go up; when the big guys sell, stocks go down.

When is the correct time to invest in a stock mutual fund? Any time the prime rate is below the Investor's Decision Line. During those years, no matter how widely the Dow Jones or TSE stock averages fluctuate, the stock market and stock mutual funds will grow an average of 15-20% or more for the period. During this period there will be unpredictable corrections. The Money Movement Strategy allows you to react to these corrections logically rather than emotionally. (See Dow Corrections Chart on page 294.)

DOW CORRECTIONS SINCE 1982

The greatest stock market correction in history came as a shock to the world on October 19, 1987, when in the United States the Dow dropped 508 points. During a bull market, however, major corrections are a normal part of the cycle, not a cause for panic. Although big publicity has been attached to the correction of October 19, it is only one of six major corrections since 1982. Following are the others, which attracted far less attention.

DOW CORRECTIONS SINCE 1982

Year	Duration	Dow Begin	Dow End	% Drop
1982	Nov. 3 — Nov. 23	1065	991	7%
1984	Jan. 6 — July 24	1287	1087	16%
1986	July 2 — Aug. 1	1909	1764	8%
1987	Apr. 6 — May 20	2406	2216	8%
1987	Aug. 25 — Oct. 15	2722	2413	11%
1987	Oct. 19 — Oct. 19	2246	1738	23%

The important thing to remember is that during this same period the stock market overall achieved record growth. Within months after each correction there was a major gain in the Dow average. For example, by March 1988 the Dow had recovered 60% of what it lost on October 19, 1987.

In January 1985, following the Money Movement Strategy, the U.S. members of my organization were told: "The prime rate is below 9½% (the U.S. Investor's Decision Line), move your money to stock mutual funds." Those who did made an average of 40% in 1985, 30% in 1986, and an average of 3% in 1987 even with the biggest stock market drop in history. The total three-year return was 73%, or 24% per year. That's how the Money Movement Strategy will protect you and make you a wealthy investor.

Strategy #265:
MOVE YOUR MONEY TO A MONEY MARKET FUND WHEN THE PRIME RATE MOVES ABOVE THE INVESTOR'S DECISION LINE.

How do you know when a bull market is really over? When the prime rate is rising and reaches the Investor's Decision Line. At that time move your money out of stock mutual funds and into money market mutual funds. When the prime rate is above the horizontal Investor's Decision Line, money market funds will not only give you the best return but will also be the safest investment. Can you ever make money in a money market fund? Of course. In 1981, with the prime rate as high as 20%, money market funds were paying as much as 21% interest! Of course, when the prime rate is at 11% and you are in a money market fund, you are averaging only about 11% on your money, but you are protected from the coming bear market in stocks and the radical drops in bond prices.

Strategy #266:

MOVE YOUR MONEY TO A BOND FUND WHEN THE PRIME RATE IS HIGH AND COMING DOWN.

As long as the prime rate is over the Investor's Decision Line and moving up, stay in money market funds. When the prime rate changes direction and starts downward, move your money to the third and last investment in the prime rate cycle, a bond mutual fund.

Bond mutual funds are always the best investment when the prime rate is high and coming down. During that period you will earn two profits from bonds — interest and appreciation. The appreciation can be your big profit, averaging more than 20% per year.

There are two principles that guide this aspect of the Money Movement Strategy:

1. When the Prime Rate Drops 1%, Bonds Appreciate 10%.

Prime down "one," bonds and bond mutual funds up "ten." Ten to one is the best leverage you'll ever get in a safe investment plan. A good example was 1982, when the U.S. prime rate dropped 5%, from 16½% to 11½%, and the average U.S. bond mutual fund appreciated 40%.

Why are bonds and government securities a poor investment so much of the time? Because the opposite of the foregoing principle is also true.

2. When the Prime Rate Rises 1%, Bonds Depreciate 10%.

Prime up "one," bonds and bond mutual funds down "ten." Never invest in bonds or government securities when the prime rate is going up. Your principal may be decreasing faster than you are earning interest. Most financial salespeople will incorrectly tell you to hold onto 7% or 8% bonds even when principal is falling because "you haven't lost anything unless you sell and, after all, you are still getting the interest payments." You have lost. You've lost the opportunity to reinvest your money in bonds paying 12% to 13% when the prime rate eventually goes up. Your bond or bond fund value can drop as much as 50% as interest rates rise, locking you into unwanted low interest bonds. You could only sell at a big discount.

MONEY MOVEMENT STRATEGY SUMMARY

There is always one type of mutual fund in which you will earn an average of 15% to 20% or more over time; in 1981 it was money market funds, in 1982 and 1984 it was bond mutual funds. In 1983 and the average of 1985, 1986, 1987, and 1988, the right investment was stock mutual funds. In November of 1988, money market funds were the appropriate investments through June of 1989. Bond funds then became the right investment and remained so until March of 1991, when stock funds became the best investment choice. The Money Movement Strategy will always have you at the right place at the right time and overcome the problem of short-term market drops.

The Money Movement Strategy will produce the greatest profits when the prime rate is dropping, often 30% or more per year in stocks or bonds. When the prime rate is rising, Money Movement becomes more of a defensive strategy and profits are in the 10% to 15% range. During these periods consider discounted mortgages as your source of an up-to-20% return (Chapter 28).

The Money Movement Strategy is not intended to be a get-rich-quick scheme. It is a lifelong strategy for reducing risk and maximizing investment profits. The Money Movement Strategy will allow you to average 15% per year, year after year — without having to watch your money day by day. It is a winning mutual fund strategy for both conservative and aggressive investors.

There are three investments in which you can successfully use the Money Movement Strategy in mutual fund families. Two are tax shelters; all are covered in this book.

1. No-load mutual fund families — Chapter 24
2. Your RRSP Account — Chapter 13
3. Self-directed RRSP — Chapter 26

The following chart lists the Canadian prime rate history from October 1979 to May 1991. It also lists the correct investments (money market — MM; bond fund — BF; or stock fund — SF) during this period according to the Money Movement Strategy. If you had made these investments, you would have profited by an average of 20% per year.

CANADIAN PRIME RATE DIRECTION CHANGES
1978 TO 1991

DATE	FROM	TO	DIRECTION	#OF MOS.
Jan. 1978 to Apr. 1980	8.25%	16.75%	up	28
Apr . 1980 to Sep. 1980	16.75%	12.25%	down	5
Sep. 1980 to Aug. 1981	12.25%	22.75%	up	12
Aug. 1981 to May 1982	22.75%	17.00%	down	9
May 1982 to Jun. 1982	17.00%	18.25%	up	1
June 1982 to Feb. 1984	18.25%	11.00%	down	20
Feb. 1984 to July 1984	11.00%	13.50%	up	5
July 1984 to Jan. 1985	13.50%	11.00%	down	6
Jan. 1985 to Mar. 1985	11.00%	11.75%	up	2
Mar. 1985 to Dec. 1985	11.75%	10.00%	down	9
Dec. 1985 to Feb. 1986	10.00%	13.00%	up	2
Feb. 1986 to Mar. 1987	13.00%	8.75%	down	13
Mar. 1987 to Aug. 1987	8.75%	10.00%	up	6
Aug. 1987 to Mar. 1988	10.00%	9.75%	down	7
Mar. 1988 to July 1990	9.75%	14.75%	up	29
July 1990 to Feb. 1991	14.75%	11.25%	down	6

HISTORY OF CANADIAN CHARTERED BANK
PRIME BUSINESS LOAN INTEREST RATES

DATE	PRIME LENDING RATE	CORRECT INVESTMENT	DATE	PRIME LENDING RATE	CORRECT INVESTMENT
1979			July 14	13.00	BF
Oct. 29	15.00	MM	July 17	12.75	BF
			July 28	12.25	BF
1980			Oct. 3	13.00	MM
Mar. 14	15.75	MM	Oct. 10	12.75	MM
Mar. 29	16.50	MM	Nov. 3	13.25	MM
Apr. 3	17.50	MM	Nov. 10	13.75	MM
Apr. 18	17.25	BF	Nov. 28	14.50	MM
Apr. 28	16.75	BF	Dec. 5	15.50	MM
May 5	16.50	BF	Dec. 12	17.00	MM
May 12	15.75	BF	Dec. 19	18.25	MM
May 15	14.75	BF			
May 26	13.75	BF	1981		
June 23	13.25	BF	Mar. 23	17.75	MM

DATE	PRIME LENDING RATE	CORRECT INVESTMENT	DATE	PRIME LENDING RATE	CORRECT INVESTMENT
Apr. 20	18.25	MM	Oct. 26	12.50	BF
May 1	18.50	MM	Nov. 20	12.00	SF
May 8	19.50	MM	Dec. 7	11.75	SF
June 5	20.00	MM	Dec. 21	11.25	SF
July 24	21.00	MM			
July 31	21.75	MM	**1985**		
Aug. 7	22.75	MM	Jan. 11	11.00	SF
Sep. 8	22.25	MM	Feb. 22	11.50	SF
Sep. 15	21.75	MM	Mar. 8	11.75	SF
Sep. 21	21.25	MM	Mar. 29	11.25	SF
Oct. 13	20.50	BF	Apr. 12	11.00	SF
Oct. 19	20.00	BF	Apr. 19	10.75	SF
Nov. 9	19.50	BF	May 22	10.50	SF
Nov. 16	18.00	BF	Aug. 23	10.25	SF
Nov. 23	17.25	BF	Oct. 7	10.00	SF
1982			**1986**		
Jan. 4	16.50	BF	Jan. 7	10.50	SF
Mar. 26	17.00	BF	Jan. 14	11.00	SF
June 4	17.50	BF	Jan. 31	11.50	SF
June 18	18.25	BF	Feb. 7	12.25	MM
July 16	17.75	BF	Feb. 14	13.00	MM
July 23	17.25	BF	Mar. 14	12.50	BF
Aug. 6	17.00	BF	Mar. 21	12.00	SF
Aug. 20	16.00	BF	Apr. 7	11.75	SF
Sep. 3	15.50	BF	Apr. 11	11.25	SF
Sep. 24	15.00	BF	May 2	10.50	SF
Oct. 8	14.50	BF	May 16	10.25	SF
Oct. 15	13.75	BF	July 18	9.75	SF
Nov. 12	13.00	BF			
Dec. 17	12.50	BF	**1987**		
			Jan. 23	9.25	SF
1983			Mar. 13	8.75	SF
Jan. 7	12.00	BF	Apr. 24	9.25	SF
Feb. 18	11.50	SF	May 22	9.50	SF
Apr. 19	11.00	SF	July 31	10.00	SF
			Oct. 9	10.50	SF
1984			Oct. 23	9.75	SF
Mar. 23	11.50	SF			
May 9	12.00	SF	**1988**		
June 25	12.50	MM	Apr. 22	10.25	SF
June 29	13.00	MM	June 3	10.75	SF
July 6	13.50	MM	Aug. 26	11.25	SF
Aug. 10	13.00	MM	Sep. 16	11.75	SF

DATE	PRIME LENDING RATE	CORRECT INVESTMENT	DATE	LENDING RATE	CORRECT INVESTMENT
Dec. 9	12.25	MM	Aug. 17	14.25	MM
			Sep. 21	13.75	BF
1989			Nov. 23	13.25	BF
Feb. 17	12.75	MM	Dec. 21	12.75	BF
Mar. 23	13.50	MM			
			1991		
1990			Jan. 18	12.25	BF
Feb. 16	14.25	MM	Jan. 31	11.75	SF
Apr. 23	14.75	MM	Feb. 19	11.25	SF

Strategy #267:
INVEST IN U.S. EQUITIES THROUGH CANADIAN FUNDS.

One of the most obvious trends over the past few decades is that, regardless of the economy, U.S. equities tend to outperform Canadian equities by about 40% to 75%. For the Canadian investor, the disadvantages of investing in a U.S.-based fund are:

1. Business is being done with a foreign entity. Though the legal system in the two countries is similar, it is much easier to enforce your rights in the event of a problem with a Canadian company than a U.S. one.
2. Some U.S. toll-free numbers may not fully access all 10 Canadian provinces.
3. U.S. funds will expect to have their accounts settled in U.S. dollars. If you don't already maintain U.S. dollar holdings, you will find there is a hidden "fee" in converting funds back and forth from one currency to another — the so-called "bank spread," usually about 5% on each conversion.
4. U.S. funds are required by U.S. law to deduct some U.S. taxes at source when you settle your account. The Canada-U.S. treaty ensures you will get full credit for such withholdings on your own yearly tax return, however.
5. Canadians who hold U.S.-based funds may get entangled in U.S. estate tax laws if they allow such holdings to remain in their estates after death. This creates additional costs and complications for the heirs. (One method of circumventing this is to hold U.S. securities through a Canadian holding company. However, this means that the individual capital gains exemption is no longer available, and creates more accounting and reporting problems down the road.)

6. Canadian-based funds can "flow-through" the tax benefits of capital gains and dividends to unit holders.

Here are a number of no-load Canadian funds that hold primarily U.S.-based securities. Such funds show a history of strong returns:

	1 YR	2 YR	3 YR	5 YR	10 YR
Crown Life Pen U.S. Eqt	5.2	6.2	8.2	6.4	11.2
PH&N U.S.	19.9	19.2	15.7	7.4	13.9
Canada Trust					
American Equity	22.1	2.4	8.6	18.7	15.1
National Trust Pooled					
Non-Canadian	19.5	-1.5	7.1	18.7	15.5
Royal Trust Am. Stock	28.9	4.0	12.4	17.3	14.6

Chapter 24

MUTUAL FUND
WINNING
STRATEGIES

There are two times in a man's life when he should not speculate: when he can't afford it, and when he can.

Mark Twain, *Following the Equator*, 1897

Objective: Earn a safe 20% per year with no commissions in a liquid investment.

Strategy #268:
**USE THE MONEY MOVEMENT STRATEGY IN
NO-LOAD MUTUAL FUND FAMILIES.**

One of the easiest investments in which to apply the Money Movement Strategy is a no-load mutual fund family. A mutual fund is an investment company registered with a provincial securities commission in Canada or the S.E.C. (Securities and Exchange Commission) in the U.S. and managed by a professional fund manager. The mutual fund buys a portfolio of stocks, bonds, or money market instruments, and you, as an investor, own a share of the entire portfolio. Mutual funds are open-ended, that is, they can sell unlimited numbers of shares to new investors. The mutual fund promises to redeem shares upon notice at the current net asset value (NAV). A mutual fund family is a group of mutual funds all under the same management.

MUTUAL FUND DEFINITIONS

To profit from mutual fund investments, there are several terms and definitions you must understand. These are the mutual fund terms that allow you to manoeuvre your investment.

Account

Your investment arrangement and record with the mutual fund. Your account is initially the amount of your investment minus any front-end commissions. Your account increases in value when the fund's assets increase or when you invest more money. Your account decreases in value when the fund's assets decrease, you withdraw money, or the fund's management expense is deducted. You receive a periodic statement of your account.

Adviser

An organization or person employed and paid by the mutual fund to give professional investment advice to the fund.

Asked Price

The price at which you can buy shares in a mutual fund, also known as the offering price. This price is the current net asset value per share (NAV) plus any sales charge.

Bid Price

The price at which the mutual fund will buy back your shares. The bid, also called the redemption price, is the current net asset value per share (NAV). Back-end loads or commissions, if any, are subtracted from the total amount you receive when you sell.

Capital Gains or Losses

For most investors, your profit or loss from the sale of your mutual fund shares. Capital gains and losses may be created when investments are sold by either you or the mutual fund, or when you sell your shares in the fund or move to another fund. If your mutual fund is tax-sheltered — for example, if you hold it through an RRSP — tax will be deferred until you receive the money from your plan. If you are a "trader in securities," for example, by virtue of past history, knowledge, or otherwise, your profits from a mutual fund could result in income, rather than a capital gain.

Cash Position

The amount of the fund's assets that are not invested in stocks or bonds but are put in the bank or in short-term investments. If a stock fund manager thinks stocks may go down, he will sell stocks and maintain a bigger "cash position" with the intent of buying stocks at a reduced price later. If the stock goes up and the fund maintains a big cash position, it will be out-performed by those funds that stayed more "fully invested."

Certificate

The printed record showing ownership of mutual fund shares, similar to a stock certificate. Because of a unique computerized record of your account maintained by the fund, certificates are seldom issued unless the shares are going to be pledged for a loan or margin account.

In some cases, if you purchase your fund through your own broker, the fund will be registered to your broker and not you. Although this will not cost you any money directly, there are indirect costs. For example, you may be cut off from any newsletters, reports, or bulletins the fund issues. (If the fund has free switching privileges within its family, you may be cut off from this as well.)

Distributions

The payments to shareholders of capital gains or dividends in the form of cash or additional mutual fund shares.

Capital gains distributions are payments made to mutual fund investors representing profits earned by the fund when stocks or bonds are sold. These profits are generally paid at the shareholder's option, in cash or as additional shares or units in the fund. Capital gains are normally distributed once per year in the United States and either yearly or quarterly in Canada. Most Canadian mutual funds are eligible for special tax rules that allow the tax benefits of capital gains and dividends to be "passed out" to individual investors. Most U.S.-based mutual funds do not contain this feature; however, there are a number of Canadian-based mutual funds specializing in U.S. or other foreign investments which enjoy these tax benefits.

Although the total net asset value of the fund remains the same before and after a distribution, the per share NAV drops as more shares are issued to each shareholder representing the capital gains per share.

For example:

BEFORE DISTRIBUTION

1,000,000 shares at $11 per share = $11,000,000 net assets of fund

Capital gains distribution $1,000,000

AFTER DISTRIBUTION

1,100,000 shares at $10 per share = $11,000,000 net assets of fund

The total assets remain the same but the number of shares and the NAV per share change proportionately.

Dividend Distributions are the distribution of dividends and interest from investments to the mutual fund shareholders. The distribution methods are the same as with capital gains distributions.

The ex-dividend date is the date on which declared distributions are deducted from the fund's assets. On that day the share price drops but since each shareholder receives more shares, the amount in the shareholder's account remains the same.

Exchange Privilege

The right of a mutual fund shareholder to transfer his money from one fund to another within the same family. The two types of exchanging are:

1. Telephone or Wire Switching — Your money can be moved by a phone call or a telegram.
2. Mail Exchanging — You write to the fund to move your money.

An exchange is actually the sale of shares in one fund and the purchase of shares in another. The transaction is taxable unless your investment is protected by a tax shelter like an RRSP.

Management Company

The entity that manages the fund. Often a fund family will have different officials than those who actually manage the fund. The "advisor" described earlier gives investment advice; in Canada, the management company gives the advice and must be a registered advisor.

Net Assets

A mutual fund's total assets minus current liabilities.

Net Asset Value per Share (NAV)

The mutual fund's total assets minus current liabilities, divided by the number of shares outstanding.

Payroll Deduction Plan

A plan where mutual fund contributions are deducted from your paycheque and sent by your employer directly to the fund.

Performance

The percentage change in a fund's net asset value per share (NAV) over a period of time. Performance is a method of comparing different mutual funds.

Portfolio

All the securities owned by a mutual fund.

Portfolio Turnover

The percentage of a mutual fund's investments that were changed during the year (sold and the money reinvested). The total can be from 0 to over 100%. Most aggressive funds have higher portfolio turnovers.

Prospectus

The official brochure issued by a mutual fund that describes how the fund works, how it manages its money, the objectives of the fund, how you invest and withdraw your money, and how much the fund charges in fees and commissions. Much of the information is required by the Securities and Exchange Commission in the United States and the Provincial Securities Commission in Canada.

Reinvestment Privilege

The right of a mutual fund shareholder to have interest, dividends and capital gains automatically used to purchase additional shares of the fund.

In addition to these terms, you must know the three categories and many subcategories of mutual funds. Knowing the difference and when to use each is the basic secret of mutual fund investment success.

MUTUAL FUND CATEGORIES

All mutual funds fall into three basic categories:

1. Stock mutual funds
2. Bond mutual funds
3. Money market mutual funds

STOCK (EQUITY) MUTUAL FUNDS

A stock represents ownership of a portion of a company's assets. Individual stocks are bought and sold through stockbrokers who are connected by computer to the major exchanges, such as the New York or American Stock Exchanges. Stocks not listed on the exchanges are traded broker-to-broker through the National Association of Securities Dealers (NASD) in the United States or the Canadian Over-the-Counter Automatic Trading Systems (COATS) in Canada. The brokers receive commissions for handling investors' stock trades. The per share price of a company's stock increases or decreases based on supply and demand. If there are more buyers than sellers, the price goes up. If there are more sellers than buyers, the price drops.

A mutual fund that invests primarily in stocks is a stock or "equity" mutual fund. Stock mutual funds are classified into many sub-categories and are named by their investment objectives and the type of stocks in which they invest. Since few stock funds use the term "stock" in the fund name, you, as the investor, must understand the terms that identify a stock fund and its investment philosophy.

These are the most common sub-categories of the stock funds:

Growth Fund

A stock mutual fund that invests primarily in common stocks with good growth potential, as determined by the fund manager.

Aggressive Growth Fund

A stock mutual fund that uses aggressive and sometimes volatile techniques in an attempt to increase profits. These aggressive techniques include leverage, short selling, and buying warrants and options.

Growth and Income Funds/Dividend Income Funds

A stock fund that attempts to give investors capital growth and income at the same time. The fund invests in stocks that are lower in price so that the dividend yield is higher. Dividend yield is the amount of dividends paid per share divided by the price of one share. The lower the price, the higher the yield.

Equity Income Funds

Combination stock and bond funds that have a primary goal of income and a secondary goal of long-term growth. If you want to share in the growth of Canadian companies, these funds are a good choice. You may also invest in common stocks of foreign companies through equity funds.

The equity income funds perform well when the prime rate is dropping because both stocks and bonds are appreciating, and the stocks and bonds are earning interest and dividends. Equity income funds are poor performers when the prime rate is going up because any stock gains are automatically wiped out by bond losses.

SPECIALTY STOCK MUTUAL FUNDS

Specialty stock mutual funds buy stock using a special selection process, leverage, or other type of investment formula not used by the regular stock funds, and are generally for only more knowledgeable and speculative investors. The following is a description of major categories of specialty stock funds.

Option Fund

A mutual fund that buys stock options instead of stocks. An option is the right to buy or sell a specific number of shares of a stock at a fixed price by a specific date. Some option funds buy stocks and then attempt to hedge against a price drop by purchasing "puts" or options to sell on the same stock. Option funds have not been particularly successful during the past ten years and should be avoided.

Index Fund

A mutual fund that theoretically owns all of the stocks in the Standard and Poor's 500 or other index, for example, the Toronto Stock Exchange 300 Composite Index. The growth, therefore, is the same as that of the index. For example, the Toronto Dominion Bank offers both a U.S. and a Canadian "pure" index fund. During the past five years, the S&P 500 average has outperformed the average growth and aggressive growth mutual funds. Investors who guess at which mutual funds will be good performers will generally earn less than an index fund. Investors who use knowledge and good mutual fund advice like that in this book will nearly always outperform the S&P 500 and the index funds.

Balanced Fund

These mutual funds invest in a combination of stocks, bonds, and preferred stocks and violate the rule: "Every economy has one best investment." Knowledgeable investors avoid the overdiversified balanced funds, which are big losers when interest rates are rising.

Closed-end Fund

Sometimes called investment trusts in the United States, closed-end funds issue a fixed number of shares and are publicly traded on the stock exchanges. These closed-end funds in Canada are set up as corporations. Unlike the open-ended funds, which are the more familiar mutual funds, closed-end funds do not issue or redeem shares from investors. The current share price of a closed-end fund is not the NAV (net asset value per share), but a price based on supply and demand. Poor overall performance is the best reason to avoid the closed-end funds.

Social Conscience Fund/Ethical Fund

There are two no-load funds that invest in stock of companies organized for social good, or that seek to avoid companies involved in war materials, liquor, tobacco, gambling, or South Africa. Two such U.S stock funds are PAX World Fund and Dreyfus Third Century. These funds have had an average to poor track record and should be used only by those whose social consciences match the objectives of the funds.

Industry Fund

Funds that purchase stocks related to only one industry are called industry funds. Some industry funds, like the health funds, have been great performers because of the overall growth or profits of that single industry. Others, like the high-tech funds, have been at times the big losers.

Industries represented by industry funds include: high-tech, computer software, drugs, computers, biotech, health, chemicals, energy, financial, housing, leisure, defence, restaurants, life insurance, automotive, paper, broadcast media, banking, air transport, and industrial materials.

Sector Fund

When you put several industry funds under one mutual fund family and allow switching between these as well as money market funds, you have sector funds. Sector fund investing allows the choosing of more specific stocks with the safety of diversification. In the United States, the Fidelity family has 35 sector funds called "Select" funds, and Vanguard has five sector funds it calls "Special" funds. Sector funds are good choices for aggressive investors.

Emerging Company Growth Fund

Stock funds that buy shares in new companies with good future potential. These funds are volatile and far riskier than regular stock funds because of the unpredictability of small-company performance, and should be avoided by conservative investors.

Precious Metal Fund

These funds buy the stocks of mining companies involved in the extraction of gold, silver, platinum, and other precious metals. They are volatile funds and should be used only by more aggressive investors. Overall, the performance of the gold funds has been greater than the growth or aggressive growth stock funds even with some bad years. The increase or decrease in value of precious metal funds follows the market price of the metals and not the prime rate, and makes these funds unpredictable. Invest in precious metal funds only with good, dependable advice.

Multi-Fund

A multi-fund is a mutual fund that invests in shares of other mutual funds. An example is the U.S.-based Vanguard's Star Fund, which invests in other Vanguard stock, bond, and money market funds. These funds have a poor track record because of overdiversification. Multi-funds are sometimes classified as "balanced funds," discussed earlier.

Multi-funds have become popular recently in Canada because they are being offered on a "no-load" basis by load mutual fund families.

These versions do have back-end loads to the investor and the investor pays again when the multi-fund buys shares of a load fund. "Popular" does not make an investment any better.

BOND MUTUAL FUNDS

A bond investment represents a loan made by an investor to a corporation or government agency for a term ranging from one to 30 years. Bonds normally pay guaranteed interest rates like certificates of deposit, but unlike CDs, bond values go up and down daily due to changes in marketplace interest rates. A bond may sell at a premium (more than its face value) or at a discount (less than its face value). At the end of the term, the issuer guarantees to pay the investor the face value of the bond.

A mutual fund that invests primarily in bonds is a bond mutual fund. These can be classified into several subcategories:

High-Yield Fund

A bond fund investing in corporate bonds with supposedly higher than usual interest rates and often lower than usual ratings.

Fixed-Income Funds

A bond fund that invests most of its assets in long-term bonds.

MONEY MARKET MUTUAL FUNDS

Money market funds are mutual funds that invest in short-term, supersafe, interest-bearing instruments. The maturity date of these securities is between one day and one year. The interest paid to a money market fund is then divided up as dividends to investors and is a composite of all the earnings on the money market instruments held by the fund. Money market rates in the past few years have ranged from a low of 6% to a high of over 20% annually. Money market funds are good investments when interest rates are over 10% and on the rise and poor investments when interest rates are less or coming down.

Money market funds are not the same as money market accounts available at banks. Money market account is a fancy name for bank savings plans that pay variable instead of fixed interest. The banks use the name in an effort to confuse investors and to lure money away from the money market funds. Money market accounts pay an average of 3% less per year than money market funds.

Money market funds were originally created in 1972 in the United States with the birth of the Reserve Fund. The objective was to offer small investors the opportunity to get better-than-bank rates on money market instruments, formerly available only to investors with $100,000 or more. In 1974 the Fidelity Daily Income Trust, also in the United States, pioneered the concept of cheque-writing in a money market fund. Many money market funds now allow you to write up to three cheques per month, with a $250 to $500 minimum.

The per-share value of a money market fund is always $1 in U.S. funds and $10 in Canadian funds. Your principal value does not increase or decrease. The dividends earned by your shares are added to your account as additional $1 shares in U.S. funds or $10 shares in Canadian funds. Newspapers quote money market funds in terms annualized by daily interest paid.

Money market funds have been created both by mutual fund families and stock brokerage firms. The following descriptions centre on those no-load money market funds that are part of mutual fund families.

Regular Money Market Funds

Invest in:

1. **Government Securities**. Short-term debt instruments issued by government agencies.
2. **Bank Jumbo Certificates of Deposit.** Loans of $1,000,000 or more made to banks.
3. **Bankers' Acceptances.** Short-term bank guarantees designed to finance imports and exports. The importer does not want to pay a foreign company until goods are received. An exporter does not want to ship the goods until he is guaranteed he will receive his money when the goods are delivered. Bankers' acceptances are the guarantees and are risk-free.
4. **Commercial Paper.** Unsecured, but virtually risk-free, short-term notes issued by large credit-worthy corporations and finance companies. Maturity dates are up to nine months.
5. **Re-purchase Agreements**. A security sold by a brokerage firm to finance its transactions with a written guarantee to re-purchase the security on a specific date, at the same price, plus interest. Re-purchase agreements have a maturity of less than one week.

Asset Management Accounts

The natural outgrowth of money market funds are the asset management accounts, which have unlimited chequing and offer other financial services such as "debit cards."

As explained in Chapter 22, Canadians are generally free to trade in either U.S. or Canadian funds as they choose.

The best reporting on mutual fund performance in Canada is done by the Southam Corporation through a report called *The Mutual Fund Sourcebook*. Portions of the report appear every third week in the *Financial Times* and contain all mutual funds, not just the ones that are members of the Investment Funds Institute of Canada that are shown in the *Financial Post*. The sourcebook has broken down all the Canadian funds into the following specific categories:

1.) Balanced — Funds that invest in a mix of both equity and debt instruments.

2.) Bond — Funds that invest almost exclusively in bonds.

3.) Bond/mortgage — Funds that invest almost exclusively in a mix of bonds and mortgages.

4.) Canadian equity — Funds that are almost exclusively invested in Canadian equities.

5.) International equity — Funds that are almost exclusively invested in non-Canadian equities. This may or may not include some U.S. equities as part of the mix.

6.) Money market — Funds that invest exclusively in short-term debt instruments such as Treasury bills, certificates of deposit, bankers' acceptances, etc.

7.) Mortgage — Funds that invest almost exclusively in mortgages.

8.) Preferred dividend — Funds that invest almost exclusively in preferred shares.

9.) Real estate — Funds that invest exclusively in income-producing real estate properties.

10.) Specialty equity — Funds that are invested in a particular market segment or have an equity investment philosophy that sets unique investment restrictions on fund managers. Examples of the former would be gold funds or natural resource funds. Examples of the latter would be option equity funds or funds that restrict investment to stocks with small capitalizations ("small cap" funds).

11.) U.S. equity — Funds that invest almost exclusively in U.S. equities.

Now that you have an overall picture of the diversity of mutual funds available, let's look at the strategies that will put these funds to work for you.

Strategy #269:
INVEST ONLY IN FUNDS THAT HAVE MORE THAN
$25 MILLION AND LESS THAN $3 BILLION IN ASSETS.

The size of a mutual fund should be considered in your investment strategy. If a fund has under $25 million in assets there is a good chance it cannot afford to hire or keep the best of the fund managers. You do not want your capital used to provide the training ground for a new fund manager.

Getting too big also has a downside. If a stock mutual fund has over $3 billion in assets, it loses flexibility. Much of the success of a stock fund in beating the stock indices is created by portfolio turnover — moving money in and out of cash positions in anticipation of market drops or gains. A fund manager can't move money fast enough if the fund is too large.

Big mutual funds have an option. They can close the existing fund to new investors and start a new one with new management but an identical investment philosophy.

Strategy #270:
INVEST IN GOOD PERFORMING NO-LOAD FUNDS
WITH TELEPHONE SWITCHING.

Choosing the right fund and fund family is easy once you know what you are looking for. All the information you need is at the end of this chapter. Following is a step-by-step process for choosing your mutual fund:

1. Choose for convenience a fund that is part of a family with at least one:
   A. Stock fund

B. Bond fund

C. Money market fund

2. Choose a no-load or low-load fund. Check for exit fees and early withdrawal fees.

3. Choose a mutual fund that has a minimum required initial deposit within your investing limits.

4. Choose the right type of mutual fund for the current economy by using the Money Movement Strategy (Chapter 23).

5. Choose a fund with assets of more than $25 million, less than $3 billion.

6. Choose a fund based on its track record for the type of economy in which you intend to use it, not its five-year or ten-year total performance record.

7. If you want income, choose a fund that offers a periodic withdrawal plan. All types of funds have periodic withdrawal plans.

8. If your account is an RRSP, make sure the fund you choose qualifies.

Check the Fund Family Fact Sheets for minimum required investment and yearly fee.

Strategy #271:

USE THE FUND FAMILY FACT SHEETS TO CHOOSE THE BEST FUND AND FUND FAMILY FOR YOU.

From the Fund Family Fact Sheets at the end of this chapter, choose two or three mutual fund families that meet the above criteria and your own special needs and objectives. There is no one right choice, so don't waste time trying to find it.

Call the mutual fund family's number and request a prospectus for each fund by name. Most of the recommended fund families have toll-free numbers (shown in the Top 25 Mutual Funds list at the end of this chapter). The prospectus will tell you everything about the fund, including the investments owned. It is not necessary to read through all the required technical gibberish, but read carefully the instructions pertaining to investing, moving, and withdrawing your money. To save you countless hours of researching the mutual fund families, you will find all of this information in the Mutual Fund Family Fact Sheets. To open an account, complete and send the application with your cheque to the address listed in the prospectus. Specify by name the fund in which you want your money initially invested.

Although past performance is no guarantee of future performance, a mutual fund's track record should be an important factor in your choice. Use the performance histories in the Mutual Fund Family Fact Sheets along with the Prime Rate Direction Changes chart in Chapter 23 to compare fund performance. For instance, if you want to know what would have happened to the value of your shares in any fund during 1985 and 1986, first determine where your money should have been invested according to the Prime Rate History chart in Chapter 23. Both were years of declining interest rates and a time for stocks, so you would check only stock fund performance. The Canadian prime rate fell from a high of 11.5% to a low of 9.7% during 1985 and to 8.3% by December 1986. As you might expect from your understanding of the Money Movement Strategy, one of the greatest surges in stock market history began and lasted until October 1987. When the smoke cleared, recommended stock funds appreciated approximately 40% in 1985, 30% in 1986, and about 3% in 1987, even after the stock market drop of October 19.

Strategy #272:
LEARN TO TRACK BOTH CANADIAN AND U.S. MUTUAL FUNDS TO FIND THE BEST OPPORTUNITIES.

You will want to learn to read the mutual fund performance for both Canadian and U.S. mutual funds in order to always have the option of the best alternatives.

The current value in dollars of one share of a mutual fund is known as its net asset value per share (NAV). You have daily access to the net asset value of any fund through the financial pages of major newspapers. The NAV is listed under "Mutual Funds" near the stock market quotes. The mutual funds are listed by family. For example, all of Value Line's funds are listed together alphabetically under "V," all of the Fidelity funds are listed alphabetically under "F."

To read current U.S. mutual fund quotes, look to the right of the fund name and you'll find two price columns. Load funds will have a price in both columns. The higher figure is the price at which you could purchase one share, the lower figure represents the price at which you could sell one share. The difference between the two prices represents the commission charged by loaded funds. If the commission is 8%, there will be an 8% difference between the two prices. No-load funds have no commissions and only one column will show a price. The other column will contain a dash (–) or "N.L." (no-load).

The process for Canadian funds is even simpler. Only the daily closing NAV is shown. The salesman and investor negotiate any commissions separately. You will also find some funds whose NAV is quoted weekly or monthly rather than daily. If you purchased your shares at $10 each (100 shares for each $1,000 you invested), and the share price increased over the next six months to $12 per share, you have made a 20% profit on your money. When dividends are earned for one or more stocks in your stock fund, or interest is earned and re-invested in a bond fund, you will be credited with more shares unless you request a cash distribution.

Make note of how many shares you receive when you first invest. Even if it appears you have made only 10% on your money from the price change alone, you may discover that you now have 15% more shares and have actually earned 25% total return. The current net asset value per share (NAV) is not enough information to determine your profit or loss. Profits from capital gains distributions, dividends, and interest are usually given to investors as additional shares. On the distribution dates, the number of shares owned by each investor will increase, but if you look at NAV per share alone, your profit from distributions will not be reflected. To find the true value of your investment, multiply the number of shares shown on your last statement by the current NAV and compare to the amount of money you originally invested. On many statements, the total current value of your account is shown.

Each month, you will receive a complete statement showing your status in the fund at the end of the previous month. The statement is easy to use, easy to follow, and is one major benefit of investing through a mutual fund family.

A no-load mutual fund family investment is a must investment for everyone. Get yours started or reorganized today.

TOP 25 MUTUAL FUNDS
(ANNUALIZED 5-YEAR RETURN, FOR YEAR ENDING DECEMBER 31, 1990)

1. Imperial Growth Equity	15.1
2. Universal Pacific	14.0
3. Bullock American	13.7
4. Counsel Real Estate	12.5
5. AGF Japan	12.3

6. Cambridge Growth   11.7
7. MD Realty A   11.7
8. First City RealFund   11.4
9. MD Realty B   11.3
10. Elliott & Page Money   10.6
11. Investors Japanese Growth   10.5
12. Investors Pooled Mortgage   10.5
13. Guardian Short Term Money   10.4
14. Allied Income   10.3
15. First Canadian Mortgage   10.3
16. Bolton Tremblay Money   10.2
17. Green Line Mortgage   10.2
18. PH & N Bond   10.2
19. Viking Money Market   10.2
20. Altamira Income   10.1
21. Crown Life Pen Short   10.1
22. Industrial Cash Management   10.1
23. CDA RSP Money Market   10.0
24. Investors Trust Bond   10.0
25. AGF Money Market   9.9

MUTUAL FUND FAMILY FACT SHEETS

CIBC SECURITIES, INC.

Toronto Mutual Funds Centre
P.O. Box 51
Commerce Court Postal Station
Toronto, Ontario M5L 1A2

In Toronto: 980-FUND
In Vancouver: 685-FUND
In Montreal: 866-FUND
In Regina: 757-FUND

In Calgary: 261-FUND
Toll Free: (800)-465-FUND
Fax: (416) 362-1967

Name	Type	Eligible for RRSP	Assets	Front	Back	1 Yr.	2 Yr.	3 Yr.	5 Yr.	10 Yr.	Minimum Initial Investment	Additional Investment
Balance Income & Growth	BAL	Y	58.0	0.0	0.0	11.8	9.1	9.8	NA	NA	500	50
Canadian Equity	CDN	Y	32.0	0.0	0.0	2.5	5.6	NA	NA	NA	50	50
Canadian T-Bill	MM	Y	185.0	0.0	0.0	NA	NA	NA	NA	NA	3,500	500
Fixed Income	BND	Y	31.1	0.0	0.0	18.9	11.5	9.5	NA	NA	500	50
Money Market	MM	Y	857.3	0.0	0.0	12.2	12.2	NA	NA	NA	3,500	500
Mortgage Investment	MOR	Y	120.3	0.0	0.0	14.7	12.8	9.5	10.1	11.7	500	50

FUTURLINK

Central Guaranty Trust Co.
Funds Services
Toronto, Ontario N5G 2C2
The Atrium on Bay, Tower C

(416) 345-5911
Fax: (416) 345-4906

Name	Type	Eligible for RRSP	Assets	Front	Back	1 Yr.	2 Yr.	3 Yr.	5 Yr.	10 Yr.	Minimum Initial Investment	Additional Investment
Canadian Growth	CDN	Y	124.7	0.0	0.0	1.7	3.9	6.4	NA	NA	500	25
Government Bond	BND	Y	36.2	0.0	0.0	17.5	9.8	8.6	NA	NA	500	25
Money Market	MM	Y	267.2	0.0	0.0	12.2	12.0	NA	NA	NA	1,000	500

GREAT WEST LIFE ASSURANCE CO.

Great West Life Assurance Co.
100 Osborne Street, N.
Winnipeg, Manitoba R3C 3A5

(204) 946-1190
Fax: (204) 946-8622
Toll Free: (800) 665-0551

Name	Type	Eligible for RRSP	Assets	Front	Back	1 Yr.	2 Yr.	3 Yr.	5 Yr.	10 Yr.	Minimum Initial Investment	Additional Investment
Bond	BND	Y	289.1	0.0	0.0	18.1	10.4	8.5	7.8	11.1	1,000	0[1]
Diver RS	BAL	Y	45.3	0.0	0.0	9.0	7.6	7.4	6.8	NA	1,000	50[1]
Equity Index	CDN	Y	201.4	0.0	0.0	-1.9	0.8	3.7	4.4	NA	1,000	50[1]
Equity Invest	CDN	Y	123.5	0.0	0.0	2.4	5.1	5.7	NA	NA	1,000	50[1]
Money Market	MM	Y	159.8	0.0	0.0	12.0	11.8	10.9	9.5	10.7	1,000	1,000[1]
Mortgage	MOR	Y	302.4	0.0	0.0	15.7	11.5	9.2	8.7	11.2	1,000	1,000[1]
Real Estate	RE	Y	325.7	0.0	0.0	-3.7	4.0	6.0	7.3	8.4	1,000	1,000[1]

1 – With autotransfer

MARITIME LIFE ASSURANCE COMPANY

Maritime Life Assurance Company
2701 Dutch Village Road
Halifax, Nova Scotia

(902) 453-4300
Fax: (902) 453-7041

Name	Type	Eligible for RRSP	Assets	Front	Back	1 Yr.	2 Yr.	3 Yr.	5 Yr.	10 Yr.	Minimum Initial Investment	Additional Investment
Balanced	BAL	Y	62.1	0.0	0.0	12.7	8.0	8.0	NA	NA	Varies	500[2]
Bond	BND	Y	26.0	0.0	0.0	18.9	NA	NA	NA	NA	Varies	500
Growth	CDN	Y	165.6	0.0	0.0	-0.6	1.2	3.6	3.2	7.7	Varies	500
Money Market	MM	Y	46.3	0.0	0.0	11.4	11.0	10.2	9.1	NA	NA (Varies)	500

2 – Minimum investment of $500 under the Capital Accumulation Plan (CAP).

MD MANAGEMENT LTD.

MD Management Ltd.
1867 Alta Vista Drive
Ottawa, Ontario K1G 3Y6

(613) 731-4552
Toll Free: (800) 267-4022
Fax: (613) 526-1352

Name	Type	Eligible for RRSP	Assets	Front	Back	1 Yr.	2 Yr.	3 Yr.	5 Yr.	10 Yr.	Minimum Initial Investment	Additional Investment
Bond Fund	BND	Y	299.4	0.0	0.0	18.1	11.7	NA	NA	NA	None	500
Equity Fund	CDN	Y	1059.7	0.0	0.0	0.1	2.1	5.8	7.8	12.7	None	500
Growth Investments	INTL	N	794.4	0.0	0.0	-2.7	1.5	5.2	6.3	14.2	3,000	None
Money Fund	MM	Y	212.7	0.0	0.0	12.1	11.5	10.5	9.4	10.6	None	None
Realty A	RE	Y	250.1	0.0	0.0	2.8	8.8	10.8	11.5	NA	None	None
Realty B	RE	N	160.0	0.0	0.0	2.4	8.5	10.6	11.1	NA	3,000	3,000

MONTREAL TRUST COMPANY

Montreal Trust Company
Place Montreal Trust
1800 McGill College Avenue
Montreal, Quebec H3A 3K9

(514) 982-7000
Fax: (514) 982-7069

Name	Type	Eligible for RRSP	Assets	Front	Back	1 Yr.	2 Yr.	3 Yr.	5 Yr.	10 Yr.	Minimum Initial Investment	Additional Investment
Money Market	MM	Y	39.4	0.0	0.0	12.1	11.9	11.2	NA	NA	10 Units	No Minimum
RRSP Equity	CDN	Y	63.9	0.0	0.0	2.9	5.5	5.3	6.1	7.8	230	25
RRSP Income	BND	Y	59.4	0.0	0.0	16.9	10.3	8.2	8.5	12.5	180	25
RRSP Money Market	MM	Y	38.2	0.0	0.0	12.3	11.9	11.0	NA	NA	10 Units	No Additional
RRSP MOR	MOR	Y	49.1	0.0	0.0	13.6	11.6	9.9	9.7	11.6	520	25

PHILLIPS, HAGER & NORTH, LTD.

Phillips, Hager & North, Ltd.
1700-1055 West Hastings Street
Vancouver, British Columbia U6E 2H3

(604) 684-4361
Toll Free: (800) 661-6141
Fax: (604) 684-5120

Name	Type	Eligible for RRSP	Assets	Front	Back	1 Yr.	2 Yr.	3 Yr.	5 Yr.	10 Yr.	Minimum Initial Investment	Additional Investment
Balanced	BAL	N	64.7	0.0	0.0	13.8	11.4	NA	NA	NA	3,500	1,000
Bond	BND	Y	161.2	0.0	0.0	18.8	12.5	10.8	10.2	13.9	3,500	1,000
Canadian	CDN	Y	52.3	0.0	0.0	4.7	8.2	9.6	8.2	10.1	3,500	1,000
Money Market	MM	Y	120.9	NA	0.0	12.8	12.6	11.5	NA	NA	10,000	2,000
Pooled Pension	CDN	Y	73.5	NA	NA	5.0	6.6	8.2	7.4	10.0	Corp. only	Corp. only
RSP/RIF Equity	CDN	Y	26.1	0.0	0.0	4.9	8.6	9.8	7.5	9.9	3,500	1,000
U.S.	US	N	70.6	0.0	0.0	19.9	19.2	15.7	7.4	13.9	3,500	1,000
U.S. Pooled Pension	US	Y	230.0	NA	NA	21.2	20.5	16.8	8.5	15.4	Corp. only	Corp. only

ROYAL TRUST COMPANY

Royal Trust Company
Suite 3900, Royal Trust Tower
Toronto-Dominion Centre
Toronto, Ontario M5W 1P9

Toll Free: (800) 463-3863
Fax: (514) 876-2762

Name	Type	Eligible for RRSP	Assets	Front	Back	1 Yr.	2 Yr.	3 Yr.	5 Yr.	10 Yr.	Minimum Initial Investment	Additional Investment
Adv. Balanced	BAL	Y	128.7	0.0	0.0	11.1	9.4	10.4	NA	NA	500	25
Adv. Income	BAL	Y	72.1	0.0	0.0	13.6	10.6	9.3	NA	NA	500	25
American Stock	US	N	50.1	0.0	0.0	15.7	17.8	14.6	7.9	10.5	500	25

ROYAL TRUST COMPANY (CONTINUED)

Name	Type	Eligible for RRSP	Assets	Front	Back	1 Yr.	2 Yr.	3 Yr.	5 Yr.	10 Yr.	Minimum Initial Investment	Additional Investment
Bond	BND	Y	408.1	0.0	0.0	18.5	11.5	9.3	8.3	12.7	500	25
Canadian Stock	CDN	Y	230.4	0.0	0.0	1.7	2.1	5.6	4.5	6.3	500	25
Canadian Money Market	MM	Y	945.7	0.0	0.0	11.9	11.6	10.7	NA	NA	5,000	1,000
Energy	SPEC	Y	26.7	0.0	0.0	-5.8	7.4	3.6	9.4	-0.1	5,000	1,000
Mortgage	MOR	Y	901.3	0.0	0.0	14.3	12.6	10.2	10.3	12.3	5,000	1,000
U.S. Money Market	MM	N	116.8	0.0	0.0	NA	NA	NA	NA	NA	250	25[4]

4 - U.S. Dollars

ROYAL BANK OF CANADA

Royal Bank of Canada
4th Floor, North Tower
Royal Bank Plaza
Toronto, Ontario M5J 2J2

(416) 974-0616
FAX (416) 974-4076

Name	Type	Eligible for RRSP	Assets	Front	Back	1 Yr.	2 Yr.	3 Yr.	5 Yr.	10 Yr.	Minimum Initial Investment	Additional Investment
RoyFund Balanced	BAL	Y	66.7	0.0	0.0	6.7	7.1	7.2	NA	NA	100	15
RoyFund Bond	BND	Y	223.2	0.0	0.0	18.0	11.2	9.0	8.2	11.0	100	15
RoyFund Equity	CDN	Y	686.0	0.0	0.0	-6.4	-0.2	2.0	2.7	7.3	100	15
RoyFund Money Market	MM	Y	353.1	0.0	0.0	12.4	12.1	11.1	NA	NA	5,000	15

Chapter 25

BUILDING BIG PROFITS
WITH MARGIN ACCOUNTS

How I made my fortune? It was really quite simple. I bought an apple for five cents, spent the evening polishing it, and sold it the next day for 10 cents. With this I bought two apples, spent the evening polishing them, and sold them for 20 cents. And so it went until I had amassed $1.60. It was then that my wife's father died and left us a million dollars.

Anonymous capitalist

Objective: Use OPM (other people's money) to increase the earning power of mutual funds.

One of the most powerful uses of credit is to borrow money at a low interest rate and invest at a higher rate. The difference between the cost of the money and your investment return is your profit. Most businesses, investment fortunes, and even countries have been developed on borrowed money, and yet investing with borrowed money, or leverage, is still a foreign concept to most Canadians. If your objective is to build wealth in the shortest possible time, with the least effort and greatest return, then investing borrowed money is a must.

> *Strategy #273:*
> **MARGIN MUTUAL FUND SHARES TO INCREASE
> YOUR INVESTMENT CAPITAL.**

Mutual fund margin accounts should be considered by every investor wishing to maximize profits in a minimum amount of time. Used correctly, they are one of the safest wealth-building accelerators.

A margin account is a line of credit with a broker, bank, or trust company that allows you to borrow money for investing or other purposes using your existing investments — stocks, bonds, or mutual fund shares — as collateral. A mutual fund margin account allows you to increase your mutual fund shares with borrowed money.

How do margin accounts work? You can borrow up to 50% of the current market value of your investments. If your shares of stocks, bonds, or mutual funds decrease in value past the minimum 50% margin requirement — the amount of collateral you must maintain on your loan — you will receive a "margin call" requiring you to put up more collateral, which could be more securities or cash.

Following this strategy, you will borrow against your existing mutual fund shares and buy more shares in the same or other funds. Reinvesting money borrowed from a margin account in this manner is far less risky than reinvesting in stocks directly. On the average, a mutual fund will drop no more than 10% even during downward cycles.

The average stock mutual fund in the United States, during the worst stock market drop in history (October 1987), dropped only 16%. In Canada, reinvesting borrowed money in stock or bond mutual funds gives you the upside profit potential of 12% to 20% per year without the risk of individual stocks or bonds. The interest rate you pay on a margin account at a brokerage firm is the broker's loan rate, which is only 1% or 2% above the prime rate. If the margin account interest rate is 10% and you are earning an average of 15% per year in your mutual fund family, your net profit is 5% after paying the interest on the borrowed money. Your interest on the margin account should be tax deductible. One thing you should be careful of, though, is the fact that interest deductions may increase your "investment loss" account. As you'll see in the next chapter, this may interfere with your ability to claim tax-exempt capital gains. You do not have to repay the principal or interest as long as the market value of your pledged shares is within the margin limits. Interest is generally charged to your account and compounded monthly.

MUTUAL FUND MARGIN ACCOUNT DEFINITIONS

Current Market Value (CMV): represents the total value of the securities held in the account on a given day based on the amount of cash that would be credited to the account if all the securities were sold.

Borrowed Capital (BC): represents the amount borrowed to make purchases either in or out of the margin account. Borrowed capital also includes accrued interest.

Equity (EQ): represents actual net value of the margin account, taking into account the amount owed to the brokerage firm. EQ=(CMV – BC).

Margin Call: is a brokerage firm's or bank's legal demand that a margin account holder deposit more cash, or sell a portion of the portfolio.

Strategy #274:
USE A MUTUAL FUND MARGIN ACCOUNT TO FREE UP CAPITAL FOR OTHER INVESTMENTS.

You can transfer your mutual fund shares into a margin account where you can borrow up to 50% of the market value of your shares (depending on current stock exchange margin regulation or your bank's internal margining policy). For example, if you own 1,000 shares of a mutual fund whose NAV (net asset value per share) is $10 per share, the market value of your shares is $10,000. You may borrow up to $5,000 to buy more shares of the same or a different fund.

If you own shares of a mutual fund and want to use the shares as collateral for a personal loan for purposes other than buying investments, you may borrow up to the same 50% of the market value of your existing shares.

You cannot open a mutual fund margin account with a mutual fund directly, but you can through most brokerage firms, including discount brokerage firms, and most banks or trust companies. As mentioned before, holding mutual funds through a broker may have hidden costs, however — such as the loss of free switching or true "no-load" purchasing.

COMPARING INVESTMENTS WITH AND WITHOUT THE MARGIN ACCOUNT

EXAMPLE 1: You own or buy $10,000 worth of shares in a stock mutual fund. The collateral value of your shares is 50% of market value once they have been transferred into a margin account. You now buy an additional $5,000 worth of mutual fund shares. During the year, the fund's shares do very well and increase in value by 20%. What is your profit with and without the margin account if the broker's margin account interest is 10%?

WITH MARGIN ACCOUNT		WITHOUT MARGIN ACCOUNT	
ORIGINAL SHARES	$10,000	ORIGINAL SHARES	$10,000
FINANCED SHARES	$ 5,000	FINANCED SHARES	$ 0
TOTAL INVESTMENT	$15,000	TOTAL INVESTMENT	$10,000
20% PROFIT	3,000	20% PROFIT	$ 2,000
MINUS 10% INTEREST	— 500	INTEREST	$ 0
NET PROFIT	$ 2,500	NET PROFIT	$ 2,000
PROFIT PERCENTAGE	25%	PROFIT PERCENTAGE	20%

The profit in both cases is calculated on your original $10,000 cash investment. Using the mutual fund margin account, you have increased your net profit to 25% in a mutual fund that returned only 20%. You earned an additional $500 or 25% profit (5% + 20%) on your $10,000 investment. The interest you pay can be claimed as a tax deduction.

EXAMPLE 2: Let's say you own the same $10,000 in shares during the same time period, but instead borrowed 50% of the value to buy a piece of rental real estate. You borrowed $5,000 and used the money for the down payment and closing costs on a real estate investment property you purchased for $80,000. Tax savings from depreciation on the building (80% of the cost of the real estate investment) are calculated using the 4% per year CCA rate (subject to the "half-year" rule) for a person in the 40% combined federal and provincial tax bracket (federal and provincial surtaxes are ignored). Appreciation is calculated at 5% for the year. The appreciation of the mutual fund shares is assumed to be 20%. Assume rental income is sufficient to pay the mortgage and provide for expenses, including CCA. You cannot claim the CCA when there is income enough to cover it.

MUTUAL FUND PROFITS

Total Investment	$10,000
	× .20
20% Profit	$ 2,000

REAL ESTATE PROFITS — $80,000 PROPERTY

Your Own Investment	0
Borrowed Money Invested	$ 5,000
Total Investment	$ 5,000

Tax Savings — Depreciation	$ 512
Appreciation (5%)	$ <u>4,000</u>
Real Estate Profit	$ 4,512

COMBINED PROFITS AND COSTS

Profit — Mutual Fund	$ 2,000
Profit — Real Estate	$ 4,512
Minus: Margin Interest 10%	$ <u>−500</u>
Net Profit	$6,012
Profit Percentage	60%

Upon the sale or other transfer of the real estate, tax will be payable in respect of its appreciation in value.

By using borrowed money from your mutual fund margin account to buy a piece of rental real estate, you have achieved a 60% return on your original $10,000 capital in one year! As is the case with example 1, deductions can be claimed for the margin interest. Although investments other than mutual funds can be used in a margin account, margin accounts are used in our examples because your future strategy is to get rid of riskier individual stock investments and use mutual funds.

Strategy #275:
USE A MARGIN ACCOUNT TO AVOID LOSSES WHILE PUTTING YOUR AVAILABLE CAPITAL BACK TO WORK.

If you sell an investment that is losing big right now, you eliminate the opportunity to gain back your losses. If, on the other hand, you keep the investment, thinking that it may recover the losses eventually, you lose the opportunity to invest in something you know will make you money now.

A margin account gives you the best of both worlds.

By "parking" your losing stocks or bonds in a margin account, you can borrow 50% of the current market value to reinvest in mutual funds (using the Money Movement Strategy).

Here is an example:

You paid $20,000 for stock that is currently worth only $14,000.

You think the stock will recover and don't want to take a capital loss now.

You borrow $7,000, or 50% of the current $14,000 market value of your shares, and put the money into a mutual fund.

Over the next three years, your mutual fund earns a yearly average of 18% after taxes, and your stock recovers to the full $20,000 original value. The margin interest is 10%, but since you are in the 40% bracket you are paying a net of only 60% of the total interest after your deduction.

MUTUAL FUND EARNINGS

Three years at 18% (without compounding)	$3,780
Margin interest (net after deductibility)	−1,250
Net profit	$2,530

Instead of just breaking even on the recovery of your stock, the margin account enabled you to earn an additional before-tax profit of $2,530.

Strategy #276:
USE A MARGIN ACCOUNT TO AVOID CAPITAL-GAINS TAXES WHILE MAKING INVESTMENT CAPITAL WORK HARDER.

Eventually, as a successful wealth builder and investor, you will face a situation where you have appreciated investments but have used up your total $100,000 capital-gains exemption. Now if you sell at a profit you will pay tax at your full rate on the taxable portion of the gain (which is now 75%).

If, using the Money Movement Strategy (Chapter 23), you determine the growth cycle is at an end for a while and you want to invest in something else but don't want to pay the taxes on the profits, use your margin account instead.

You can borrow 50% of the current market value of your investment, including 50% of the non-taxed profits you have earned to invest in mutual funds according to the Money Movement Strategy or other investments.

Your money is still working harder for you and you have avoided all of the capital-gains taxes. (Because the capital asset is unsold, there is no "gain.")

Here is an example:

You invested $20,000 in stocks a few years ago and their value has now grown to $30,000. Your capital-gains exemption is used up. You know that the growth cycle for stocks is coming to an end but you don't like the idea of selling and paying up to $4,000 in taxes on your $10,000 profit (40% tax bracket).

What do you do? By putting your $30,000 worth of shares into a brokerage or bank mutual fund margin account, allowing you to borrow $15,000, or 50%, you invest the $15,000 in a piece of rental real estate, which appreciates by $5,000.

Your total profit before interest charges is 33% for the year on the $15,000 borrowed money. You paid $1,500 tax-deductible interest at 10%, which amounts to only $900 the first year after your tax savings of $600 (40% bracket).

Appreciation on investments at 33%	$5,000
Net interest	− 900
	$4,100

Even if you experience a paper loss on your original stocks for the next couple of years, you are still earning $4,100 per year on the $20,000 original investment, an investment that would have shown no profit if left as it was.

In addition, you would not pay any taxes on the appreciation from your real estate investment until you actually sell or otherwise transfer the investment.

Chapter 26

RRSP INVESTMENT
SUPER STRATEGIES

*A banker is a fellow who lends you his umbrella when the
sun is shining and wants it back the minute it rains.*

Mark Twain

**Objective: Earn over 20% per year in non-traditional RRSP
investments.**

As we have already seen, the RRSP remains Canada's most powerful tax
shelter. In fact, cynics have suggested that if Ottawa gets any more tax
hungry, the RRSP might end up being Canada's only tax shelter!

Here are some slightly more sophisticated strategies for maximizing
your savings with RRSPs.

Strategy #277:
SET UP A SELF-ADMINISTERED RRSP.

Most RRSP-qualified investments offer pre-packaged investment portfolios. So if you don't like the way your plan is run, your only alternative is to switch plans — if you can do this without incurring big
close-out fees or other restrictions.

The smarter alternative is the so-called "self-administered RRSP"
(also referred to as a "self-directed RRSP"). This is an RRSP where
the financial institution holding the RRSP plays a passive role so you
may select the investments that are to be made by your own plan.

Most financial institutions now have these self-administered RRSPs
available.

When you set up a self-administered plan, you will be able to choose any combination of "qualified" investments that are allowed under current income tax regulations. These regulations offer considerable flexibility.

Strategy #278:
LOOK FOR THE LOWEST FEES.

You can minimize the fees you have to pay for a self-administered RRSP by shopping among financial institutions and brokers that offer these plans. In many cases, a financial institution or brokerage house will reduce its fees so that its self-administered plans become "loss leaders" to get your business. These can be a bargain. But check carefully for hidden fees. Avoid RRSPs that charge fees based on the value of your plan instead of a flat fee.

Also check carefully whether you will be charged a fee for each transaction in your plan, or whether you will be allowed a certain number of transactions on a fee-free basis. Watch also for "close-out" fees, additional charges for special types of transactions (e.g., investments in private mortgages), and so on.

Strategy #279:
PAY YOUR ADMINISTRATION FEES SEPARATELY.

A number of self-administered RRSPs allow you to pay administration fees separately instead of deducting them directly from the balance in your plan. In the former case, but not the latter, the fees you pay for a (non-spousal) RRSP may be tax deductible. By paying the administration fees separately and claiming a tax deduction, you can often cut these costs by up to 50% because of the tax breaks.

Strategy #280:
HOLD "HIGH-TAX" INVESTMENTS IN YOUR RRSP.

Not all investments are taxed in the same manner. Some, such as stocks and real estate, are eligible for special tax benefits. Interest-bearing investments, on the other hand, are fully taxable.

If your investment portfolio is too large to be held by your RRSP — remember that the size of your RRSP is based on your earned income from year to year — it is best to hold your low-tax investments personally and your high-tax investments in your RRSP. You will get the benefits of tax breaks on the low-tax items, while the high-tax items will be tax sheltered in your RRSP. Once the RRSP is established, you can substitute or swap property of equal value into your RRSP. Therefore, if you have an RRSP with $100,000 cash value in low-tax (capital gain) equities, and you hold $100,000 in high-tax (income) GICs, you may swap the two by filling out a few forms. Note: Certain penalties may apply if the properties being swapped are not considered to be of equal fair market value. Also, there is a "deemed sale" at fair market value when assets are transferred into an RRSP. This could result in tax exposure if the assets have appreciated, but capital losses will be disallowed.

Strategy #281:
MAKE THE MOST OF DEPOSIT INSURANCE.

If your RRSP is invested in financial institution savings accounts, GICs, and so on, make sure that these investments are fully covered by Canada Deposit Insurance.

Many think our financial institutions are rock-solid. The truth is that, if there were a bank run, most of them would be in deep trouble because of bad loans. It has happened in the United States — it can happen here. As the Standard Trust fiasco in the early '90s demonstrated, Canada is not immune to financial mismanagement on a large scale.

If you put your RRSP money into the type of investment that qualifies for deposit insurance, the investment will be insured to a maximum of $60,000 per financial institution that is a member of the Canada Deposit Insurance Corporation. Limit your investment to $50,000 or less so that the interest earnings are also covered by deposit insurance. If this coverage isn't adequate, you should invest your RRSP with a number of different institutions.

Your RRSP and personal investments are considered to be separate for the purposes of deposit insurance. So you and your RRSP can effectively obtain protection of up to $120,000 per financial institution.

Financial institutions that are members of the Canada Deposit Insurance Corporation display their membership sign at each branch.

Strategy #282:
CONTRIBUTE EARLY IN THE YEAR.

Most people wait until the last minute to make their RRSP contribution. If this means that you're simply letting your money sit in the bank in the meantime, you're paying taxes needlessly, since the interest will be taxable.

Instead, make an RRSP contribution early in the year. The interest you earn will then be tax sheltered.

The difference this simple strategy makes can be astounding. Suppose, for example, that you are eligible to make a $5,000 RRSP contribution. If the money simply earned interest at 12% for the year, you could end up paying nearly $300 or more of tax on this interest income each year. You can save the $300 by making a contribution early in the year. Effectively, the $300 tax saving would be reinvested in your RRSP. After 25 years, the taxes you saved on your early deposits will accumulate to more than $40,000 if your tax saving is invested at only a 12% return.

Strategy #283:
INVEST IN A
PRIVATE MORTGAGE.

You can usually add at least three points to your investment return by holding a private mortgage through your RRSP, instead of investing with a financial institution. You can find private mortgages by getting in touch with a good real estate lawyer or mortgage broker.

There is no requirement that it be a first mortgage as long as it is secured by Canadian real estate. In fact, it might even be possible to invest in a "participating mortgage." This is a mortgage that, in addition to the stated interest rate, may carry a bonus based on cash flow or re-sale profits.

Here's another lucrative possibility: you can purchase discounted mortgages for your RRSP and increase your yield even further. For more on discounted mortgages see Chapter 28.

To show how effective the private-mortgage strategy can be, let's see what difference a mere 3% can make. Suppose that you invest $10,000 at 10%. After 25 years, this will grow to about $108,000 in your RRSP. Invest at 13%, and your $10,000 will grow to more than $212,200 — a profit of more than $100,000!

The bottom line is that, by investing in a private mortgage, you could be able to double your money, compared to conventional financial institution investments.

Strategy #284:
MAKE AN RRSP MORTGAGE LOAN TO YOURSELF.

A number of financial institutions have special plans that allow your RRSP to make you a personal mortgage loan provided that it's properly secured by your real estate and is insured. Participating financial institutions include Royal Trust, Merrill Lynch, Dominion Securities, Burns Fry, the T-D Bank Greenline Investors Service, and Montreal Trust.

This manoeuvre will make particular sense if it allows you to pay down a personal mortgage loan or other non-deductible interest expenses. In this case, you will be able to pay your RRSP the money you would have paid to your mortgage company. While it's true that you will forgo the return you could have made on a conventional RRSP investment, the manoeuvre can still be worth it if the interest you pay yourself is several points higher than what you could have made with a conventional RRSP investment.

As a rule of thumb, the loan-to-yourself strategy may make sense if you have at least $25,000 in your RRSP. If your RRSP is smaller, the set-up and administration costs may be steep, relative to your financial gain.

Strategy #285:
INVEST IN MUTUAL FUNDS.

Mutual funds have been some of the top investment performers. It is often possible to earn 15% to 20% or more per year by moving your money among stock, bond, and money market funds. Most Canadian mutual funds have RRSP options and low trustee fees.

RRSPS — QUALIFIED INVESTMENTS

- Canadian money, and deposits in a bank or trust company.
- Canadian government bonds, debentures, and similar obligations.
- Shares listed on the major Canadian stock exchanges.
- Trust company GICs.
- Debt obligations of corporations listed on the Canadian stock exchanges.
- Foreign shares listed on the major U.S. exchanges, NASDAQ, as well as the London and Paris stock exchanges. (Note: The cost of all foreign investments in your RRSP is, in essence, restricted to an amount equal to 10% of the cost of all investments held in your RRSP.)
- Warrants or rights listed on a major Canadian stock exchange or the Toronto futures exchange, provided that upon exercise of the right or warrant, the property acquired would itself be a qualified investment for an RRSP.
- Mortgages secured by Canadian real estate. Generally, the loans must be to "arm's length" persons.

NON-QUALIFYING INVESTMENTS

- Foreign currency.
- Real estate.
- Art.
- Stamps and coins.
- Precious metals.

Note: It is sometimes possible to hold these investments indirectly through special RRSP-eligible mutual funds.

Strategy #286:

TRANSFER YOUR RRSP FUNDS TO AN RRIF
INSTEAD OF ANNUITIES.

Unless you want to pay tax on the balance in your RRSP, you must convert it to a "maturity option" no later than the end of the year in which you turn 71.

Most people transfer their RRSP to an annuity at this point. What they don't realize is that they become part of the Great Insurance Company Rip-off. Insurance companies make big bucks on annuities — at your expense!

Fortunately, there's another alternative, called a Registered Retirement Income Fund. These special investment funds, which are offered by most financial institutions, allow you to select from a wide range of investment alternatives. In fact, it's even possible to set up a self-administered RRIF (this is quite similar to a self-administered RRSP) that allows you to choose from a wide range of qualified investments.

RRIFs may also allow you the flexibility of making emergency withdrawals if you need the money. While this should be avoided if possible because of the tax bite, annuities often have it worse — most of them build in hefty penalties for withdrawals or even forbid them completely.

One drawback of an RRIF, relative to an annuity, is that it does not afford you the assurance that you will receive payments as long as you live. But like any other insurance, you will pay a premium for this — no pun intended! — when you purchase the annuity. Also, if you have followed the Charles J. Givens financial strategies, this type of insurance will probably not be necessary!

Where does the money in the RRIF come from? In most cases, the funds in the RRIF will be the same funds you built up in your RRSP — plus accumulated tax-free earnings. Although the RRIF can be started earlier, most people will likely collapse their RRSP at the mandatory age — 71 — and create the RRIF. In this way the earnings in your RRSP tax shelter remain tax free until, little by little, you actually take the cash out of your RRIF over the following years.

Note that, with the RRIF, you are required to take certain minimum amounts out in cash each year. You may take more than the minimums if you choose (although you must pay tax on the withdrawals, of course). However, the RRIF vehicle does have one flaw — it is designed to exhaust all your funds, following its minimum payout formula, by age 90. To avoid the unpleasant possibility of living past this age and having no funds left, a portion of your RRIF account should be converted to a life annuity. Any portion in excess of the minimum amount for the year may be transferred as suggested as a tax-free rollover with no penalties.

Strategy #287:
CHOOSE YOUR MINIMUM RRIF PAYMENTS CAREFULLY.

A complex formula is used to determine the minimum amount that must be removed from the RRIF — at full tax rates — each year until age 90. (Note that you can start an RRIF at any age. In the year you start the RRIF, it is not necessary to take out any amount, but for each subsequent year, you must take out the minimum payout.)

Generally, the payments set by law are small to start with and grow with the RRIF itself. For example, at age 65 with $100,000 in your RRIF, you must withdraw about $4,000 that year. Assuming that your RRIF was invested at 12% a year, compounded, then at age 75 you must withdraw at least $20,000 from that same plan; about $42,000 at age 85; and so on.

This approach — taking less in the early years of retirement, and more as you age — may not truly meet the needs of Canadians. You can instruct the institutions holding your RRIF precisely how much you want each year. An "indexed" payment based on inflation can also be arranged in advance.

Strategy #288:
LEARN REVENUE CANADA'S TRANSFER RULES FOR RRSPS AND RRIFS.

As you reach retirement you may find yourself with cash tied up in a number of investments: RRSPs, RRIFs, annuities, etc. If you transfer from one to the other, be sure to do so with little or no tax consequences. Some general rules for tax-free transfers are:

1. You can transfer from one RRSP to another. There may be a fee for this and it is usually small. Even though RRSPs are hardly new, many companies and financial centres still have trouble with the paperwork involved. If you are doing an RRSP-to-RRSP transfer, it is a good idea to regularly phone the transferring company to verify the progress of the transaction. At certain times of year — such as "RRSP season" between January and March — even simple transfers may drag on for weeks or even months.
2. From an RRSP or RRIF to another RRIF — see previous strategy. (Note that the RRIF itself can be funded only from an RRSP, another RRIF, or a commuted annuity purchased with RRSP funds.)
3. From an RRIF to an RRSP — this unusual situation would arise only if you had inadvertently taken more money from your RRIF than you wanted, and you are still eligible to have an RRSP plan.

Chapter 27

THE CAPITAL-GAINS
EXEMPTION TAX BONUS

Wealth — any income that is at least one hundred dollars more a year than the income of one's wife's sister's husband.

H. L. Mencken

Objective: To make the most of your lifetime capital-gains exemption.

The $100,000 lifetime capital-gains exemption enacted in 1985 can save you up to $35,000 in taxes under the current rules and should definitely be a part of your overall investment plan.

"Capital gain" is a fancy term describing the profit you make when you sell a qualifying investment or investment property for more than you paid for it. The gain is the difference. A capital loss results when you sell an investment for less than you paid.

There are two types of capital gains and losses to consider: "cash" and "taxable." Your cash gain or loss is the easiest to understand and is best described as cash flow, or total cash in minus total cash out. It's also known as profit.

Your capital gain for tax purposes, however, is based on a formula created by tax rules as to what part of the actual gain is taxable and what part of a capital loss is actually deductible.

For example, if you buy something for $10 and sell it for $20, you have $10 profit. However, under current rules, you only made 75% of that gain, or $7.50 for tax purposes. The $7.50 is then declared as if it were regular income and you pay your normal tax at your regular rate. The hidden benefit, however — what makes capital gains special — is the $2.50 component on which you pay no tax at all.

What are the qualifications for capital-gains status?

Not all resale profits qualify for a capital gain. The criteria for determining whether a particular sale will qualify for capital-gains status has been established by a large number of court cases over the years. Basically, the question is this: Are you realizing on your basic investment capital which itself is used to generate income, or is the sale itself part of an overall business or profit-making scheme (in which case, the gain will generally be fully taxable). Another way to look at it is to ask whether you are, in effect, in the business of buying and selling the particular item. If so, capital-gains status will not apply.

In order to determine these issues, there are a number of factors to be considered:

- Did you earn income from the property? If so, this favours capital-gains status.
- Is it apparent that your main motive was not to make a quick resale profit? If so, capital-gains status may be available.
- Is this the only property you have bought and sold of the same type lately? If so, capital-gains status may be available.
- Do the circumstances of the sale indicate that you are not in the business of buying and selling? If so, capital-gains status may be available.
- Is the transaction not related to your regular business? If so, capital-gains status may be available.
- Did you hold the property a long time? If so, this will tend to favour capital-gains treatment.

As a practical matter, most smaller-scale investors will tend to be successful in claiming capital-gains status on such investments as stocks, bonds, shares in limited partnerships, art and other collectibles. However, Revenue Canada may give you a tougher time when it comes to real estate, especially when you have an active track record in buying and selling properties, or when raw land is involved.

Strategy #289:
USE YOUR CAPITAL-GAINS EXEMPTION TO SAVE UP TO $35,000 IN TAXES.

To see how you can pocket an extra $35,000 of investment profits, let's look first at the tax rate and the amount you pay on capital-gains.

Taxable Income	Your Federal Tax Bracket (ignoring surtaxes)	Federal Capital-Gains Rate +5% 1991 Surcharge	Combined Federal & Provincial Capital-Gains Rate
First $28,784	17%	13%	20%
Next $28,785	26%	20%	31% (B)
Above $57,569	29%	23%	35% (A)

(Rates shown assume provincial taxes of 52% of the federal tax and do not include the 3% high-earner surtax or any provincial surtaxes.)

When you combine federal and provincial taxes you would normally pay $35,000 in capital-gains tax on $100,000 worth of capital gains. Your $100,000 personal capital-gains exemption will therefore save you up to $35,000 (A) if you are in the 29% tax bracket, or about $31,000 (B) if you are in the 26% tax bracket.

Strategy #290:
KNOW YOUR CAPITAL GAINS "BILL OF RIGHTS."

In addition to the break on capital gains that, generally, all taxpayers get at all times, each individual taxpaying resident in Canada gets an additional break on his or her first $100,000 of gross capital-gains profits — there are no taxes on this at all! Corporations and trusts (other than as noted in item #11 below) are not entitled to this tax break. Here is a summary of the rules:

1. Capital Gains and Loss rules can apply to all levels of investments and property, including:

Stocks	Personal Property
Bonds	Boats
Partnership Shares	Antiques
Depreciable Business Property*	Collections
Cars	Books
Machinery	Art
Buildings	

*Note that previous years' capital cost allowance may be required to be included income as "recapture" upon the sale of depreciable property.

2. Capital gains or losses are created only when you sell a property, not from the appreciation or depreciation while you still hold it.

3. If you emigrate from Canada, you are deemed for tax purposes to have sold your properties, subject to certain exceptions (the main one being real property located in Canada and shares of private corporations), at fair market value even if you still own them. This can create a substantial tax bill. The same rule, again subject to certain exceptions (where property is left to your spouse or a trust for your spouse), applies to death — only this time it's your heirs who have to worry about settling the taxes.

4. Beginning in 1990, 75% of any capital gain is subject to tax. The amount is called your taxable capital gain. This taxable amount is included in the income you report on your tax return and is subject to the same tax rates as your normal employment or interest income.

5. To determine your "net" taxable gain or loss for any one year, you first must subtract all allowable capital losses (75% of your capital losses) from your taxable capital gains. This situation will occur when you sell more than one investment or property during the same year and one or more is sold at a loss.

6. If your allowable capital losses are greater than the amount of your taxable capital gains in any one year, you may apply the excess losses to the three previous tax years to reduce up to 100% of the taxes on taxable capital gains for those years. In this case, you will get a refund for the taxes you paid. This process is called "loss carry-back." In all cases, capital losses can only offset capital gains, not general income.

7. If you had a particularly bad year for losses and have already offset the previous three years' gains, or had none to begin with, you may carry your unused losses forward indefinitely to reduce your future taxable capital gains.

8. If you have allowable capital losses that occurred before May 23, 1985, that are not yet used up, the remainder is subject to the old tax rules that allow you to use part or all of each year to offset the taxes on up to $2,000 of any other income.

9. The $100,000 personal exemption is available on all capital gains, whether from investments in Canada or elsewhere.

10. Trusts cannot use the exemption directly, but it can effectively be passed on to the individual beneficiaries of the trust. Of course, this means nothing unless your rich relatives have set up a trust for you!

11. The lifetime capital-gains exemption created in 1985 was to grow over the years to a maximum of $500,000. Those in power suffered tax panic

and capped the exemption at $100,000. Small business corporation owners and farm owners, however, are potentially eligible for an exemption allowing up to the full $500,000 when they sell shares of their business corporation or farm.

12. You must be a resident of Canada to claim the exemption.

13. In addition to the above rules, your allowable capital-gains exemption for the year is reduced by:
    a. Allowable business investment losses you are claiming.
    b. Capital losses from other years you are claiming this year.
    c. Cumulative net investment losses (called CNIL).
    If these calculations reduce your ability to take the ability to take the gain, the effect is not permanent. In most cases, the ability to claim the exemption is simply deferred to a future year.

14. Every member of your family is entitled to the full $100,000 personal capital-gains exemption. (See income-splitting strategies, Chapter 12, to take advantage of this rule.)

Strategy #291:
USE THE CAPITAL-GAINS EXEMPTION AS QUICKLY AS POSSIBLE.

"Out with the old, in with the new" applies both to politicians and tax laws. Beneficial tax laws, like the $100,000 personal capital-gains exemption, can be wiped out as quickly as they are introduced. It is, therefore, in your best interest to use your capital-gains exemption as soon as possible with the realization that it may eventually disappear. To maximize your gains:

A. Invest in appreciating assets such as mutual funds and real estate.

B. Become more aggressive using leverage (borrowed money) in investments to increase your potential capital gains (although this will also increase your CNIL — see Strategy #299).

C. Don't let your gains pile up in investments past the date you begin to hear rumours about the exemption being reduced or eliminated. Remember that the maximum personal capital-gains exemption was originally proposed to be $500,000 but was later reduced to to $100,000!

Strategy #292:

**SELL SHARES IN YOUR APPRECIATED SMALL BUSINESS
TO FAMILY MEMBERS TO CLAIM EXEMPT CAPITAL GAINS.**

If you own a profitable business, you can take advantage of the extra $400,000 capital-gains exemption by selling or giving shares to your family members, including your spouse. Of course, if you wouldn't trust your kids or other family members with a credit card or even lunch money, this strategy is not for you. However, you may be able to utilize the exemption by transferring shares to a holding company. The tax credit on the extra $400,000 of capital gains can save you as much as $120,000 in taxes, however.

The $400,000 extra exemption for small business applies only to capital gains realized on the sale or disposition of shares in a small business corporation (SBC) where the shares are held only by the taxpayer and related family members for the entire 24 months preceding the sale.

An SBC is an active Canadian-controlled private corporation in which substantially all of the value of its assets is used in an active business carried on in Canada.

In addition to the fact that the corporation must be an SBC on the date of sale or disposition, there are certain pre-conditions which must be met:

1. The shares must have been held only by the taxpayer or a related family member for the entire 24 months preceding the sale. It should be noted that shares issued from the treasury of a corporation during this 24-month period may not qualify for the exemption (see below).
2. During the entire 24-month period, more than 50% of the value of the corporation's assets must have been used in an active business carried on in Canada. There are more stringent tests which must be met where a holding company is involved.

It is not very easy to meet these qualifications, and this enhanced exemption may be more the exception rather than the rule. It is important to ensure that your shares qualify before taking advantage of the rule, as the tax consequences of failing to meet the requirements can be onerous. Where the corporation has built up a surplus of non-qualifying assets, it may be difficult to "purify" these assets from the corporation on a tax-deferred basis where an arm's-length sale of shares is contemplated. In addition, there are provisions in the Income Tax Act which are designed to restrict the use of the capital-gains exemption to "strip" profits from the corporation on a tax-free basis. These rules will have potential application where the exemption is used through a transfer of shares to a holding corporation.

There are a number of other provisions in addition to those discussed above which can affect the availability of the capital-gains exemption.

Where you carry on a small business which is not incorporated, it may be possible to incorporate such business prior to its sale in order to take advantage of the $400,000 capital-gains exemption. Where you transfer substantially all of the assets used in an active business to a corporation, the shares which you receive from the corporation on such transfer may not have to be held for 24 months prior to their sale in order to use the exemption.

If you trigger the exemption through a transfer of shares to your spouse or other family members, their cost base for taxes will be higher than yours at the time when they dispose of such shares by the amount of the capital gain you realized on the transfer to them. In the case of your spouse, however, any capital gain which he or she realizes on a subsequent disposition of the shares will be attributed back to you unless your spouse pays fair market value for the shares. In the case of other family members, a transfer of shares to them may provide an ability to do some capital-gains splitting (see income splitting strategies, Chapter 12, to take advantage of these rules).

Strategy #293:
TRIGGER CAPITAL GAINS WHEN NEEDED BY SELLING INVESTMENTS OF ALL KINDS TO FAMILY MEMBERS.

You can keep your assets and investments in the family while triggering gains to be made tax free, or to beat a potential elimination of the capital-gains exemption, by selling or giving to family members at fair market value.

These appreciated investments can include stocks, bonds, mutual fund shares, or your vacation home.

Say you have a painting you purchased for $10,000 that now has a value of $40,000. Selling the painting to your spouse changes the cost base (in your spouse's hands) to $40,000, giving you $30,000 that you can immediately apply against your $100,000 exemption.

Strategy #294:

**WHEN POSSIBLE, CHOOSE CAPITAL INVESTMENTS
OVER INTEREST INVESTMENTS.**

Revenue Canada seems to have a policy by which it more aggressively taxes investments depending on how safe the initial investment is. This policy is reflected in the fact that generally income payments (as opposed to capital gains) are taxed at full rates and, furthermore, income accrued but not paid is considered earned each year whether or not the investment is cashed in (unlike capital investments where the tax liability is deferred until disposition).

Consider the following:

Joe invests $50,000 in a vacation home in Northern Ontario. After 10 years he sells his investment and shows a $75,000 profit. That $75,000 is taxable at capital-gains rates (currently 75% of the gain × Joe's marginal rate) in the year in which it is obtained. And if Joe had any capital losses (losses sustained on bad capital investments in previous years) he could deduct those from the $75,000 to reduce the total amount of the tax liability.

Instead, assume Joe had put his money in a reliable and high-performing money market mutual fund, with instructions to let his earnings compound in the fund from year to year. After 10 years Joe determines that he has earned about $70,000 interest on his principal. At first glance, it looks as if Joe is almost in the same position but has avoided the "risk" of real estate.

In fact, this is not correct. First, the yearly interest in Joe's money market fund are taxed 100% at his full marginal rate, whereas with the capital gain, only 75% of the gain was ultimately taxed. Second, with the capital gain, Joe was able to defer paying taxes until he actually sold the property. In the case of the mutual fund, Joe will discover that, even though he has instructed the fund to compound his earnings, Revenue Canada will still expect him to declare (and pay taxes on) his interest earnings each year.

If Joe is compounding his interest within the fund, where does he get the money to pay his taxes on money he never actually received?

From other sources, that's where. In effect, Joe is borrowing money to prepay his taxes on his income — from himself!

Strategy #295:
UNDERSTAND CNIL — CUMULATIVE NET INVESTMENT LOSSES — AND USE IT TO PROTECT YOUR INCOME.

Although most tax advisors will tell you the CNIL rules are complicated, in reality, we can make them easy to understand and apply by simplifying many of the technicalities.

1. Theoretically the CNIL rules were created to prevent taxpayers from "double dipping" — taking a deduction for both the capital-gains exemption and the interest expenses involved in getting the gain in the first place. The new rules do their job, but make tax time just a little more complex than it used to be.
2. Here's a shortcut: consider CNIL as an account where you simply accumulate all (post-1987) investment-related expenses net of investment-related income (other than capital gains), then subtract the total in your CNIL account from the maximum capital-gains exemption you would otherwise claim.
3. Any CNIL (either positive or negative) not used in the current year is carried forward and used the next year.
4. Note that CNIL reduces the amount of capital-gains exemption you can claim in any one year, but not your lifetime allowable personal exemption of $100,000. In other words, the more CNIL you have, the longer it will take you to use up your exemption.
5. CNIL does not affect the deductibility of your investment-interest expenses or other investment losses, only your ability to use your capital gains exemption.
6. Once you have used up your personal capital-gains exemption, the CNIL rules no longer apply. Of course, by then you would also be paying taxes on 75% of your capital gains.
7. Some of the items you add to your CNIL account total for the year:
   a. Interest paid on loans to buy investments that pay income, such as interest income, dividends, and rent.
   b. Interest paid on a loan to buy an interest in a partnership where you are not active in the business.
   c. Your share of any taxable loss in such a partnership.
   d. 50% of your share of most deductions from a corporation or partnership involved in Canadian resource exploration in which you are not actively involved.

e. Net losses from rental property.

You then subtract income items including the following from your CNIL balance to determine your net investment loss for the year.

a. Interest and taxable dividends plus other investment income.
b. Income from a partnership in which you are not actively involved.
c. Income from rental properties — rents, lease payments.
d. 50% of income from a partnership involved in Canadian resource exploration.

The basic formula described above simply amounts to finding the difference each year between your investment income and your investment expenses. If your investment expenses exceed your income, your CNIL account balance is increased. You will notice most or all of the items involved in the calculation of your CNIL account likely don't apply to you anyway, only to those who are aggressively seeking tax shelters to protect large amounts of income. However, the CNIL rules can apply to you any time you use leverage to acquire investments — for example, if you take out a mortgage on your home in order to buy investments and deduct the interest on the mortgage. (The following worksheets contain simplified calculations; your actual CNIL may differ.)

COMPUTATION OF CNIL ACCOUNT

1. Investment income for the year
   A. Interest, taxable dividends, other
      investment income $_____
   B. Limited partnership income $_____
   C. Rental property income $_____
   D. 50% of resource property income $_____

   Total Investment Income   (A)$_____

2. Calculate investment expenses for the year
   A. Interest paid on investment loans $_____
   B. Other expenses of investment property $_____
   C. Carrying charges, including interest, with
      respect to limited partnerships $_____
   D. Limited partnership losses $_____
   E. 50% of resource property expenses $_____

   Total Investment Expenses   (B)$_____

COMPUTE CNIL

Net investment gain or loss for the year
(A) − (B) = (C)   (C)$_____

Net investment gain or loss of previous years after 1987 (i.e.,
aggregate of amounts determined under (C) for 1988 and subsequent year)   (D)$_____

Cumulative net investment gain or loss at end of this year.
(C) + (D) = (E)   (E)$_____

If (E) is a loss, you have a CNIL balance which will have an effect on the calculation of the capital-gains exemption available.

COMPUTATION OF CAPITAL-GAINS EXEMPTION AVAILABLE

The capital-gains exemption available is the least of three amounts:

1. Capital-gains exemption you have left;

2. Your annual gains limit;

3. Your cumulative gains limit.

Calculate Annual Gains Limit

Taxable capital gains for this year (including reserves
from property disposed of after 1984)   (F)$_____

Allowable capital losses for this year (excluding
allowable business investments losses)   (G)$_____

Net Capital Gains or Losses
(F) − (G) = (H)   (H)$_____

If (H) is a loss, enter 0 in (H), skip from here to (P) and enter
amount of loss carryover. Then get out your previous three years'
returns and, going back one year at a time, use this year's losses
against the three previous years' capital gains. You will be entitled to a refund if you paid tax on capital gains in previous years
and can carry any unused loss forward indefinitely.

Any capital loss carryover claimed in year   (I)$_____

Allowable business investment losses for year   (J)$_____

Annual Gains Limit   (H) − [(I) + (J)] = (K)   (K)$_____

If (K) is a loss enter amount in (K), and disregard remainder of
section.

Calculate Cumulative Gains Limit

Aggregate of amounts determined under (K) for this year and
each year ending after 1984 (L)$_____

Amount of capital-gains exemption used to date
(i.e., aggregate of amounts determined under (O) for previous
years) (M)$_____

CNIL at end of this year (E)$_____

Cumulative Gains Limit
(L) − [(M) + (E)] = (N) (N)$_____

If (N) is less than 0, enter 0 in (N) and disregard the balance of
this section.

Capital-gains exemption available is amount not exceeding the
least of:

A. Capital-gains exemption you have left (If you used the exemption before 1990, the amount previously claimed must be
grossed up to 75% rate)

B. (K)

C. (N)

CAPITAL GAINS EXEMPTION UTILIZED (O)$_____

Capital Loss carryover — back three years, then forward
indefinitely (P)$_____

Strategy #296:
CLAIM DEFERABLE INTEREST NOW TO OFFSET UNUSED CUMULATIVE NET INVESTMENT LOSSES.

On specific investments acquired before 1990 you have a choice of
claiming the earned income by deferred interest yearly or waiting for
up to three years.

As a general rule, your objective is to defer taxes as long as possible, but there are times when exceptions can be profitable.

The greater your CNIL, the less of your capital-gains exemption you
can use. The greater your investment income, the less your CNIL ac-

count increases. By claiming deferred interest this year instead of waiting an extra year or two, you can reduce your CNIL and the result could be to increase your allowable capital-gains exemption dollar for dollar by the interest you claim.

Investments that qualify for the maximum three-year deferral rule include:

A. Deferred interest Guaranteed Investment Certificates (GICs).

B. Compound interest Canada Savings Bonds (CSBs), and

C. Stripped coupons (also known as stripped bonds).

For investments acquired after 1989, the three-year deferral no longer applies. Also note that if the term of an investment is extended or otherwise materially altered, it is treated as if it were acquired after 1989.

Let's say you have $2,000 taxable capital gains (profits) from your investments, which would normally be tax free because of your personal capital-gains exemption, but your CNIL account (see Strategy #295) has a balance of $1,500. You could only claim an exemption of the difference of $500. But you also have compound interest CSBs bought before 1990, which will earn you $1,000 in interest that you won't receive — nor do you have to claim — for another two years. By claiming the $1,000 interest this year you reduce your $1,500 CNIL account by $1,000, allowing you to claim an extra capital-gains exemption of $1,000.

Strategy #297:
SPLIT THE PROFITS OR LOSSES ON BONDS INTO INTEREST AND CAPITAL GAINS/LOSSES.

If you buy or sell debt securities like bonds between the issue date and the maturity date, part of your profit or loss may be "capital" in nature as opposed to purely interest.

When you buy after the issue date you may either pay a premium (more than the face value) or buy at a discount (less than the face value). The difference between your purchase price and what you receive at maturity — or what you sell for before maturity — may represent your capital gain or loss, assuming you meet the requirements for capital-gains status and the bond was issued at a commercially reasonable interest rate.

Many people report the gain or loss as part of the interest. Usually, reporting such a gain/loss as income will cost you big tax dollars.

Remember, you pay tax on capital gains at only 75% of the rate you pay on interest, and you may be able to claim the capital-gains exemption.

What about losses? Here, you would actually prefer not to take the loss as capital losses — which can then be offset only against other capital gains — but as a general loss, although there must be a reasonable basis for doing so.

You are allowed to make an election using Form T123 to have all of your capital gains/losses from qualifying Canadian securities treated, but this election, once made, is irrevocable. If you have not made the election, you could conceivably treat such losses or gains in a different manner from year to year to maximize your tax strategy, provided, of course, that it is reasonable to do so.

Strategy #298:
USE THE CAPITAL-GAINS RESERVES RULES
TO DELAY PAYMENT OF TAXES ON PROFITS
YOU HAVE NOT YET RECEIVED.

This strategy applies to profits from the sale of properties, such as real estate, where you take part of the money and profit now and the balance in future years. You end up financing the sale yourself!

A capital-gains reserve, according to the tax law, is the amount of the sale price that you do not receive until after the end of the current year. The reserve is only available to residents of Canada and cannot be used when you sell property to a corporation you control.

You must report the full sale price in the year you sell, but you are allowed to subtract the amount of the reserve from the total to determine the amount on which you will be taxed this year. The reserve is only available to residents of Canada and cannot be used when you sell property to a corporation you control.

You can postpone your taxes on the gain for no longer than a total of five years.

To determine your total gain, subtract the purchase price from the selling price (net of selling costs). For tax purposes, you must recognize each year for taxes the greater of 20% of the total gain or the actual percentage you received of the sale price times the total gain.

Let's make these calculations even simpler:

1. If you received less than 20% of the sale price the first year, you still must recognize for taxes a minimum of 20% of the gain because of that five-year rule.
2. If you received more than 20% of the sale price the first year, let's say 30%, then you must pay taxes on 30% of the gain.
3. The total gain claimed must be a minimum of 20% per year. In the third year, for instance, you must have claimed a total of 60% (three years × 20% per year minimum).
4. The five-year deferral rule is extended to 10 years if you are selling qualified farm property or shares in a small business to your children or grandchildren.
5. You can, of course, apply your capital-gains exemption to your gains as you report them.

Example:

You sell for $500,000 a piece of land for which you originally paid $100,000. The buyer pays $100,000 a year for five years.

1. Your total gain is $500,000 − $100,000 = $400,000.
2. Using the capital-gains reserve rules, since you were paid 20% down and 20% a year, you must recognize 20% of the total gain each year.
3. Therefore, you take into account the following amounts as yearly capital gains:

Year #1	$80,000
Year #2	$80,000
Year #3	$80,000
Year #4	$80,000
Year #5	$80,000

Chapter 28

DISCOUNTED MORTGAGES

A broker is a man who runs your fortune into a shoestring.

Alexander Woollcott, *Wit's End*

Objective: Earn 30% per year guaranteed and secured.

Strategy #299:
**INVEST IN DISCOUNTED MORTGAGES FOR A
GUARANTEED 30% RETURN.**

What if there was an investment that paid a guaranteed interest rate of 30% each year, in which your principal was 100% secured? There is such an investment, but you'll never find it at brokerage firms, banks, or financial planners. The investment is discounted mortgages — usually second mortgages — that you locate, negotiate, and purchase yourself.

Occasionally, an investment opportunity arises, created by unusual economic conditions. During the late '70s and early to mid-'80s, the years of super-high interest rates, homeowners who wanted to sell found there were not many willing buyers. High interest rates meant that the buyer's payments would be too high if a new mortgage was obtained. "Creative financing" replaced location as the most important words in real estate. In order to entice a purchaser and help that buyer avoid the costs of refinancing, the seller would allow the buyer to assume the existing low-interest first mortgage, and then take back a second mortgage for a large part of the down payment. There were thousands of properties in every area sold in this manner.

Sellers normally do not like mortgages; they want cash, and as a result, tire quickly of owning a mortgage that is paid in periodic payments. The seller's desire to get cash out of a mortgage creates an unequalled investment opportunity.

Discounted mortgages are one of the best investment choices for reinvesting equity you have borrowed from your own home. The high guaranteed and secured investment return of discounted mortgages certainly qualifies them for our list of the "eight best investments."

Strategy #300:

WHEN MAKING AN OFFER FOR A MORTGAGE, BEGIN BY OFFERING NO MORE THAN 60% OF FACE VALUE.

Because there is no ready-made market for mortgages, sellers are forced to sell mortgages at a discount of 30% to 50% from the face value, and the price is determined by agreement between the seller and buyer of the mortgage. When making a cash offer for a mortgage, begin by offering 60% of the face value. You may either stick to your 60% offer or negotiate up to 75%, but usually not more. You'll be surprised by how many good mortgages you can buy for 60 cents on the dollar.

BUYING A DISCOUNTED MORTGAGE

For example, if a seller sold his home two years ago and took back a $10,000 interest-only 12% second mortgage for seven years, and you purchase the mortgage for 60% of face value, you pay $6,000 for the mortgage. When the mortgage term is up in five years, you receive the entire face value, $10,000, which is $4,000 more than the $6,000 you invested. Until maturity, the interest of 12% is paid to you.

The 12% interest, remember, is based on the $10,000 face value of the mortgage and amounts to $1,200 each year. Since you have only $6,000 invested, but still receive the full $1,200 interest annually, your return is 20%. Your total annualized return from the interest plus the discount is 30%.

Face value	$10,000
Purchase price	$ 6,000
Balance of term	five years
Original Interest Rate	12 %

Return on Discounted Mortgage as a Percentage

Your interest rate	20.00%
Earnings from discount (annualized)	<u>10.75%</u>
Annual return	30.75%

Return on Discounted Mortgage in Dollars

Interest ($1,200 year × 5 years)	$ 6,000
Discount	<u>4,000</u>
Total profit	$10,000

In this example, you would have earned $10,000 during five years on a $6,000 investment or about 30% per year — guaranteed. Once you get the hang of it, you'll wonder why every investor isn't looking for and buying discounted mortgages.

You won't buy discounted mortgages at financial institutions, nor will you normally find them advertised in the newspaper. Where do you look?

Strategy #301:

**USE THE REGISTRY OFFICE AS A
DISCOUNTED MORTGAGE SOURCE.**

The easiest method of locating unlimited numbers of mortgages that you can buy at a discount is at the Registry Office. If you inspect the transfers that have recently been registered, or the fee book that the Registrar maintains at the Registry Office, you'll be able to get the names of the sellers of houses and the property addresses. You can then call the seller's solicitor for further information, e.g., the seller's current address, whether a mortgage was given back, and whether or not the seller would be interested in selling the mortgage.

Relevant terms you will need to understand are:

Mortgagor — person responsible for the payments.
Mortgagee — person to whom the money is owed.
Address of the property — so you can evaluate it.
Mortgage Amount — the face value.
Mortgage Terms — payments, interest, due date.

Make a list of 10 or 20 that look promising and are within your investment capital range. Your goal is to buy a mortgage at 30% to 40% less than face value. When you get home, look up the telephone numbers of the mortgagees. If you can't find one, call the mortgagor and ask for the phone number of the person to whom they make their second mortgage payment. Call the mortgagee and use these words to open the conversation:

Hi, Mrs. Smith? My name is [your name] and I understand you are holding a mortgage for $[amount] on the property located at [address]. Is that correct? Well, Mrs. Smith, I'm an investor and I would like to buy your mortgage for cash. Does that interest you? (Four out of five will say "yes" at this point.)

Set up an appointment with the mortgagee and negotiate the discount amount by beginning your offer at about 60 cents on the dollar or $6,000 for a $10,000 mortgage. The longer the mortgage has to run, the more receptive the mortgage holder will be to your offer.

Why would a person sell a mortgage to you at a discount? Because most Canadians are such poor money managers, they need cash now far more than they need payments over time, even if the payments will produce more income. You'll find that one out of three mortgageholders will sell to you at a 30% to 40% discount.

Strategy #302:
RUN NEWSPAPER ADS IN SEARCH OF MORTGAGES YOU CAN BUY AT A DISCOUNT.

You can spend a few tax-deductible dollars running ads to search for people who want cash for their mortgages. The ads can be placed in the classified section or as a larger display ad with such captions as:

"Cash for your mortgage."
"I buy mortgages."
"Investor wants to buy first and second mortgages."
"Want to sell your second mortgage?"

Most who have tried the newspaper route find it a long, slow, but eventually successful process, generating one to five calls per week and one or two mortgage purchases a month.

Strategy #303:
BUY DISCOUNTED MORTGAGES WITH NO MORE THAN AN 80% LOAN-TO-VALUE RATIO.

Every commercial mortgage company has an upper limit on how much money it will lend on a first or second mortgage. The formula for calculating the maximum loan amount is known as the loan-to-value (LTV) ratio. You will want to adopt your own LTV, I recommend you use 80% as your loan-to-value ratio, as I do.

The LTV is the maximum percentage of the market value of a property you would be willing to finance. The maximum amount you would pay for a mortgage should be no more than 80% of the market value of the property, less any other mortgage amounts. If a property is appraised at $100,000, the sum of all mortgages including yours would have to total less than $80,000 or you would not want to purchase the mortgage. If the first mortgage is $60,000 and the mortgage you are purchasing is $10,000, the total of the mortgage amounts would be $70,000. This would be perfectly acceptable because $70,000 is less than the $80,000, 80% maximum.

If the mortgage on the property is $75,000 and the mortgage you wanted to buy has a face value of $15,000, the loan-to-value ratio of 80%, or $80,000, would be exceeded and you would not purchase the mortgage.

Strategy #304:
MAKE FRIENDS WITH REAL ESTATE PROFESSIONALS WHO WILL CALL YOU WHEN THEY LEARN OF A MORTGAGE FOR SALE.

You can cultivate a mortgage garden of real estate agents and brokers. Since there is no ready-made market for discounted mortgages, the first person a mortgage holder would think to call about selling a mortgage is someone in the real estate business.

By making friends with several real estate professionals and letting them know of your interest in purchasing discounted mortgages, you'll discover a never-ending supply.

Many years ago, when I was first getting into investment real estate, I enrolled in an adult night-school course called "Real Estate Financing." The people I met in that one class, mostly real estate professionals, were worth thousands of dollars to me. From friendly conversations that ensued on class breaks, I bought several properties at a bargain, found a property manager, a handyman for inexpensive repairs, got several new clients for my printing and publishing companies, and bought several discounted mortgages.

The Toronto Real Estate Board and its equivalent in other large centres issues a book of listings monthly. You can find out from a real estate agent which properties have been sold. Then, call the sellers who may have agreed to take back a second mortgage on closing (which would not, as yet, have occurred). Arrangements could be made with the second mortgagee (seller) to purchase the mortgage when the transaction has been completed.

Strategy #305:

WHEN BUYING DISCOUNTED MORTGAGES, EXPECT THE BEST, ARM YOURSELF FOR THE WORST, AND TALK TO YOUR LAWYER FIRST.

Your "worst case" risk when buying discounted mortgages is that the mortgagor won't make the payments and you may have to foreclose on the property or put the property up for sale under "power of sale" to protect your investment — not a problem if you plan effectively.

Before you buy a discounted mortgage, have a chat with a competent real estate lawyer who is familiar with the real estate laws and practices in your area. Develop a contingency plan for how he will handle collection if the mortgagor is late with the payments. If the mortgage is in default 35 days or more, your solicitors should serve notice that you intend to sell under power of sale or to foreclose. You will seldom have a real problem if you act immediately. As a holder of a mortgage, never get into the welfare business by allowing other people's problems to influence you into letting them be late with their payments. No matter how you feel emotionally, the only 100% sure method of protecting yourself and collecting every dime is to act, act immediately, and act in the strongest way possible. Once you learn to act immediately and consistently, the mortgagor will find a way to make the payments on time — because he knows you mean business.

HOW TO HANDLE A MORTGAGE FORECLOSURE OR POWER OF SALE

If, in a rare case, the property does begin to proceed to foreclosure or power of sale (court-supervised sale) because payments either weren't made on the first mortgage or on your second mortgage, you and your lawyer will want to choose one of three options:

1. Nip things in the bud by bringing the payments current on the first mortgage to prevent the first mortgage holder from foreclosing while you are handling the situation. When you buy a mortgage, always send a certified letter to the first mortgage holder stating that you are the holder of a second mortgage and want to be notified any time a payment is late. Although not required by law, the first mortgage holder will generally comply with your request.
2. Convince the mortgagor he should immediately deed the property to you using a Quit Claim Deed to avoid the embarrassment and ordeal of a foreclosure, and to preserve his credit standing. This alternative is often the best.
3. If the property goes to power of sale or auction, bid an amount equal to the existing first mortgage plus the amount of your second mortgage. If someone outbids you, they will have to pay every cent owed to you. If you win the bid with the highest offer, you may have to put a portion of the bid into escrow and will then have about 30 days to produce the balance. Check the rules for your area. Your bank will help you with some short-term financing while you re-finance or sell the property to get your money back. In this case, the worst that can happen is that you have purchased a property worth, at a minimum, 20% more than you bid at foreclosure.

Strategy #306:

CHECK THE CREDIT HISTORY OF THE MORTGAGOR BEFORE BUYING A DISCOUNTED MORTGAGE.

Carefully check the credit rating and credit history of the mortgagor, the person who will be responsible for making the payments. Good credit habits are likely to continue; poor credit habits on the part of the mortgagor may come back to haunt you. Since the mortgagor has been making payments to the mortgage seller for some time, obtain proof of the timeliness of the payments. Mortgages that have a payment history are called "seasoned" mortgages.

If you have over $15,000 of total investment capital, discounted mortgages should be a serious consideration. You will find mortgages available between $10,000 and $50,000. Begin immediately by going through the motions of locating possible mortgage purchases even if you don't intend to buy one just now. You'll get a feel for the process without being required to make a commitment. Even if you grow to love discounted second mortgages as an income and wealth producer, invest no more than 30% to 50% of your capital into real estate mortgages, since your investment is tied up from two to ten years.

The final step in purchasing a mortgage is to have your lawyer handle the mortgage transfer and record the mortgage at the registry office, giving you a priority claim against most other subsequent loans or mortgages.

Chapter 29

THE BARTER ALTERNATIVE

I've been rich and I've been poor. Believe me, rich is better.

Sophie Tucker, entertainer

Objective: Buy goods and services without middleman mark-ups.

In 1990 the McDonnell-Douglas helicopter company had a problem. Through an error in planning, the company had allowed over $16 million worth of nuts, bolts, washers, and screws to accumulate in its warehouse. Selling off the overstock would have meant taking distress prices — something like three cents on the dollar. Instead, the company arranged, via a "barter" organization, to swap the goods for barter credits. The company would not receive cash, but instead would get $16 million worth of goods and services from traders and merchants who dealt with the same barter broker.

What do you have in common with a helicopter company? You can use bartering to give you more financial clout while spending less money.

Strategy #307:
MAKE IT, BUILD IT OR REPAIR IT YOURSELF.

Due to the tax laws there is always an extra set of hands in every transaction — the government's! Say that your new house needs a dining-room set, and that, although you are a bookkeeper by trade, you also work with wood as a hobby. For $500 in raw materials, and several evenings of your time spread over a period of weeks, you ultimately build yourself a fine dining-room set that would normally sell in the stores for $5,000. If you are in the 45% tax bracket, the real cost of that set to you, if you paid cash, would have been over $9,000. Instead you paid only $500 — which, in your tax bracket, meant you first had to earn $900 — all told, that's a saving of over $8,000!

Retail price	$5,000
Income you must earn	$9,000
(in 45% tax bracket) to purchase $5,000 item	
Cash to buy materials	$500
Income required to buy materials	$900
Savings ($9,000 − $900) = $8,100	

Strategy #308:
SWAP FOR IT, ONE ON ONE.

The official viewpoint of Revenue Canada is that barter transactions can result in income or expenses, capital gains or losses, etc., depending on the circumstances of the persons who are bartering and what is bartered.

You and your neighbour Harry are both managers at the same office. Your hobby is carpentry and Harry's is plumbing. You agree to swap services; you will build Harry a dining-room table in return for Harry's fixing up your new basement shower. Assume you are both in a 45% tax bracket.

Dining-Room Table

Cost of materials Harry provides	$500
Market value, including taxes	$1,500
Harry's pre-tax cost ordinarily, in a 45% bracket	$2,700

Basement Shower System

Cost of materials you provide	$500
Market value, including taxes	$1,500
Your ordinary pre-tax cost, in a 45% bracket	$2,700

In this example, both you and Harry had to purchase $500 worth of materials to make the swap of services. At the 45% tax level, these materials would have required you to earn about $900 in income to have $500 left over to make this purchase. In return, you each received a product — not just services for which ordinarily you would have to earn, pre-tax, about $2,700 — for a net saving from your income of approximately $1,800.

Even if you don't take into account an allowance for pre-tax and after-tax dollars, you each have an absolute cash saving: $1,500 − 500=$1,000.

Assuming that, for tax purposes, you and Harry are not considered to do "for a living" the activity that you swapped and that each of you provided your own materials so that the other person could provide the services, you could take the position that there are no tax consequences. However, if Revenue Canada considered that you earned your living as a carpenter, and Harry as a plumber, or that this was "an isolated business venture," things would be slightly different. In this example, Harry would be deemed to have made a sale of services — for a taxable profit of $1,000 that he must declare at income tax time. The same situation would apply to you, too. Also, if you and Harry start bartering your services with each other on a frequent basis, you might become eligible for taxation on the services as "income."

Strategy #309:

IF YOU ARE IN BUSINESS, JOIN A LOCAL, INTERPROVINCIAL, OR NATIONAL BARTER EXCHANGE AND SWAP FOR ITEMS YOU NEED TO RUN YOUR BUSINESS.

A barter exchange works like a bank. And, like any bank, it uses its own currency — barter credits. When you join a business barter exchange, you generally pay a one-time membership fee for registration in their computer system. You are then given a list of all the other businesses in the exchange. The better exchanges will have hundreds, if not thousands, of active members with whom you can barter. Other members will offer a wide range of goods and services that they will "sell," at retail, to any other member in return for barter credits. These members in turn use the barter credits to buy other merchandise from other members. How does a barter exchange make money?

The exchange itself makes money in a number of ways. The membership fee is an obvious one. There may be other fees as well — such as statement-issuing fees and newsletter fees. The main way an exchange makes money, however, is by brokering — that is, by taking a commission on each transaction. A typical business barter commission structure is 3% "each way" — that is, 3% on both the buy and the sell.

For example, if you barter a box of typewriter paper with a $100 retail value to another barter member, you incur a cash transaction cost of $3. In return you get $100 of barter credits that you use to purchase, on barter, $100 of adding machine paper to be used in your office from another member. You are "even" in that you swapped one item worth $100 for another of the same value, but you also have a cash expense of $6, $3 on the buy and $3 on the sell.

Revenue Canada treats a barter exchange between businesses the same as buying and selling for cash. In the example above, if both the adding machine paper and typewriter paper cost $60 and the exchange price for each was $100, the taxable profit would be $40. The tax treatment of the asset you acquire depends on its nature and role in the business. Some (as in the example) may be deductible. In many other cases the asset can be depreciated (e.g., if you barter for office equipment, a business automobile, etc.).

In simplified accounting, not allowing for overheads or barter broker fees, here is how the ledger would look for both seller and buyer, assuming the same costs as in the example above:

Sale of item

Purchase unit for inventory	$60
Deemed "sale"	$100
Deemed profit	$40

Purchase of Item

"Deemed" expense	$100
Net Result ($40 − $100)	$ 60 (loss)

So in this instance, each party in the transaction shows a loss of $60 ($40 net income, $100 expense). Add to this the brokerage cost of barter — $6 for each party — and the actual loss to each is $66. In fact, both parties are actually ahead because each swapped something he did not need for something he did!

Strategy #310:

TURN THE HIDDEN ADVANTAGES OF BUSINESS BARTER INTO "VISIBLE PROFITS."

As the example above illustrates, the two businesspeople who bartered the supplies ended up with a paper loss for tax purposes. If each could readily have sold their merchandise for cash at retail, then the paper loss might be considered a lost opportunity to make profit.

In the world of business, however, a number of factors make barter attractive even when the net result seems to be a loss.

For one thing, the goods may be time-sensitive. A grocer with a large stock of chickens may want to move those chickens while they are still fresh and firm.

For another, inventory turnover — the speed at which old goods replace new goods — is often a factor. Barter may provide a good opportunity to move merchandise that would otherwise remain idle and non-productive. For those in the service trades, this may mean extra hours that you are prepared to work but which, in ordinary circumstances, you might not be able to fill.

Finally, barter transactions are an excellent and cost-effective way to promote a business and bring in new customers — customers who may choose to pay cash the next time around!

Strategy #311:

IN BUSINESS BARTER, AVOID TAX PROBLEMS BY MAKING SURE YOU ARE ALWAYS BUYING MORE THAN YOU ARE SELLING.

It is possible to avoid showing taxable profits through your business barter transactions by making sure your account is at all times in a slight debit or negative position — i.e., you have made more deductible barter purchases than profitable sales. Barter brokers actually encourage this practice to entice new members — who can resist the old hook "Buy now, pay later"?

Most brokers will immediately arrange a line of barter credit for new members when you join. The typical line is about $1,000 and, generally, there is little or no interest charged. By keeping track of your barter account, and making sure that you are usually either even or making good use of your credit line, you may be able to stay out of a profitable position. In fact, in some circumstances, you could even end up generating tax losses if you swap for high-write-off items.

For example, Brian owns the Happy Florist. In his first year with his barter exchange, Brian was given a $10,000 credit line. His own margins are about 50% — it costs him 50 cents for every dollar's worth of flowers he sells.

During his first months in the exchange, Brian went wild. He used the exchange to provide, travel (excluding meals), legal consulting, market consulting, fax paper, computer paper and some office supplies. Within a few months, he ran up a barter bill of $6,000, upon which he had to pay a brokerage fee of $180. ($6,000 × 3% brokerage fee = $180.)

Then came Valentine's Day. Brian called every one of the hundreds of members of the exchange and, in a 24-hour period, managed to sell $10,000 worth of roses. (With a broker's fee of $300.)

Brian's tax situation looks like this:

"Deemed" Sale	$10,000	
Cost of sale (50% markup)	$5,000	
Barter fee on sale	$300	
"Deemed" profit	$4,700	
Barter "expenses"	$6,000	
Fee on expenses	$180	
Total Expenses	$6,180	
Net (profit-expenses)	($1,480)	loss

Brian is out-of-pocket the cash cost of his supplies ($5,000) plus his brokerage fees ($480), for a total of $5,480. In return he has obtained $6,000 worth of goods and services plus created a loss for tax purposes of $1,480 to offset against his other revenue. (In fact, when you include Brian's business overheads, you would probably find his out-of-pocket costs are the same, but his allowable tax loss even higher.)

Is Brian happy? In fact, he is. Although it looks like he is only about $500 ahead on the renovations ($6,000 − $5,480 = $520), Brian is quick to point out that flowers are perishable and, if he hadn't moved his stock via barter, he would have had to write them off anyway. In addition, Brian picked up literally hundreds of new customers during his Valentine's Day "blitz" — customers who will remember him and possibly use his business on a cash basis sometime in the future. And then there is that $1,480 tax loss, an extra "bonus" for a day's work well done!

Strategy #312:
ALWAYS PAY SALES TAXES ON BARTER.

When you do barter, don't forget sales taxes. Provincial and federal legislation requires sales taxes to be paid on the transactions. The barter "sale" price of any merchandise must be adjusted to include provincial sales tax and federal GST where applicable. Note that in certain circumstances an exemption from GST may apply. When the business completes its sales tax return, the tax that would have been collected must be remitted to the appropriate government offices: PST to the provincial tax collector, and GST to Revenue Canada, Excise Department. In certain circumstances, an exemption from GST may apply. Policies among barter exchanges vary on the subject of sales taxes. Some exchanges insist their members settle the tax portion of their transactions in cash at the time of the transaction, protecting both parties. Other barter groups request that all transactions be "cashless," leaving it to their individual members to settle their obligations with the government.

MAJOR BARTER EXCHANGES IN CANADA

Barter Atlantic Limited	Dartmouth, N.S.	902-462-2274
BarterCard	Vancouver/Burnaby, B.C.	604-521-7911
BarterPlus	Toronto, Ont.	416-250-6064
ThunderBay Barter	Thunder Bay, Ont.	807-623-5244
System Troc	Montreal/Quebec City, Que.	418-622-7214
System Troc	Trois Rivières, Que.	819-375-8482
System Troc	Chicoutimi, Que.	418-696-1447
Barter Pro	Toronto, Ont.	416-299-4349

Note: System Troc is the largest trade group in Canada. They also have an office in Hollywood, Florida (305-923-2444).

Chapter 30

COPING WITH GST —
THE "7% POLLUTION"

The promises of yesterday are the taxes of today.

W.L. Mackenzie King

Objective: Reduce the devastating impact of Canada's toughest new tax.

In 1990 Canadians were shocked to discover that their country had joined the ranks of those nations that use a "value-added" consumption tax levied on most goods and services as a supplementary revenue-gathering tool. For most goods and services sold in Canada, the Goods and Services Tax (GST) officially "kicked in" in January of 1991.

After months of bickering, the provinces ultimately refused to join with the federal government in creating a unified value-added system, so the feds were forced to go it alone. As a result, there is currently no uniformity (Quebec excepted) in the way GST interacts with provincial sales taxes from province to province. The resulting two-tier value-added system is, in fact, unique in the world.

Initially, Canadians were promised that the GST would be the "simple solution," but it turned out to be anything but. By mid-1991, the government itself was prepared to admit that the actual cost to Canadian consumers was approximately double what was originally projected and, at the same time, GST revenues for government use were much higher than originally expected.

The 7% GST tax can make quite an impact on your wealth because of the wide variety of goods and services on which it is paid. Canadians now enjoy the dubious distinction of being among the highest-taxed citizens in the Western world.

The strategies following allow you as both consumer and business-person to minimize the effects of the tax.

What is the GST?

The Goods and Services Tax is a broad-based tax collected on "taxable or zero-rated supplies" of most goods and services produced in Canada for consumption in Canada.

Note that this definition includes a secondary definition that takes some getting used to: "zero-rated supplies." Zero-rated supplies are items for which there is GST collectible — but only in theory! Since the GST tax rate for these zero-rated items is automatically set to zero (that's where the name comes from!), then, practically, there is really no GST on a zero-rated item. (The definition is the result of some technical drafting problems within the legislation.)

Generally, GST tax is collectible — and refundable — at each level of commercial activity in the ongoing manufacturing or distribution chain.

The GST tax is paid by each company at each step in the manufacturing and distribution chain. When a company sells a product to another processor, wholesaler or distributor, the new owner pays 7% on what they paid for the goods, and files for a refund of the tax it paid. As goods are marked up in price along the chain, the tax becomes higher and higher. When the goods are finally bought by the non-commercial end user, a consumer or company, the tax is paid but not refundable since the goods will not be used for commercial purposes.

For example, Jake is in the wood-furniture-making business. When Jake buys the wood, the nails, the tools, the varnish, and the other provisions that make up his furniture, he will pay 7% GST on each purchase. Jake is allowed to reclaim all the GST he paid out by filing a GST return. Jake can claim the refund immediately, even if he does not sell the finished product until months or years later. If Jake keeps any of the furniture for his own personal use, he is not entitled to a refund on those pieces.

How is the GST paid?

For most businesses, 100% of the tax paid on purchases for re-sale, with some minor exceptions, can be claimed as a GST credit. Consider the making of a coffee table. The sawmill takes the trees right from the forest, converts them to lumber, and sells enough lumber to make one coffee table for $100 to the cabinetmaker. The cabinetmaker will pay $7 GST on the wood, which is recoverable — generally, he will net it out (subtract) on his GST return for the period in which he purchased the wood. Next, the cabinetmaker, in the same return period in which he purchased the wood, turns the $100 of wood into a $1,000 cabinet, which he next sells to a "consumer" for cash, plus $70 GST, for a grand total of $1,070.

Therefore, in this GST return period, the cabinetmaker would show that he paid $7 GST and collected $70 GST. On the return, he would remit to Ottawa $63 ($70 – $7).

What does the GST cover?

There are some goods and services which are not subject to the GST tax. Some are known as "zero-rated" goods and services and include prescription drugs, medical devices, basic groceries, agriculture/fishery products, exports — including exported "financial services" which, otherwise, would be "exempt" if destined for Canada only — international travel services, and international transportation services.

"Exempt" goods and services are the second exception to the GST regular rules. These categories include residential housing, health care, educational providers, supplies relating to child/personal care, legal aid, public sector services, certain supplies from charities and non-profit organizations, financial services, and road tolls.

Suppliers of exempt goods or services are required to pay GST on purchases from other businesses, but they do not collect GST when they sell anything. They may not, however, obtain a refund for the GST they themselves have paid.

Strategy #313:
AVOID THE GST BY BARTERING YOUR SKILLS
FOR EXEMPT SERVICES.

Remember from our discussion of bartering in Chapter 29 that if you trade your job-related services such as electrician, carpenter, or mechanic, the government requires that GST be collected as if the sale had been made for cash. You would pay 7% of the fair retail value of whatever you traded your time and services for.

Here are two more rules to keep in mind, however:

1. If you trade for goods and services that are exempt or zero-rated, you turn

your time or products into something you need and avoid the dreaded 7% GST.

2. If you trade or barter for services that you would not ordinarily sell or provide in a day-to-day business setting (as, for example, when a professional carpenter barters his services as piano tutor), then no GST is payable on the swap.

So, if a carpenter provides a dentist with a new cabinet in exchange for a root canal, the government is owed its GST on the retail value of the cabinet, but not the root canal (dental services are exempt).

If the carpenter gives the dentist swimming lessons in return for the root canal, then no GST is payable at all!

Strategy #314:
AVOID GST BY BUYING NON-TAXED GROCERIES.

There is no GST collected on certain types of groceries. You can save a hundred dollars or more of unnecessary tax each year by buying groceries in the non-taxable "basic groceries" category when possible. Baked goods are expensive enough without the GST to worry about. If you are buying any baked goods, buy six or more at a time and you have circumvented the GST.

Nuts are a nutritious and economical food, but salted nuts are taxed. Shop at bulk-food depots and select only unsalted nuts — they are healthier anyway and tax free.

Carbonated drinks are taxable and so are fruit drinks, i.e., fruit beverages with less than 25% fruit juice content. There are a number of inexpensive "carbonators" on the market that allow you to add fizz to anything from apple juice to plain water. Although these devices will have GST added when you buy them, it is cheaper to carbonate your own drinks. By substituting fruit juices in the family diet or buying a low-cost carbonating device, you drink tax free.

Don't buy groceries in a restaurant. Even groceries that ordinarily don't attract GST (milk, butter) will have GST added if sold in a shop where the majority of the food is prepared, such as a restaurant.

Strategy #315:

TAKE ADVANTAGE OF THE "$40 RULE" WHEN ORDERING FROM THE UNITED STATES.

You can import by mail an infinite number of items with a value of up to $33 U.S. ($40 Canadian) without having to pay any duties or taxes, including GST. When purchasing several items less than $40, use separate orders and avoid taxes and duties.

Strategy #316:

IF YOU ARE TRAVELLING OUTSIDE CANADA, HAVE YOUR CANADIAN PURCHASES MAILED AHEAD TO AVOID THE GST.

If you are vacationing abroad or living in the United States part of the year, you normally buy clothes and other items to take with you. Have the merchant mail your purchases to an address across the border and pick them up when you arrive, and you have saved not only the 7% GST, but also any applicable retail sales tax plus extra packing. There is no tax on goods shipped out of the country.

Strategy #317:

THINK "USED" AND SAVE AN ADDITIONAL 7%.

Buying used goods privately gives you a double saving — one for the price you pay, two for the taxes you save.

A housewife from Vancouver admits to buying all her household electronics from the want ads. She simply looks for people who are in the process of relocating ("CONTENTS SALE") and then drops by to make an offer. She will only buy almost new equipment that is in good condition with the owner's manual still on hand.

For example, consider that 12 months ago a four-head stereo VCR would have sold for $499 in the store. Add federal and provincial sales tax, and you might have spent $575 for the item new. A year later that same VCR is worth only 50% of its original net selling price, or $250. This means a savings of 56% over the original cash outlay (including taxes) for an item that is still in excellent working condition. After you've owned an item for an hour it is used anyway.

Note also that used cars sold privately do not incur GST, but if sold through a dealer they do. Therefore, for a $6,000 used car, you can save at least $500 by making your purchase from the original owner!

Strategy #318:
IF YOU ARE NOT IN BUSINESS, START A BUSINESS.

If you are in business and registered for the GST, you may ask for a refund of all GST paid on items that are used in or by the business. This includes travel, meals (limited to 80% of GST paid, however), car expenses (see Strategy #322), and equipment purchased to use in your office. For more information on starting a business, see Chapter 18.

Note that to get back your GST credits you must first register into the system as a GST collector. All businesses that gross over $30,000 a year must register. However, businesses doing less than $30,000 may or may not choose to register.

THE FOLLOWING STRATEGIES APPLY TO GST-REGISTERED BUSINESSPEOPLE ONLY:

Strategy #319:
IF YOU ARE IN BUSINESS, FILL OUT YOUR GST THE REGULAR WAY — AVOID SHORTCUTS.

Most of the shortcut methods offered by the government to "assist" merchants in preparing their GST returns are biased in the government's favour.

Consider the so-called Quick Method:

Assume that your business operates on a 30% margin, i.e., what you buy for $70 you sell for $100. Under the ordinary ("track each item") method, you would pay your supplier $4.90 in GST and collect $7 on sale, leaving a net remittance of $2.10.

The Revenue Canada Quick Method, which is designed to make things easier for the merchant, simply tells you to collect GST on sale ($7) and remit a nominal 3% of the total collected. In this case, that would be 3% of $107, or $3.21. All you really should pay the government, according to the strict letter of the law, is $2.10. In this example, the price you paid for the convenience is $1.11, or a 50% overpayment in terms of tax owed! Multiply the difference by hundreds of times and you can overpay thousands of dollars.

Strategy #320:

TRACK YOUR BUSINESS PURCHASES CAREFULLY TO RECLAIM ALL GST DUE YOU.

If you are in business, you must track each expenditure of GST so you can claim it back when you fill out your return. Failure to track all GST expenses, no matter how small, results in two unfortunate consequences.

First, you lose the right to money to which you are entitled, which in effect raises your own costs of doing business by the amount of the lost refund.

Second, since the government system is not designed to notice that someone has neglected to claim back GST, it will happily accept the overpaid GST. The government will then have collected the same tax twice; once when you paid your supplier for the input but didn't ask for your credit back, and the second time when you charged your customer for the finished goods or service!

There are specific rules concerning the documentation that must be kept for purposes of claiming GST input credits. The following special documentation must be kept to support your returns.

GST RECEIPTS

REQUIRED INFO	< $30	$30-$150	> $150
vendor's name	x	x	x
date	x	x	x
price paid/due	x	x	x

GST amt. paid		
(or marked as "included")	x	x
vendors GST #	x	x
purchaser's name		x
terms of sale		x
description of goods or service		x

Strategy #321:
ASK FOR A RECEIPT ON EVERYTHING YOU BUY
FOR YOUR BUSINESS.

A "bug" in the GST legislation makes it difficult to track GST expenses on items purchased for $30 or less. Even though you are entitled to claim these expenses back, the law does not require the sellers of low-priced goods or services to present you with proper receipts indicating the amount of GST paid. Often it is up to you (or your bookkeeper) to look at the receipt, figure out what was purchased, figure out if GST was included, and then use the so-called "notional" formula (7/107 × amount paid) to calculate actual GST. Begin by assuming that every receipt under $30 includes GST unless the government can show differently! Track all petty cash carefully because the amounts add up. I have often said that when it comes to wealth building, there is no such thing as petty cash.

Suppose you have three employees who spend an average of $150 per week apiece, mostly for items under $30. This means that your employees are spending $18,200 a year in petty cash. Properly tracked, this could entitle you to as much as $1,190 in refundable GST input credits!

Strategy #322:
GET GST REFUNDED ON AUTOMOBILES
USED IN BUSINESS.

GST on automobiles is one of the biggest hunks of tax you can pay. By using your automobile in your small business you can avoid part or all of the GST. Here is a summary of the GST rules when you use your car in your small business:

1. When an individual or partnership purchases a vehicle, and that vehicle is not used over 90% for business, the GST amount is added to the CCA (Capital Cost Allowance — see Chapter 18), and depreciated each year. For example: If the car is used for business 40% of the time, the new automobile costs $10,000 with GST included, and the normal CCA is 30%, the CCA credit that year would be   .30 × $10,000 × .40 = $1,200. Here, the registrant could then claim an input credit of 7/107 of $1,200, or $78.50.
2. Cars purchased by corporations are subject to the "primarily" test — if the asset is used more than 50% of the time for business, 100% of the GST is refundable in the course of the normal filing of your GST returns. If the car is used 49% or less by the business, you lose the right to a GST refund.
3. Different rules apply when you lease a vehicle. You may deduct the business portion of the GST paid. If the lease is 75% for the use of the business, then 75% of the GST on the lease costs are refundable. If business use is below 10%, no GST input may be claimed.

Epilogue

*No great thing is created suddenly, any more than a bunch
of grapes or a fig. If you tell me that you desire a fig, I
answer you that there must be time. Let it first blossom,
then bear fruit, then ripen.*

Epictetus

Knowledge eliminates the two undesirable elements of building
wealth — risk and fear. With those out of the way, you become un-
stoppable.

What is financial success and how do you know when you have it?

Financial success is having the money to do the things you want to
do, when you want to do them, and, most importantly, the attitude to
enjoy them. You must, therefore, determine through your plan and
objectives what financial success means to you.

For some, financial success means having the money to pay the
bills and enough left over for a six-pack and a bag of microwave
popcorn. For a greater number it means living the good life with the
right clothes, cars, perhaps a condominium on the beach, or even
travel to exotic places. It's all available to those who are willing to
take control.

In a democracy, we are guaranteed equality of opportunity, but no
one guarantees equality of results. Results are the product of knowledge and action, and that's what eventually separates financial
winners from losers. Winners are those who see financial opportunities where others see only problems.

You can build your wealth under any economic conditions, including inflation, recession, or even depression. It's what you know and
not what's happening around you that counts. Stop worrying about
the economy, the deficit, and tax laws — they have little to do with
your personal wealth unless fear shifts you into action.

Having a lot of money does not create problems, it solves them.
Often on television talk shows the host will ask me what the downside is to having lots of money. I've never found one.

Money is only energy — a medium of exchange. It is what money
will buy that counts, and money buys freedom — the freedom to
choose alternatives not available to those without it. If you have

money you can choose where and how to live, what kind of car you wish to drive, how often you want to eat out, where you want to spend your next vacation, and when you want to quit working. Without money the freedom to choose disappears. Your alternatives are often dictated by the thickness of your wallet. Freedom is the reason that any extra time and effort required to build your wealth is worth it.

Wealth building does not require the compromise of your principles. Greed, ruthlessness, conceit, and aggressiveness are not necessary.

You will find these positive traits among most of those with a lot of self-made wealth:

- Compassion
- Discipline
- Integrity
- Decisiveness
- Sharing
- Caring
- Sense of Adventure
- Direction

Where do you begin? You already have. Now it's a matter of applying one strategy at a time. By the inch it's a cinch. Strategies don't wear out nor are they used up. Use each strategy again and again until it becomes habit. As you put one strategy into operation choose another and begin stacking them. You will soon be experiencing the momentum principle — producing 10 units of results for each unit of effort. Your friends will comment that you have developed the Midas Touch.

Guiding your momentum, and reaching the objectives you have chosen, is one of the most satisfying and exhilarating rewards of life, measurable in terms of:

Wealth Without Risk

My best for your success,
Charles J. Givens

INDEX